SuperSleep™

Family 149-154 151
146 Exercise
15 bottom good general script
- adapt this

SuperSleep™

The Ultimate Power to Change Your Life

TERI D. MAHANEY, Ph.D.

CITADEL PRESS
Kensington Publishing Corp.
www.kensingtonbooks.com

This book presents information based upon the research and personal experiences of the author. It is not intended to be a substitute for a professional consultation with a physician or other health care provider. Neither the publisher nor the author can be held responsible for any adverse effects or consequences resulting from the use of any of the information in this book. They also cannot be held responsible for any errors or omissions in the book. If you have a condition that requires medical advice, the publisher and the author urge you to consult a competent health care professional.

CITADEL PRESS BOOKS are published by

Kensington Publishing Corp.
850 Third Avenue
New York, NY 10022

All Kensington titles, imprints, and distributed lines are available at special quantity discounts for bulk purchases for sales promotions, premiums, fund-raising, educational, or institutional use. Special book excerpts or customized printings can also be created to fit specific needs. For details, write or phone the office of the Kensington special sales manager: Kensington Publishing Corp., 850 Third Avenue, New York, NY 10022, attn: Special Sales Department, phone 1-800-221-2647.

Citadel Press and the Citadel Logo are trademarks of Kensington Publishing Corp.

First printing: September 2002

10 9 8 7 6 5 4 3 2 1

Printed in the United States of America

Library of Congress Control Number 2002100666

ISBN 0-8065-2336-0

This book is dedicated to you
and the adventure you are embarking on
when you use the *Change Your Mind* SuperSleep™ program
to change your life.

Contents

Introduction   xi

1. The Creation of the *Change Your Mind* SuperSleep™ Program:
   The Beginnings and the Pioneers   1

2. Writing Your Emptying-the-Cup Scripts   12
   The Emptying-the-Cup Script Formula   *13*
   How to Clear Your Past   *14*
   How to Clear Your Present   *18*
   How to Play Detective   *19*
   Sample Emptying-the-Cup Script   *21*
   The Quick Script   *24*
   Questions and Answers   *26*

3. Writing Your Filling-the-Cup Scripts: Positive
   Affirmation Suggestion Statements   32
   Your Filling-the-Cup Scripts Guidelines   *33*
   How to Use the A to Z Scripts in Chapter 8   *35*
   How to Use the Self Talk Technique   *36*
   How to Use the So What? and Why? Technique   *37*
   How to Use Filling-the-Cup Stems   *39*
   Questions and Answers   *40*

4. Recording Your Voice to Music: Simple Technical
   Instructions   49

Your Tools   *49*
You're Ready to Record   *53*
SuperSleep™ to Your Tape   *54*
Questions and Answers   *54*

5. What Can I Expect?   59
Clearing and Processing   *59*
Processing by Past Experiences   *60*
Processing Time Frames   *61*
Processing by Emotional Style   *62*
Processing by Hemispheric Dominance   *63*
Processing by Gender   *63*
Questions and Answers   *64*

6. What Is SuperSleep™ and How Does It Work? Understanding
    the Research   68
Brainwave States   *68*
SuperSleep™ and Changing Your Mind   *70*
Mommy and I Are One   *71*
Music and Cadencing   *72*
Subliminals and Supraliminals   *73*
Questions and Answers   *74*

7. Go-to-Sleep Introduction Scripts   78
Progressive Relaxation: Muscle Relaxer   *79*
Progressive Relaxation: Back and Neck   *80*
Meditation Relaxation: The Escalator   *82*
Meditation Relaxation: Releasing   *83*
Meditation Relaxation: Forgiving   *84*
Meditation Relaxation: Emotional Healing   *85*
Meditation Relaxation: Physical Healing   *86*
Meditation Relaxation: Inner Peace   *86*
Meditation Relaxation: Manifesting   *87*

8. A to Z Scripts: Clearing and Affirmation Suggestion
    Statements   89
Action *90* • Aging *92* • Anger *93* • Assertiveness *96* • Betrayal *99* •
Boundaries *101* • Budgeting *103* • Careers *104* • Change *107* •
Childhood *109* • Commitment *110* • Communication *112* • Com-
pleting: Projects/Tasks *115* • Concentration *116* • Confidentiality *118*
• Conflict Resolution *120* • Conscious Evolution *122* • Control *125* •

Creative Problem Solving *127* • Creativity *130* • Dating *132* • Debt *135* • Delegation *137* • Deserving *139* • Divorce *141*

Exercising *145* • Expectations *147* • Family Dysfunction *149* • Family—Loving *151* • Fear *154* • Feedback 157 • Feelings *160* • Forgiving *164* • Global Citizenship *166* • Goals *168* • Gratitude *171* • Grieving *173* • Guilt *174* • Healing: Christian *176* • Health: General 178 • Holographic Universe *182* • Humor *183* • Inner Peace *186* • Intelligence *189* • Intimacy *192* • Intuition *195* • Letting Go *197* • Listening 2*00* • Manifesting 2*03* • Meditation *206* • Moving On *208* •

Neatness 2*09* • Negativity *212* • Passive-Aggression *213* • Perfectionism *214* • Performing Well *216* • Personal Power *218* • Prayer *220* • Prejudice *222* • Prosperity *223* • Public Speaking *225* • Quit Smoking *227* • Sales Calls/Cold-calling 231 • Self-love *235* • Shame *238* • Spirituality *240* • Strategic Thinking *242* • Struggle *245* • Studying *246* • Sufi Code *248* • Taxes *249* • Test Taking *251* • Time Management *254* • Truth *257* • Twelve Steps *260* • Wealth *264* • Weight Loss *268* • Weight Loss: Dieting *271* • Weight Maintenance *273* • Working *274* • Wrestling *276* • Writing *279*

Bibliography   281
Index of Scripts   289

Introduction

The SuperSleep™ state is your mental/emotional closet, and it works very much like your physical closet. Suppose you have an old coat in your closet. Where do you have to go to get that coat? (This is not a trick question.) Of course, you have to go to the closet. And what happens if you keep putting new clothes in the closet and never clean out the old clothes? The new gets lost in the old, and you still don't have the right things to wear.

Think of SuperSleep™ as your mental/emotional closet where all your old "clothes" are stored—your memories, thoughts, feelings, patterns, programs . . . The old is crowding out the new. No matter how many new things you try to put into your mental/emotional closet, you still don't have the right thoughts, feelings, and actions.

To clean out the old, establish the new, and have the right things to think, feel, and do, you must go to your SuperSleep™ closet. And that is easy to do, because you go there every night while you sleep. You can clean out your SuperSleep™ closet then with recordings you make yourself, using this book as a guide. Or you can use a premade recording of mine, or you can combine the two.

In 1985, I discovered my SuperSleep™ closet by accident when I fell asleep listening to a tape I had made to improve my time management, goal setting, and delegation skills—and it worked anyway. Unwittingly, I had accessed the brainwave doorway to the source of my thoughts, feelings, and actions.

I began teaching others how to tap into their SuperSleep™ closets. We learned together as I developed clearing statements to remove old "clothes" and positive affirmation statements to replace them. I watched my clients change their lives. Four years and four hundred clients later, I realized it was my life's purpose to expand and perfect the way to clean out the Super-Sleep™ closet and refill it. Eleven years of research, experimentation, and observation—and thousands of scripts later—I had created a program that transcended the existing limits.

My working with the *Change Your Mind* SuperSleep™ program has been like any successful relationship, full of passion, intensity, change, tedium, joy, adjustment, hard work, learning, drama, frustration, laughter, blocks, self-observation, analysis, disappointment, doubt, astonishing realizations—and the ultimate reward of understanding, inner peace and certainty. And like most relationships, it has been sustained by my passion for it, my willingness to do whatever it took to make it work, and my stubborn belief that all my efforts would be rewarded.

I have experienced much of that reward along the way. The process of creating a script—researching, philosophizing, conjecturing, writing, endlessly revising—nourishes my mind and emotions. Experiencing the resulting transformation nourishes and heals my mind, body, and soul.

When I am working on a new topic, I become single-mindedly focused. I immerse myself in the subject, reading five to ten books a week and questioning everyone I know about their related issues. I relentlessly revise and refine script approaches, formulas, and words. I write thousands of "test" sentences. My friends call this my "take no prisoners" mode. Three faithful friends have listened, discussed, debated, corrected, edited, proofread, commiserated, cheered, championed, celebrated—and in all appropriate ways supported my process. They have my total gratitude. Thanks to DeAnna LoCoco, Steve DeSoer, and Mary Rose.

Some scripts come together in a year; some take a decade or more. It took thirteen years to complete the *Loving Yourself* script; it took ten years to complete the *Taking New Directions* script and another four years to revise it as *Transcending Cause and Effect*. The scripts that deal with my personal issues are the easiest and most fun to write, as I am undergoing self-discovery and self-transformation along the way. *Trusting Your Guidance* was one of the most difficult scripts to write, as that topic is so automatic for me that I couldn't think of anything to say.

During my various phases and stages of developing the *Change Your Mind* SuperSleep™ program, I was supported with descriptions like healer, visionary, and pathfinder. For balance, I was called crazy, a fraud, and "woo-woo." Of all my labels, I prefer "a woman who walks her talk."

I've walked, plodded, trudged, pushed, tramped, slogged, stamped, and stomped my talk through the development of this program—playing detective with my issues, following the script formulas, and SuperSleeping to tapes.

I created the program, and using the program re-created me. All in all, it has been quite a journey. My intention is for it to support you in your personal journey as well. Enjoy the book, enjoy the process, enjoy your changes!

1

The Creation of the *Change Your Mind* SuperSleep™ Program:

The Beginnings and the Pioneers

Life is what happens when you're making other plans.
—Betty Talmadge, American meat broker (b. 1924)

I've always been curious about people who *make it* and people who don't. I probably wasn't supposed to *make it*, but I did, and I always wondered why. I was a bright teen who questioned authority and only followed rules that made sense to me. Consequently, I got kicked out of one high school and two colleges. Each "disciplinary action" was for the same reason—not living where the school administrators wanted me to, in a particular district or a particular dormitory. Of course, the same rules I was punished for breaking were changed a short time later, which made me even more determined to do things my way! I was a stubborn independent thinker. I was self-validating and believed in learning and experiencing. I was destined to struggle.

Characterized as a Type A overachiever, I went on to earn a Ph.D. and a six-figure income. Along the way, I alternated focusing on my career, raising my daughter on my own, traveling abroad, rafting a thousand miles of whitewater rivers, living in Alaska, and enjoying close relationships with many wonderful friends. I read voluminously, averaging a hundred books a year, and sampled many groups, schools, and movements. While studying the Edgar Cayce materials, I analyzed my dreams, discovered my soul's purpose, used castor oil packs, and focused on "mind is the builder." I read Ram Dass and concentrated on being here now. I read Shakti Gawain and taped affirmations to my bathroom mirror and created treasure maps. I meditated, fasted, and cleansed. Each experience helped me, and my life improved. But I continued to struggle.

I struggled with jobs—so I formed my own businesses, ultimately becoming a consultant. I struggled with relationships—and discovered true intimacy and feminism. I struggled with my daughter's dyslexia, which created

1

years of frustration for both of us—and moved into brain research, hypnosis, and acupuncture. I struggled with my own development, and got into past-life regressions, rolfing, Reiki, and releasing what didn't work. Each step felt better, so I kept going. *Where, I didn't know.*

I never intended to make my own supraliminal (or subliminal) tapes, much less help other people make theirs. It all happened coincidentally (if you believe in coincidences).

In the 1980s, I was a business instructor for the community college in Anchorage, Alaska, and developed *Supertraining,* a management consulting and training company. I specialized in developing new courses, new topics, new perspectives, new materials. Denis Waitley's Psychology of Winning (POW) program was new, and, of course, I wanted to take it. The college personnel director liked the idea and flew up a POW trainer to present the course to college teachers. I took the course and began teaching it myself.

Via video, Waitley introduced me to the accelerated learning concept of relaxing to baroque music to learn rapidly. He suggested changing my self-image using these same techniques, which was "new" to me. I read *Super-learning*® which explained one accelerated learning process developed by Bulgarian, Georgi Lozanov. Lozanov relaxed students with baroque music and repeated material to be learned three times to an eight-second cadencing. Intrigued, I attended the Lozanov Institute's five-day training program and was certified in his Suggestopedia method.

Change Your Mind developed as I put it all together—combining self-help with Suggestopedia. I wrote a positive affirmation script on goal setting, time management, and delegation (the self-help part). I recorded the script on an audiotape with baroque music in the background, repeating each statement three times to an eight-second cadencing (the Suggestopedia part).

Skeptical but curious, I began listening to the tape each afternoon in a relaxed state. But instead of relaxing, I kept falling asleep. After falling asleep three days in a row, I threw the tape away, certain I had wasted my time. Ten days later, I realized the tape was working! In ten days, I had organized my office, delegated two major projects that had been on hold for a year, written long-term goals, and adopted a day planner system. Intrigued, I began studying subliminal research.

My account of these results interested my friends, and many began experimenting with me. Everything we tried worked, and my friends sent friends who sent friends. I began charging a fee for consulting, which involved helping clients write their own personal scripts. At this stage, everything was experimental, and every script was completely individualized and unique. The scripts worked, and the word spread. More people came, and I raised my fees.

At this point, the program was called Superperformance, and I was helping people with their business issues—selling more insurance or real estate, getting a promotion, improving communication with a business partner, passing a licensing exam, etc. Within these issues, some common themes, such as self-esteem and change, came up repeatedly. I developed a notebook of generic scripts on the common issues so my clients could spend their sessions with me working on their personal and specific issue. They took the notebook home to work on the common issues later. As clients requested scripts on goal setting, test taking, assertiveness, feeling guilty, etc., I added them to the notebook. In this way, my clients were cocreators—contributing a new question or insight or reaction that led me to add a script or revise a procedure. *We taught each other as we went!*

Throughout this process, I studied subliminal research and talked with subliminal tape producers. I found the research to be mainly technical and argumentative; it didn't deal with behavior change (except for Silverman's work; see Chapter 6). And tape producers didn't get long-term follow-up and feedback from their clients as I did, so they didn't know what worked and what didn't.

For instance, I quickly learned that subliminal tapes made with a male voice didn't work for many women. Abused women often became angry listening to a subliminal male voice, even though they couldn't hear it consciously. Conversely, all men I worked with accepted the female voice in their subconscious. Yet most of the commercial subliminal tapes were being made with a male voice, limiting their effectiveness.

Because of this, I began questioning the effectiveness of the prerecorded subliminal tapes on the market. So I experimented. I purchased the scripts one subliminal tape company used (now out of business, fortunately). I recorded tapes using those purchased scripts with my methodology. Many didn't work, and some created or intensified the condition they were designed to eliminate. For instance, one client had been a sporadic nail biter since childhood. I made a tape for her using the purchased stop-nail-biting script in my voice with the Suggestopedia format. The language was very commanding and said things such as *"Stop, Stop, Stop Biting Your Nails Now!"* By the third day listening to that tape, my client was compulsively biting her nails to bleeding every day, asking me why she was doing it. As soon as she stopped listening to the tape, she returned to "normal," which meant biting her nails when she was anxious.

I instantly became more aware of the responsibility involved in making tapes that "program" minds. So I wrote a script "programming" my mind to use the *Change Your Mind* technology in appropriate ways and to write scripts for people that promoted their highest good and perfect healing.

I tried new scripts on myself and a group of willing guinea pig friends, and we compared our processes and outcomes. I learned that current issues were usually rooted in the past, and resolving the present issue required forgiving and releasing the related issues from the past. I constantly modified scripts to create more complete clearings of the past. Once the past was cleared, the future could be redirected with positive affirmations. I worked to refine the affirmations to create specific and effective results.

For instance, one year, I made a tape telling my mind to make more money, and it worked. I watched like a bystander while my consulting business grew and my gross income doubled. At year's end, I was startled and disappointed to discover I had worked harder than ever to earn less *net* income, despite the impressive *gross* figures. I had made more money, but my business expenses had soared. So I shifted approaches and worked with prosperity scripts. I recorded a female success script and *changed my mind* about success, money, ambition, and prosperity. And in 1989, I wrote the first self-published edition of this book within ninety days after listening to that tape!

In 1992, I began producing tapes for the public. Of course, I had always said I would *never* make tapes for other people, as they had to take responsibility for their own lives. I served as a teacher/facilitator, but I did not record tapes. Again, life happened while I was making other plans.

A client asked me to talk with her husband very confidentially (we met in a coffee shop so it looked like a casual encounter). He was a top-level government official who had discovered a ring of officials trafficking in sex and drugs with high school girls. He was determined to expose them. Needless to say, he met strong opposition from the corrupt officials who launched a personal smear campaign to discredit him. He was grappling with taking early retirement and moving out of state to protect his family. I offered to create a decision-making script for him at no charge. He asked me to record it as well, stating he never would. This created a huge values conflict for me, as (1) my *position* was that everyone had to make their own tapes, and (2) I honored and respected him and his family and wanted to support them.

He offered to pay me for the recorded tape, and I agreed, because I knew a tape would help him. The responsibility for results shifted to me, and I felt pressured. So I made two tapes: a general decision-making tape, and a specific-issue tape for his personal situation. To assure the general decision-making tape worked, I made ten copies and sent them to a cross section of friends—from a white male California forensic psychologist to a black female Texas IRS manager to a Japanese male Hawaiian self-help workshop leader to a Jewish housewife. I asked them to listen ten nights and give me feedback. Each person called with the same response— *"This is great. When can I get another tape?"* I gave my client his decision-making tapes, and he stayed in his job and got a grand jury indictment against the wrongdoers. And I began making tapes for others.

Between 1992 and 2001, I worked intensely to research issues and create tapes on empowerment, relationships, spirituality, success, and money. Some of the scripts in this book are excerpts from those tapes. For instance, I worked with self-esteem issues for thirteen years before producing *Loving*

Yourself, a foundational tape, and the *Self-love* script in this book is taken directly from that tape.

In the early stages of the program, I worked with over four hundred people one-on-one. During that period, I grappled with some unsolved problems, saw some wonderful successes, had some great personal breakthroughs, and shared in a few miracles. I had the honor of working with people with courageous pioneer spirits who were willing to experiment with my unproven program and with their own mind/brains. They spent hours writing and recording scripts and reporting back what was working and what wasn't. We worked together trying new ideas to create, change, modify, and improve this system for you.

The stories and examples throughout this book represent just a few of those people, and they are real stories about real people. I worked with each of them, and I learned from each of them. Only the names have been changed; the facts are accurate.

Roger tried the program because he was always hitting his head. He felt like a bumbler. He couldn't remember when it all started, but he said it felt like forever. Under deep relaxation, Roger saw himself in a car wreck seven years before, crashing into the windshield. His wife came to the emergency room, looked down at his glass-encrusted head, and said, "That's just like Roger to hit his head." In his state of shock, her comment served as a sort of hypnotic command that started him hitting his head (see SuperSleep™ and Changing Your Mind in Chapter 6). We wrote his script to stop him from hitting his head and included some general statements such as *My head is now completely healed.*

When I saw him ten days later, his head had fresh marks on it, but he insisted he hadn't hit his head since listening to the tape. I was wondering if the tape had tricked him into believing he wasn't hitting his head when he actually was. Then he told me the reason for the marks on his head: particles of glass had been working their way out the top of his head for a week. His doctor said it was glass from his accident seven years before, and there was no medical explanation why it was happening now. Roger wondered if the tape could have had anything to do with it. Once I recovered from my surprise, I told him what I have told hundreds of people since then: "I don't know, but anything is possible." *From Roger, I learned anything is possible, and as a result, I've been willing to work with anyone on any issue, whether or not I thought it was possible.*

Joan tried the program to lose weight. We created a script one afternoon, including eating slowly, chewing thoroughly, and enjoying each meal as she would a banquet. She listened to her tape one night. The next day, as she was hurriedly fixing a low-calorie frozen dinner for quick eating, something told her to set the table, eat slowly, and enjoy it. Though she was in a hurry, she ate her meal in a leisurely and enjoyable way. I had told her the tapes took three days to work, but she had only listened to her tape once. *From Joan, I learned the system really belongs to the person using it and not to me. I learned not to predict what would happen or how long a process might take. I also learned how fast this program can work.*

Harry and Nan tried the program because they were given a session as a gift. Harry was a handyman with his own remodeling business, and his wife, Nan, kept the books. A depressed economy was destroying all they had spent a lifetime building, and the self-confidence and health of both were beginning to fail along with their business. They were both skeptical about the program but were willing to listen and try it. Nan started with *Self-esteem* and *Personal Power* scripts, and Harry started with *Health and Success.* Within sixty days, Harry had stopped smoking, changed his eating habits, started taking supplements, and lost twenty pounds. Nan was doing equally well. Both completely changed their lives and felt back in control. They made hard decisions about their finances and started over, building from scratch. *From Harry and Nan, I experienced the power of having support during tough times. They made changes quickly in positive ways, supporting each other throughout the process. I wrote a script for receiving and being supported to help others develop that kind of support, which I incorporated into the tape,* Your First Step.

John tried the program to improve his wrestling team. An experienced coach, John was creating a new college team. Together, we developed a wrestling script (see Chapter 8, *Wrestling*), and several of his key players listened to it along with self-esteem affirmations. Even though the team became number two in the nation and John got the coach of the year award, the results from the tapes weren't consistent. One of the wrestlers found the tapes worked better for his grade point average than for his wrestling point average. Another player was on a winning streak all season and then gave up in the final qualification meet. In subsequent years, however, the wrestling script was tried again when two high school wrestlers' mothers recorded tapes for their sons. Both wrestlers won the state championship. *From this, I learned the power of the mother's voice. I also learned sports performance is altered by mental programming, but personal and family patterns can sabotage success. I spent twelve years refining the clearing script to dissolve those elements of sabotage.*

Gladys tried *Change Your Mind* for her telephone addiction. She stayed on the phone so many hours each day that she didn't get anything done. She had purchased a very expensive set of subliminal tapes that didn't help and actually seemed to be making the problem worse. We created a simple script that stated *I talk on the phone at the appropriate times. I talk on the phone for the appropriate length of time,* etc. I never heard from Gladys again, but her best friend,

Sue, came in the next month to try the program. Sue had seen the change in Gladys and couldn't believe it. Sue told me Gladys felt she hadn't changed at all and argued with her friends that she was exactly the same way she had always been. *From Gladys, I learned how the power of this program compared with commercial programs. I also learned about the role of denial in the change process, and that others often see the changes we make before we recognize and accept them ourselves.*

Greg tried the program to develop better social skills. He traveled weekly and wanted to meet people more easily. He was quiet and shy and sat scrunched down in his seat, never making eye contact as we worked. We wrote an assertiveness script, including affirmations about meeting people easily, being interesting, and being a good conversationalist. A month later, when we met to discuss his script, he sat erect and spoke clearly and directly, making eye contact the entire time. Greg told me of his displeasure with the script we had written, because he had never needed to work on those issues. He had always been an interesting man and a good conversationalist. What he had needed was self-esteem. *From Greg, I learned how totally our self-images and actions can change with no conscious recall of what we were before, and how quickly and easily that can happen.*

Diane tried the program because she wasn't getting along with her supervisor, and she wasn't being promoted. She had great vocational skills and was very creative in writing grants to generate millions of dollars, yet she was being moved down in the ranks of her organization. She was also steadily gaining weight. We worked on a script for all those issues except the weight, and included sections on self-esteem and receiving and being supported. Six months later, she left her job to set up her own grant-writing and consulting business. She realized she had been sabotaging her own career because she resented financially supporting her husband. By clearing that issue, she lost thirty-plus pounds and felt great. *From Diane, I learned the issues we think we are working on are rarely the real issues. Consequently, many seemingly unrelated problems will dissolve when a core issue is cleared. I also learned to start with the clearing script for weight loss programs.*

Peter tried the program for test-taking anxiety. He wanted to be an air traffic controller but failed the test the first time around. Together, we wrote a script on the FAA exam, and I developed a test-taking script (see Chapter 8, *Test Taking*). We discussed his father's expectations of him and wrote some affirmations about Peter being at peace with his father and living his life his own way. He passed his exam in the highest percentile and was invited to attend the FAA school in Oklahoma. He declined the invitation, however, after realizing he had chosen a secure career to please his father, not himself. For himself, he chose his artistic love, video production. Within two years, he had developed a fully equipped video studio and a comfortable though modest income. *From Peter, I learned how powerful a parent's scripting can be in our important decisions, and how easy it is to reverse that scripting and gain control of our own lives.*

Bob tried the program because he wanted to go back to school. Bob was in his mid-forties, ready for a career change. He had been a policeman and was working as a state investigator, but he really wanted to be a counselor for troubled youth. For that career, he needed a master's degree. Twenty years earlier, he had barely made it through undergraduate school, and he was afraid he wouldn't be able to "cut it" at the graduate level. We developed a personalized script for him with sections on self-esteem and his father's limiting definition of "manliness." One year later, he graduated with a double master's degree and was applying for counselor's positions. *From Bob, I learned fear, not ability, is the major block to success, and I began dealing with the underlying causes of fear.*

Suzanne tried the program because she was tired of fighting with everyone. She was a successful real estate agent, but her personal life wasn't working. She was fighting with her ex-husband, her teenage son, and her boss. She used a clearing script on male domination and success. She became very angry. Three days later, she went into her boss's office and yelled at him, demanding he pay her the money he owed her. She was surprised at her behavior, but glad she stood up for herself. Within ninety days, she had reevaluated her life and her goals and quit her job. She took a year off to enjoy herself and her teenage children. *From Suzanne, I learned that anger can be a healthy part of the change process. I began to see it as a normal part of clearing and processing* (see Chapter 5, What Can I Expect?).

Robert tried the program for stress management for his multiple sclerosis (MS). He had five years until he could retire from his top executive position for a national firm. He was experiencing blurred vision and migraines at work, and he was afraid he wouldn't last the five years to qualify for his pension. We created a script for his tiredness, blurred vision, and tension, as well as his performance until retirement. And we tried a script for MS, telling his body *to carry the electrical impulses down his spinal cord in rhythmic ways, natural ways, healthy ways,* etc. Six months later, he was vibrant and full of energy and enthusiasm. His MS appeared unchanged, but the tension and migraines were gone. He was busy making his retirement plans, stress free. *From Robert, I began to learn the difference between less successful responses to physical disease and the mind/brain issues that do respond to the program.*

Linda tried the program for stress management during chemotherapy. She had undergone surgery to remove a cancerous ovary and was in chemo treatments every ten days. She was a doctor herself and didn't really believe in subliminals, but she was desperate and willing to try anything. Her chemotherapy was debilitating. She had several days of illness after each treatment, one or two days of ease, and then several days of anxiety before the next treatment. Because of that pattern, she was unable to work, and her clinic was facing severe financial trouble. We wrote a clearing script for chemotherapy and added affirmations such as *I am at peace with my chemotherapy. I flow with my chemotherapy treatments. My body handles my chemotherapy treatments with ease. My body handles my chemotherapy treatments in peace.* She was losing her hair, so we added *My hair is thick and luxurious,* etc. She recorded her tape and called me back after one night of listening to report it worked. She told me she had tried very hard to work up anxiety about her next chemo treatment, telling herself how terrible it would be, but she didn't generate any stress. She was surprised by the success of the tape, and I was touched by her openness. She continued to lose her hair, however, until the chemo treatments stopped. The last time I saw her, she was happy, healthy, and busy in her clinic. *From Linda, I learned the program works for stress reduction (whether or not you believe in it).*

Kevin tried the program for his cerebral palsy (CP). He was convinced the tapes would cure him; I wasn't. We wrote a personalized physiological script and added a clearing script for CP. I added *I am at peace with CP, I embrace CP.* He became angry just hearing the words and didn't want to say them, much less record them, but he did. When he started sleeping to the tape, he had two days of intense anger. He called me each morning and reported, "Doc, I'm chewing nails and just waiting for someone to come by so I can pick a fight." Within three days, the changes started. He had a soft drink addiction and kept two refrigerators fully stocked with cases of Cokes. He sold one of the refrigerators and began maintaining a normal week-long supply of soft drinks. His physical appearance improved, and he transferred to a new location with his job. His CP symptoms weren't changing, but he was doing well. *From Kevin, I learned that reversing the physical symptoms may not be as important as having the courage to try. While he didn't get what he wanted—a miracle healing—he did get purpose and self-esteem.*

Of course, I've tried the program for all aspects of my life, using most of the scripts in this book, all of my prerecorded tapes, and uncounted personalized tapes for specific situations. I use tapes when I'm feeling blocked or in conflict or just to experiment with a new topic. I've made as many as six tapes in one month. The script-writing process has become a natural and enjoyable part of my self-exploration and problem solving. I now "think" the script language automatically, whether or not I write out a script or make a recording.

For transformational change, the clearing scripts have been the most effective (see Chapter 2). My personal patterns changed completely when I cleared my childhood programming of *being a good girl* and *putting myself first.* I made an easy midlife career transition by clearing *financial security, keeping commitments, and staying to get the job done right,* which were my family issues. I maintained calm and peace throughout a deposition after I cleared *the legal system and attorneys.*

When I was striving to be more spiritual, the prerecorded tape *Grounding Your Spirituality* was significant (see Chapter 8, *Spirituality*). I expected to become quieter, more subdued, and less involved in the material world. It had the opposite effect. I returned to my direct, outspoken, high-energy ways, and my management-training contracts for the Department of Defense increased dramatically. I realized I could be fully spiritual, living a very material life, and that the management training I conducted on military bases could be fulfilling a spiritual purpose beyond my conscious knowledge.

The sections on clearing romance, fantasy, and illusion and attracting a loving partner from the tape *Loving Courtship* (see Chapter 8, *Dating*) have saved me lots of time and energy. Now, I am clear when I meet someone if I am interested in developing a relationship of any kind—friendship or more. If not, I bring simple closure and bow out gracefully.

Working on the prerecorded tape *Opening to Wealth* (see Chapter 8, *Wealth*) brought out my unresolved issues around maintaining wealth. I had created it and accumulated it in the past, but I had not maintained it. Now, I am certain my future years will be very different financially from my previous years.

And like my clients, I'm often surprised. I once recorded a grieving script for a friend who had lost a loved one (see Chapter 8, *Grieving*). I made a copy for myself just to experiment. After listening two nights, I became very angry with my personal relationship and made major changes in it. Though I don't know the connection between my friend's grieving tape and that relationship (most likely, it was the section on transcending denial), I was delighted with the effect!

Another surprise came while I was listening to the prerecorded tape *Attaining Inner Peace* (see Chapter 8, *Inner Peace*), which obliquely addresses addictive behavior. I expected it to change my "workaholic" ways. Instead, I changed my daily routine of morning showers, and nightly bubble baths. Now I am flexible about my bathing and dressing schedules, sometimes going to my computer or working on a project for hours before getting "made up." In addition, I lost my feelings of attraction for a certain movie star. In contrast, my work schedule went unchanged. I can only guess that makeup, baths, and the movie star were addictive behavior, while work was for the love of it. This experience reminds me that the unconscious is just that—unconscious. Any ideas I have about unconscious causes—mine or yours—are just educated guesses!

It has been a great adventure to develop this program, use it myself, and share it with others. In some ways, it's like other self-help systems; it deals with self-limiting beliefs. But it provides very different results. It integrates Suggestopedia and brainwave and subliminal research with traditional and nontraditional approaches to self-help, psychology, and healing. The scripting formulas—meticulously developed and refined over a fifteen-year period—work to dissolve patterning at the deepest levels so the new can take root and blossom.

But the most important difference is you. You make the program different when you become a working partner with your own nonconscious mind. You make the program different with your self-exploration and experimentation. By taking the time and energy to play detective with your issues and to create your own personal scripts and tapes, you direct your change, growth, and healing.

After fifteen years, I have come to realize that this program is my life's work and purpose. I developed it for me and you. Personalize it, change it, and make it yours. Use it to support your living your purpose as well.

I wish you the best,
and I know you will change your mind and your life
when you SuperSleep™.

2

Writing Your
Emptying-the-Cup Scripts

In China, a prestigious university professor devoted his life to learning. He traveled to every library and read every book. Having mastered all written knowledge, he turned to the monasteries to learn what had not been written. He began with a pilgrimage to the oldest and wisest living monk and told him his goal: to learn all that the monks knew.

The monk asked if the professor had time for tea before the lesson began. The monk handed the professor a cup and saucer, and began pouring the tea. He continued to pour until the cup was full, and continued to pour until the cup was overflowing into the saucer; still he continued to pour until the tea overflowed into the professor's lap.

The professor leaped up, demanding to know what the monk thought he was doing. Surely he could see that the cup was already full, and yet he continued pouring.

"The cup is like your mind," replied the monk, speaking gently. "It is already too full to add what I know."

The emptying-the-cup script empties your cup so you can refill it. It empties your mind of negative messages, programming, and scripting so you can refill it with the things you want to be, do, and have. It is a powerful technique to clear your mind and life of old programming that obstructs your well-being mentally, emotionally, physically, and spiritually. Consequently, I call it the clearing script.

The clearing script is completely personal and is created out of your unique experiences, thoughts, and feelings. The effectiveness of your script depends on how well you play detective, so take your time creating it.

You can write your script alone, thinking and writing. Or you can think and talk into a tape recorder, making notes as you relisten to the tape. Or you can talk to a friend who takes notes for you. Combine these techniques or devise others. Find a method that suits your personal style.

12

Writing clearing scripts takes time and energy; the remarkable results are worth the effort. This process has been the basis of success for me and for my clients.

The Emptying-the-Cup Script Formula

Level One Clearing

I follow a fill-in-the-blank-formula approach for clearing scripts. When I began creating recorded tapes, I used the following script format. The tapes worked well on what I call the personality level and were effective for most behavior changes.

> _____ *and I are one.*
> *I release and forgive _____ .*
> *I release and forgive _____ for _____ .*
> *I release and forgive myself for _____ .*
> *I transcend _____ .*

Use this level of clearing (1) when you want to create or change a certain attitude and behavior for a specific situation such as a job interview, choosing the right residence, passing a test, etc., and (2) when you want to try a "quick fix" without delving deeply into the roots of an issue.

Keep in mind the results you get will be in direct proportion to the power of your clearing statements and affirmations. If you have a locked-in message controlling the issue you are addressing, the clearing script must address that message directly to transform it.

The advantage of this level of clearing is it is fast and easy. You can try it first, and if it doesn't provide the changes you seek, you can move to the level two clearing script.

Level Two Clearing

The clearing script for core level change is the following sequence of sentences:

Emptying-the-Cup Script
> _____ *and I are one.*
> *I release and forgive _____ .*
> *I release and forgive myself for _____ .*
> *I dissolve all imbalances on the soul level around _____ .*
> *I dissolve all imbalances on the soul level around fearing _____ .*
> *I dissolve all imbalances on the soul level around judging _____ .*

I dissolve my field of experience around _____.
I transform my vibrational patterns around _____.
I transcend _____, and I am at peace with it.
I surrender to _____, and I allow it in my life as appropriate.
I bring all past issues around _____ to an elegant completion in total grace.
I dissolve all future issues around _____ before they materialize.
I take total and complete responsibility for _____.
I allow and assign _____ total and complete responsibility for _____.

How to Clear Your Past

Clearing your past allows you to live a future of freedom and choice. You start with your mother. Begin with *Mommy and I are one,* and then use the name you called your mother—Mom, Ma, Moms, Mama, etc. (see Chapter 6, Mommy and I Are One).

Mommy and I are one.
I now release and forgive Mom.
I now release and forgive Mom for _____.

Let your mind wander on this statement, making notes of any images or thoughts that come to mind. If you see Mom going to work, note it and clear it with

I release and forgive Mom for going to work.

Now play detective. How do you feel about this? Identify the emotion (the *Feelings* script in Chapter 8 has a list that can serve as your reference tool). If you feel resentment, loneliness, abandonment, and anger, clear yourself for feeling those emotions.

I release and forgive myself for feeling resentment and anger when Mom left to go to work.
I release and forgive myself for feeling lonely and abandoned when Mom left to go to work.

And clear the emotions by themselves, as you may be unconsciously creating life experiences that trigger those emotions in you. It is not because you want to feel them; it is because they are part of your repeating life patterns.

I dissolve all imbalances on the soul level around resentment and anger.
I dissolve all imbalances on the soul level around loneliness and abandonment.
I dissolve all imbalances on the soul level around fearing and judging resentment and anger.
I dissolve all imbalances on the soul level around fearing and judging loneliness, and abandonment.

If you have no reaction or feelings around the statement *I release and forgive Mom for leaving to go to work,* you may have buried the feelings. You can work with that in two ways.

1. You can clear the situation without identifying the feelings:
   I dissolve all imbalances on the soul level around Mom leaving to go to work.
2. If you want to identify the feelings, you can write
   I now choose to be fully conscious of my feelings about Mom leaving to go to work as appropriate.

Note I have added my "disclaimer"—*as appropriate.* It may not be a good time to bring up buried feelings, as you may be attending Mom's sixtieth birthday party next week, or getting ready for a performance review at work, or some other situation in which you would not want to reexperience past disappointments and hurts.

The most interesting situation for me is not feeling any emotion around a statement, because it means (1) I am clear, healed, and neutral about it, or (2) it's buried so deeply I don't even know it is there. In this situation, I simply write a clearing script and monitor myself for reactions. If I have no reaction (thoughts, dreams, flashbacks, etc.), I assume I am "clear" on that issue. If I have a reaction, it brings the issue into focus, and I am alerted to look for related issues to clear.

Follow with

I dissolve my field of experience and transform my vibrational patterns around Mom.

If you have identified a major feeling—such as a feeling of abandonment—and you think it may be a core level issue for you (you feel women abandon you; you get involved with career women who are always leaving you for work, etc.), use this statement to clear that core issue:

I dissolve my field of experience and transform my vibrational patterns around being abandoned.

End the sequence with

I now transcend Mom, and I am at peace with her.
I surrender to Mom, and I allow her in my life as appropriate.
I bring all past issues with Mom to an elegant completion in total grace.
I dissolve all future issues with Mom before they materialize.
I take total and complete responsibility for my part in the relationship with Mom.
I allow and assign Mom total and complete responsibility for her part in the relationship with me.

When you've finished with Mom, repeat the process with Dad, using the same script formula.

Always include each situation that comes to mind, even if it seems minor
or silly to you. For instance, if you remember your parents were always telling
you to clean your plate as a child, include that. You may still be reacting to
that simple message today, either by cleaning your plate because you are
"supposed to," or not cleaning your plate because you are defying Mom and
Dad. In either action or reaction, you are being controlled by an old message
that you can clear and neutralize.

One client was preparing his first clearing script and kept seeing his pre-
teen little sister in her bedroom alone. He thought it was too minor and
childish to include in his script. When we discussed it, he found he resented
she had her own bedroom while he had to share a bedroom with his brother.
He included it in his clearing script,

> *I release and forgive my sister for having her own bedroom.*
> *I release and forgive myself for resenting my sister having her own bedroom.*
> *I release and forgive myself for having my own bedroom.*
> *I release and forgive myself for not having my own bedroom.*

While processing this script, he realized he had vowed to himself as an
adolescent that he would never share a bedroom again. He had created his
own programming: *don't share a bedroom.* He was thirty-nine and unmarried,
and his serious relationships always ended when the woman "shared his bedroom." If an image, event, person, or issue floats up, it is not too minor,
unimportant, or silly to include in your clearing script!

After clearing Mom and Dad, clear brothers and sisters, aunts and uncles,
grandmothers and grandfathers, and others who played a significant role in
your youth. If you are adopted, include your natural mother and natural father. If you don't know their names, say *my natural mother* or *my birth mother* or
language that is meaningful for you. If you had foster care or an alternative
living environment, include your foster parents or alternative caretakers.

Include schoolteachers, coaches, counselors, childhood friends, church
figures—anyone you remember with a negative event or feeling. Review your
childhood and teen years, and include any friends who hurt you, betrayed
you, or who you thought were better than you. Clear past relationships, hus-
bands and wives, children, in-laws, and others. Clear past employers and
other authority figures.

Perhaps you had a best friend in high school named Dana who got better
grades and had more friends than you, and your parents compared you to
Dana. Clear Dana and the situation with

> *Dana and I are one.*
> *I release and forgive Dana.*
> *I release and forgive Dana for getting better grades than I did.*
> *I release and forgive myself for not getting as good grades as Dana did.*
> *I release and forgive Dana for having more friends than I did.*
> *I release and forgive myself for not having as many friends as Dana did.*

I release and forgive my parents for comparing me to Dana.
I release and forgive myself for comparing myself to Dana.
I release and forgive myself for not comparing myself to Dana.
I release and forgive my parents for wanting me to be like Dana.
I release and forgive myself for not being like Dana.
I release and forgive myself for being jealous of Dana.
I dissolve all imbalances on the soul level around being compared to others.
I dissolve all imbalances on the soul level around not measuring up.
I dissolve all imbalances on the soul level around feeling inferior.
I dissolve all imbalances on the soul level around being jealous.

At this point, you may feel there is a connection between being compared to others and being jealous, and that is a core level issue for you. Use these sentences to clear that core level issue:

I dissolve my field of experience and transform my vibrational patterns around being compared to others.
I dissolve my field of experience and transform my vibrational patterns around being jealous of people who do better than I do.

And complete the clearing with

I transcend Dana, and I am at peace with her.
I transcend being compared to others, and I am at peace with it.
I transcend being jealous, and I am at peace with it.
I surrender to Dana, and I allow her in my life as appropriate.
I surrender to being compared to others, and I allow it in my life as appropriate.
I surrender to being jealous, and I allow it in my life as appropriate.
I bring all past issues around Dana to an elegant completion in total grace.
I bring all past issues around being compared to others to an elegant completion in total grace.
I bring all past issues around being jealous to an elegant completion in total grace.
I dissolve all future issues around Dana before they materialize.
I dissolve all future issues around being compared to others before they materialize.
I dissolve all future issues around being jealous before they materialize.
I take total and complete responsibility for my part in the relationship with Dana.
I allow and assign Dana total and complete responsibility for her part in the relationship with me.
I take total and complete responsibility for my performance.
I allow and assign others total and complete responsibility for their performance.
Being compared with others and being jealous are separate for me now.

Your level two clearing often takes more than one recording to complete. If the person/event/issue/emotion you are clearing has been significant in your life, you may experience significant processing (see Chapter 5). If your childhood was troubled, this clearing can be very emotional for you. Refer to the scripts on *Childhood, Family Dysfunction, Family—Loving, and Self-love* (Chapter 8) for script models. Take your time and relax with the process, knowing you will benefit tenfold from your efforts.

How to Clear Your Present

Clearing today's people, feelings, and conditions usually involves clearing your past, as a lot of your present is because of your past experiences and messages.

For instance, you might be considering moving but are overwhelmed by indecision, confusion, and values conflict. Start through the clearing script and see what "comes up" around moving.

Moving and I are one.
I now release and forgive moving.
I now release and forgive Mom for _____ (she might have wanted to move but didn't because she was afraid of starting over in a strange place) *being afraid to move and start over.*
I now release and forgive Dad for _____ (he might have been in the military and moved you all the time) *for moving me too much.*

Add yourself to the script and clear your move and move history. To release and forgive your present-day actions and feelings, clear them both ways: release and forgive yourself for doing it or feeling it, and release and forgive yourself for not doing it and not feeling it.

Your objective is to come to a neutral place so you can take the best action based on today's circumstances. Actions are often based on reactions to events to the past. What appears to be a positive action, such as being very stable and never moving, may be a reaction to being moved too much as a youth and associating fear or loss with moving. Perhaps your present-day situation requires you to be less stable, and a move might be the most appropriate action.

I release and forgive myself for moving.
I release and forgive myself for not moving.
I release and forgive myself for _____ (you may remember the first time you moved, you were lonely and unhappy) *being lonely and unhappy when I move.*
I release and forgive myself for not being lonely and unhappy when I move.
I release and forgive myself for _____ (perhaps you turned down a job offer because it was away from your family, and you lost momentum in your career) *not moving when it was in my best interests.*
I release and forgive myself for moving when it is in my best interests.

Or perhaps you are afraid of starting over, so you clear that.

Starting over and I are one.
I release and forgive myself for being afraid of starting over.
I release and forgive myself for not being afraid of starting over.

This process will neutralize your issues around moving so you can make the best decision for your present without interference from your past.

After writing your clearing script, add a filling-the-cup affirmation script that says what you want to happen (see Chapter 3). You might use affirmations like these:

I am at peace with my issues around moving.
I make the best possible decision about moving.
I move at the right time to the right place.
I move at the right time for the right reasons.
I make the best decisions about what to take and what to leave.
Everything I do makes the move easy.
It is easy to bring closure to all the move issues.
I release the move to a higher purpose.

It is easy to see how a clearing script can go off in all directions, and you may end up somewhere entirely different from where you started or thought you were headed. When I was creating an exercise tape for myself, I found significant issues with attending classes and playing competitive sports. I was only involved in physical activities that were noncompetitive—I rowed white-water rivers, gardened, and exercised to videotapes at home. I uncovered my discomfort over being the sister who was naturally slender. My older sister, who was forced to exercise to lose weight, compared herself to me. I felt her pain with that comparison/competition, and I created my own programming: I unconsciously decided never to be in a position in which others compared themselves to me physically. My exercise script evolved into a competition-and-competitive-sister script, and my relationship with many women changed. I got a great bonus for playing detective with why I wouldn't play tennis or racquetball!

How to Play Detective

By now, you are aware of the importance of playing detective to find your controlling memories and messages—your core level issues. The most effective scripts for domino-effect change address these core level issues.

There are several ways to play detective which include (1) doing any thought process to get closer to the issue: guided meditation, nature walks, reverie, brainstorming, etc.; (2) creating a list of questions to ask yourself;

(3) writing and recording a script instructing yourself to become aware of the core level issue:

> *I am aware of the core level issue for me in* _____,
> *I am Divinely Guided to the true issue in* _____,
> *I now choose to be conscious of my core level issue with* _____ ;

(4) combining all three; and/or (5) creating other ways. It is your process. Keep changing and modifying until it is simple and effective for you.

I use all of these processes, and each has been effective for me. I get especially clear while taking a shower and while highway driving long distances on cruise control.

I have a set of questions I mentally run through that include the following: What is the issue? Who gave me messages around this issue and what were those messages? What significant emotional event have I had around this issue? What is the difference between what I'm doing, having, and feeling now and what I want to be doing, having, and feeling? What is missing from what I want to be doing, having, and feeling?

To find a family of origin pattern, I ask myself: How is this like my childhood? What is my family's pattern around this? What was my primary caretaker doing when s/he was the age I am now? Who in the family of origin did what I am doing now? Who in the family gave me messages around this? What were those messages?

To find relationship patterns, I ask myself: Who in my family does this person remind me of? Who in my childhood does this person remind me of? Who treated me like this person treats me? Who did I respond to like I respond to this person?

To identify significant emotional events, I ask myself: Have I had a trauma or survival experience similar to this? Have I had a significant emotional event like this? Has someone close to me experienced an event like this?

To identify my self-fulfilling messages, I ask myself: What is my language around this? Is it fear-based? judgmental? negative? Do I have a saying or phrase I use all the time around this?

To identify my repeating patterns, I ask myself: Have I done this before/been in this situation before/had this happen to me before? If so, what is the first time I remember doing it/having it happen? What were the circumstances? Who was involved? How are they like who is involved now? Is there a repeating timing/rhythm/cycle of the event?

The repeating timing/rhythm/cycle is intriguing to investigate. For instance, if you change jobs every five years, ask yourself: What was I doing when I was five years old? There is a good chance you were moving. Or ask, What was my worker parent doing when I was five. Perhaps s/he was changing jobs. If you are experiencing a dramatic life-changing event, ask yourself, What was my role model doing when s/he was this age?

One of my friends was a very successful bank executive. To advance into the global banking world, she returned to school to get a master's degree in international finance and marketing. After graduation, she was unable to get a job for four years, despite her experience and new degree. She worked as a part-time retail clerk and could not pay her bills. She was facing bankruptcy. When I asked her what her father was doing when he was the age she was then—thirty-eight—she realized with a shock that he was having years of difficulty getting work in his field, and he was facing bankruptcy. She made a tape clearing bankruptcy and repeating her father's patterns. Today, she works for an international consulting firm and travels all over the world. I love simple success stories like this!

A repeating family pattern of mine is around eight years of age and cycles of eight years. I moved to Alaska for better employment opportunities and to enjoy the wilderness, or so I thought. Playing detective uncovered this pattern: I moved my daughter from Texas to Alaska when she was eight, separating her from her paternal family. My mother moved me from Texas to California when I was eight, separating me from my paternal family. My grandmother moved my mother from the East Coast to California when she was eight, separating her from her paternal family. My grandmother was moved from one town in Holland to another when she was eight, separating her from her paternal family.

In eight-year cycles, we made major moves that took us away from our support systems as well: Grandmother left Holland for America when she was sixteen; Mother moved out when she was sixteen; I moved from California to Texas when I was sixteen; I moved my daughter from Alaska to California when she was seventeen (close!). And personally, I have moved every eight years until now. I did a tape clearing the age eight, the number eight, and cycles of eight. I have lived in my present home longer than I have ever lived anywhere since birth. I love changing lifelong patterns in one simple SuperSleep™ month!

Sample Emptying-the-Cup Script

Situation: I moved into a house on a verbal lease-purchase agreement with the two elderly women owners. I began remodeling. The owners decided they wanted to move back into the house, which I learned when I received an eviction notice from their attorney (who wanted to block the sale). I had to decide if I wanted to fight for the house or let it go. So I wrote the following:

The house and I are one.
I release and forgive myself for having the house.
I release and forgive myself for not having the house.
I release and forgive myself for holding on to the house.

I release and forgive myself for not holding on to the house.
I release and forgive myself for having faith the house is mine.
I release and forgive myself for not having faith the house is mine.
I release and forgive myself for having an attachment to the house.
I release and forgive myself for not having an attachment to the house.
I release and forgive everyone who has an attachment to whether or not I get the
house.

At this point in the scriptwriting, I realized I had an issue with fighting for
what I want. I had always been a fighter for right causes, and I was trying to
walk the spiritual path of nonattachment. So fighting for what I wanted personally seemed inappropriate. Playing detective with this revealed issues in
childhood about who fought for me and who didn't. So I wrote the following:

Fighting for what I want and I are one.
I release and forgive all who block, obstruct, deny, or delay what I want.
I release and forgive everyone who did not fight for me and what I want in this
life and all others.
I release and forgive myself for fighting for what I want in this life and all others.
I release and forgive myself for not fighting for what I want in this life and all
others.
I dissolve all imbalances on the soul level around
   . . . fighting for what I want.
   . . . not fighting for what I want.
   . . . not having anyone fight for me when I was a child, woman, and mother.
   . . . anyone making me fight for myself.
   . . . anyone making me fight for my house.
   . . . needing an attorney to fight for me, my rights, and what I want.
   . . . resenting paying someone to fight for me or take care of me.
   . . . believing in limited ways to fight and fight back.
   . . . feeling the need to fight the system instead of having the system fight for
   me.
   . . . feeling tired by the thought or need to fight.
   . . . resisting the adrenaline of fighting as appropriate.
   . . . thinking fighting and being at peace are distinctly different.
   . . . anyone betraying me, my trust, and my confidence.
   . . . being a pawn or using others as a pawn.
   . . . being tricked or outmaneuvered or outsmarted.
   . . . fearing I will be outmaneuvered or blindsided.
   . . . patterns and ways of fighting that do not serve my best interests.
   . . . patterns and ways of fighting that do not serve my higher purpose.
   . . . anyone who tried to destroy what brought me ease, security, and support.
   . . . anyone who put a wedge between me and what brought me ease, security,
   and support.
   . . . myself for fighting to protect what brings me ease, security, and support.

. . . anyone using my needs and desires against me.

. . . anyone who tries to destroy my symbols of success.

. . . anyone who tries to destroy my home.

. . . anyone who goes after what is important to me.

. . . the attorney feathering his nest from the women's estate.

. . . attorneys not having honor and integrity.

. . . thinking or feeling the attorney can get the better of me.

. . . attorneys acting out their unhealed childhood with my issues.

. . . suffering silently.

. . . distrusting the system on any level in any way.

. . . doing anything to support the dysfunction of attorneys/the system.

I transcend the house and fighting for it, and I am at peace with it.

I transcend the attorney, and I am at peace with him.

I surrender to the house and fighting for it, and I allow it in my life as appropriate.

I bring all past issues around the house and fighting for what I want to an elegant completion in total grace.

I bring all past issues around attorneys to an elegant completion in total grace.

I dissolve all future issues around the house and fighting for what I want before they materialize.

I dissolve all future issues around attorneys before they materialize.

I take total and complete responsibility for my part in buying the house.

I take total and complete responsibility for my part in fighting for what I want.

I take total and complete responsibility for my part in any dealings with attorneys.

I allow and assign others total and complete responsibility for their part in my buying the house.

I allow and assign others total and complete responsibility for fighting for what they want.

I allow and assign attorneys total and complete responsibility for their part in dealing with me.

Buying the house and struggling are separate for me now.

Buying the house and worrying about paying for it are separate for me now.

I recorded this script in June 1995. In July, the eviction notice was rescinded, and I was offered a one-year lease. The following July, we executed the two-year-lease-purchase agreement. More issues around the house came up in the spring of 1998, and I did a new tape. I closed on the house August 21, 1998. I am living in it now.

During this time, I did not have the clearing statement *I dissolve my field of experience and transform my vibrational patterns around* _____. I wonder if I would have gotten faster and/or easier results with it. As it happened, the process was long and arduous. Nonetheless, I did several tapes on the issues, and I got the house of my dreams. I love happy endings.

The Quick Script

With present-day-situation scripts, I often do a "quick script." For this script, I identify the issue and type the root sentence *I dissolve my field of experience and transform my vibrational patterns around* _____ into my computer. Then I brainstorm anything and everything I think could be related to the issue. I don't follow logical lines of playing detective; I just free think and let go. Here's an example.

Situation: I was trying to get the graphics created for the *Change Your Mind* tapes and series covers. I encountered significant nonperformance by several graphic designers, for which I was being charged on an hourly rate. After months of frustration, I created the following quick script. This is as I wrote it, so you can see the random thought process.

I dissolve my field of experience and transform my vibrational patterns around
> . . . *rewarding nonperformance.*
> . . . *being soft on nonperformance when it costs me time and money.*
> . . . *going unconscious around money.*
> . . . *accommodating others.*
> . . . *being patient and understanding.*
> . . . *greed and scarcity.*
> . . . *being hyperrational.*
> . . . *the good mother archetype.*
> . . . *the victim archetype.*
> . . . *focusing on the person instead of the product.*
> . . . *my needs being heard, respected, and met.*
> . . . *people I pay performing as expected.*
> . . . *accommodating people I pay.*
> . . . *people I pay accommodating me.*
> . . . *requiring service for my money.*
> . . . *requiring appropriate quality and results for cost/price.*
> . . . *creating performance contracts for those working for me.*
> . . . *holding others accountable for the quality of products they produce for me.*
> . . . *holding people I pay accountable for doing it my way.*
> . . . *holding people I pay accountable for doing what I want when I want it.*
> . . . *holding people I pay accountable for meeting my standards and time lines.*
> . . . *allowing people I pay not to perform.*
> . . . *saving money on services provided me.*
> . . . *using my money to support me first.*
> . . . *giving myself away.*
> . . . *giving my money away.*
> . . . *protecting myself from others.*

. . . protecting my money from others.
. . . spending myself wisely.
. . . spending my money wisely.
. . . allowing people I pay to manipulate me.
. . . allowing people I pay to control me.
. . . allowing people I pay to take advantage of me.
. . . allowing people I pay to take advantage of my time and/or money.
. . . allowing people I pay to take my time and/or money.
. . . allowing people I pay to waste my time and/or money.
. . . allowing people I pay to spend my time and/or money.
. . . being clear on my objectives and requiring the people I pay meet them as appropriate.
. . . fear and judgment of running out of money.
. . . fear and judgment of others costing me.
. . . fear and judgment of others overcharging me.
. . . fear and judgment of having to carry others.
. . . fear and judgment of others' nonperformance.
. . . fear and judgment I don't have the power to get others to perform.
. . . fear and judgment I don't have the power to have my voice heard.
. . . fear and judgment I don't have the power to control my money.
. . . fear and judgment I don't have the power to confront others about money.
. . . fear and judgment of confronting about money.
. . . fear and judgment of confronting about performance.
. . . fear and judgment of confronting about the quality of my products.
. . . fear and judgment I don't have the power to have it done the way I want it.
. . . fear and judgment I don't have the power to have it done my way.
. . . fear and judgment I don't have the power to get what I want.
. . . fear and judgment I can't have what I want.
. . . false messages about getting wealthy doing what I love.

I recorded the script in May. The person I was working with at that time did almost nothing between May and September, when I fired him. A woman approached me and asked for my business, assuring me she could do the job. We worked together somewhat successfully through December. Then, finally, I found the person who could do everything I wanted done (to my standards) in the time frames I specified for a reasonable cost. HURRAH. While the results took seven months (which was not as fast as I wanted), the end result has been wonderful. That graphic designer created the CYM product covers I use today. I love to dissolve blocks while I sleep!

Note: If you choose to use this quick script format before you do a lot of clearing of your past issues, be prepared for intense processing (see Chapter 5).

Questions and Answers

Why should I take all this time to write a clearing script? I'm just interested in . . . (making money/going back to school/losing weight/improving my golf game/having more self esteem, etc.)?

It's hard to walk into the future looking into a rearview mirror. The clearing script ensures that you are focusing forward, not backward. The clearing concept and format are a major foundation piece for this program. It is one of the unique elements that make it dramatically different from other programs. Try one clearing script, and judge the results for yourself. I'm sure you'll continue using them!

Does a clearing script have to be that long or detailed or thorough to work? Do I have to dig up my past for it to work?

Yes and no. I have had some very short, simple, present-time scripts provide dramatic results. And some haven't worked at all. When I am making tapes for others, I want to assure they get the results they desire, and I strive to do that in one tape. To do that, I dig deeper and deeper and try to cover all angles on all levels.

Creating your own recording can be much easier. You can start very simply. Then, if the first recording doesn't work, you can create another one with a different approach. Do it any way that works for you. Your results are your guidelines.

Why should I say *Mommy and I are one?* (I didn't even know her/don't like her/get along with her fine/took care of that in therapy/don't have an issue with her.)

Chapter 6 explains why this exact line is included in the suggestion statements. My experience indicates that your resistance to saying it is often in direct proportion to your need for it. If you don't even notice the line as you write it, you probably don't have much need for it. If you really argue with it, you probably have a lot of unresolved issues around your mother that will benefit from clearing. If you absolutely refuse to say it, you probably need it the most!

Here are the findings from one study using *Mommy and I are one.*

At Queen's College, Dr. Kenneth Parker, an attorney and psychologist, offered extra credit to students taking his law class who agreed to participate in "a study designed to see if subliminal messages can improve academic performance." Sixty students signed up and agreed to receive subliminal programming. Three times a week just before class, the students looked through the eyepiece of a tachistoscope, a device that flashes a quick, bright light with a written or pictorial message imbedded in it (usually at four milliseconds or less). They consciously saw a flash of light while they subconsciously received a message imbedded in the light. They were divided into three groups:

> *Group 1 got* Mommy and I are one.
> *Group 2 got* The Prof and I are one.
> *Group 3 got a neutral message.*

At the end of the course, the grading was as follows:

> *Group 1 got A's.*
> *Group 2 got high B's.*
> *Group 3 got low B's.*

And after four weeks, Group 1 and Group 2 remembered more of what they had learned than Group 3 remembered.

Mommy and I are one has been researched in many other settings with similar results. A few minor exceptions have been found to its effectiveness:

1. *Mommy and I are one* doesn't work if the mother wasn't called Mommy. Then, the word *mother* must be substituted.
2. *Mommy and I are one* doesn't work for schizophrenics who have not differentiated from their mothers. (Silverman, "A Comprehensive Report")
3. *Mommy and I are one* isn't the most effective affirmation for male dart throwers in competition. In that setting, using the sentence *Beating Dad is okay* produced the highest dart scores. Conversely, the subliminal message *Beating Dad is wrong* produced lower dart scores. (If the sentences were given supraliminally, they didn't work at all.)

But I like my family and had a nice family. Why should I have to clear them?

Including people in the clearing script doesn't mean you feel negative about them. It acknowledges that they were significant in your life. If they were a positive influence, putting them through a clearing script will make you even more positive about them. And each of us is human, which means we make mistakes. Acknowledging a negative event or experience does not mean criticizing, blaming, or judging. It simply means acknowledging. If there is any question of whom to include, include that person. It only takes a few seconds, and it can't hurt.

Where did you get the clearing script?

I worked with developing scripts for over ten years before the clearing script came together in its present form. I began experimenting with an expanded script of *Mommy and I are one,* putting other words in place of Mommy. I wondered if being at-one-ment with something would bring it into *atonement.*

The first breakthrough on the expanded script was with Joan and Sue, two college roommates. Joan's mother made a tape for Joan's five college classes using the expanded *Mommy and I are one* script. It said *Calculus and I are one, western civ and I are one,* etc. for Joan's five classes. The tape was subliminal because the voice was inaudible; the college students heard only the music. Joan played the tape in her dorm room at night and her roommate, Sue, slept to it as well. At midterm, Joan got A's and high B's in all five classes, and Sue got A's in calculus and western civ, but got C's and D's in the classes she was taking that weren't covered on Joan's tape. That convinced me to add the _____ *and I are one* sequence to the program.

Concurrently, I realized most people could not fill their cups until they released their past, and most of the time, that releasing involved forgiving someone. I developed a *Releasing/Forgiving* script and added it to the program.

Separately, I was experimenting with a transcendence script. After hearing a presentation on the historical, philosophical, and religious definitions of transcendence, I wondered what would happen if I linked transcendence with issues I wanted to rise above. I did one full script of *I now transcend _____,* listing two hundred people, events, issues, and adjectives. I experienced significant processing, so I added that statement to the clearing formula.

I combined these statements and tried it. The results with myself and my clients were remarkable, so I continued to work with different concepts and approaches. For instance, in 1992, I began adding *in this life and all others* to selected statements. By 1995, that statement had evolved into *I dissolve misaligned emotions from my soul memory about _____.* Today, it is *I dissolve all imbalances on the soul level around _____.*

In 1994, I was in a "learning relationship," experiencing my first "it's all your fault" partner. I was struggling with understanding what the real problem was. To achieve clarity, I created the statements *I take total and complete responsibility for my part in this relationship. I allow and assign Gary total and complete responsibility for his part in this relationship.* Within ten days, I could see the verbal abuse patterns clearly, and I ended the relationship. Getting those two sentences for the clearing script made the relationship worthwhile!

My work grows as I grow, and I grow as my work grows. The statements change as I change, and I change as the statements change. In this way, *Change Your Mind* has offered me what no other program has ever offered me: unlimited freedom to grow and expand.

Why do the clearing scripts work?
When I started the program, I didn't know. The clearing scripts concept developed as I observed myself and others using it. I tried to understand what I observed, but I got results faster than I got understanding. When I became concerned about my inability to explain why and how clearing scripts worked, I wrote a clearing script on my own issues around having the answers. It said:

Being right and I are one.
Understanding and I are one.
I now release and forgive my family for having to be right.
I now release and forgive the educational system for stressing right versus wrong.
I now release and forgive graduate school for validating statistical research and discounting experience.
I now release and forgive myself for understanding and being right.
I now release and forgive myself for not understanding and not being right.
I now transcend understanding and being right.
Knowing the answers and I are one.
I now release and forgive myself for knowing the answers.
I now release and forgive myself for not knowing the answers.
I now transcend knowing the answers.

While I was writing this clearing script, I became aware of my negative feelings about people who don't live the principles they teach—people who talk the talk but don't walk the walk—"gurus" who aren't true to their stated principles. I had been disappointed by self-styled gurus I had met, and I didn't want to become one of them. So I cleared those issues.

Gurus and I are one.
I now release and forgive myself for seeking a guru.
I now release and forgive myself for not seeking a guru.
I now release and forgive others for seeking a guru.
I now release and forgive myself for being a guru.
I now release and forgive myself for not being a guru.
I now transcend gurus.
Walking the talk and I are one.
I now release and forgive people who talk the talk but don't walk the walk.
I now release and forgive myself for walking the talk.
I now release and forgive myself for not walking the talk.
I now transcend walking the talk.
What others have done, I can do.

This script released me from the right/wrong game that we are taught to play, and made me comfortable acknowledging and exploring the program without knowing all the answers. I became comfortable going public with the program, though I hadn't documented and footnoted my case histories. Notice how basic the script is in comparison to today's expanded version. Often, the simple script works just as well.

Since that time, more and more research has been released on the theta brainwave state and its significance. What I think I know today is summarized in Chapter 6.

When should I do the clearing script?

That depends on your personal style. If you like to plunge right into things, do the clearing script first. If you prefer establishing a comfort zone first, consider starting with the *Change Your Mind* script. Do whatever it takes for you to get a feel for the system and a comfort zone with the process. There is no rigid structure for this program. You decide the most appropriate next step in your process, and you do it on your schedule. **But please do the clearing script! It is a major key to your success with the program.**

What's the difference between creating a clearing script and using the scripts from your recorded tapes?

The clearing script you write is completely personalized. It uses your language, references your experiences, and addresses your core level issues. While I have tried to hit all the issues for each topic I have addressed in the prerecorded tapes, I cannot guarantee they address your personal issues. Of course, you can start with a prerecorded tape or script and watch your results. If you get the results you desire, there is no reason to go further.

If SuperSleep™ can effect people at a distance, can I use it to change others?

I do not recommend using this program to control, manipulate, or otherwise dominate another. If this question interests you, consider doing a clearing script for yourself on wanting to change others instead of changing yourself!

If I have positive "prayers" for another person I want to incorporate into a recording, I use the suggestion statement *I go to the highest spiritual realms to seek assistance/support for _____ according to his/her free will.*

For instance, when my dad had cancer, I used the statement *I go to the highest spiritual realms to seek assistance for Dad to die peacefully without pain according to his own free will.* When my daughter was struggling with career goals, I used the statement *I go to the highest spiritual realms to seek assistance for Jacki to pass her qualifying exam according to her own free will.*

If I would like to see a change in someone in relationship to me, I use this statement as well. When I was ending a relationship with a man who would not let go, I used the statement *I go to the highest spiritual realms to seek assistance for Gary to let go and go on according to his own free will.*

Okay, I'm going to try it. Is there an easy way to produce the script?

Yes. If you are handwriting your script, make copies of the clearing script format. Then fill in the blanks for each issue you are clearing. If you are working with a computer, use the same principle with cut and paste.

I have the clearing script format in my computer. Where there is a _____ in the script formula, I have written the word *blank* in my word-processing program. When I am doing a new script, I decide on the person/

situation/emotion to be cleared. Then I simply do a find/change command to substitute that person/situation/emotion for *blank*. For instance, if I am clearing a person before working with that person (for example, a client or a computer consultant), I use her or his name. I substitute the name for *blank*, and the basic part of my script is written with one computer command.

If you are adventurous, you can try the quick script first. As always, the only true measure of a script is the result you get using it.

Try it. Experience the results. And try it again . . . and again.

— 3 —

Writing Your
Filling-the Cup Scripts:

Positive Affirmation Suggestion Statements

Once you have emptied your cup of old patterning, messages, and programming, you refill your cup with statements of what you want. It's like asking and receiving. We so rarely ask, and we're so hesitant to receive. You ask for what you want during your powerful SuperSleep™ state, and you open to receive without your old unconscious conflicts, filters, blocks, and limits.

You ask for what you want—fill your cup—with affirmations. Affirmations are positive statements that affirm what you want to be or have or do, which may be dramatically different from what is happening in your life now. For instance, you might be alone and feeling lonely but desiring a loving, fulfilling relationship. By affirming you are in that relationship now and planting that message in your SuperSleep™ state, you direct yourself to create that situation and condition.

Often, affirmations conflict with your "self talk" and are hard to accept. Self talk is what you say to yourself—your internal dialogue, your mental conversation. Self talk thoughts, images, and feelings float through your mind/brain continually—about fifty thousand a day—and most of them are negative: *I can't. I shouldn't. I don't have enough time. It'll never work. I can't afford it.* Affirmations reverse those negative self talk statements to positive self talk: *I can. I have all the time I need to do everything I want. It works perfectly for me and for my highest good now. My income now exceeds my expenses.*

The more difficult the positive affirmations are to believe, the more you probably need them! I started using affirmations in 1976 and experienced exciting results with them, but sometimes they worked and sometimes they didn't. I didn't understand the inconsistent results until I realized my deeply

32

buried messages had to be removed equally deeply. SuperSleep™ works on those deepest levels, dissolving negative and limiting self talk and false beliefs at their origins.

You can use this program at any stage of your personal development. I've used it for years, and I'm still learning to expand my affirmations—to expand what I ask for and what I am willing to receive—and to have the courage to ask at all! Consider starting with *Self-love* (Chapter 8, *Self-love*). It took me over a decade to complete that script, which I consider a foundational script. Loving yourself carries the paradox of truth in it: the more you love yourself, the more you are willing to receive, yet the less you need in your life to be satisfied and fulfilled.

Your Filling-the-Cup Script Guidelines

Be Positive

Use positive words and positive concepts, and focus on the positive outcomes you desire. Replace negative phrases such as "I won't get into bad relationships anymore" with affirmations such as:

> *I enter into relationships that are healthy.*
> *I enter into relationships that are fulfilling.*
> *I give and receive equally as appropriate.*
> *My relationships have all positive outcomes for me now.*

If you want to quit smoking, write all the positive outcomes from being a nonsmoker. Give your subconscious positive ideas. If your goal is to have healthy lungs, use affirmations such as:

> *I breathe deeply and easily.*
> *My lungs are free and clear.*
> *My lungs are completely healed.*
> *I choose health and healthy habits.*
> *I know what is best for my health, and I do it.*

One stop-smoking subliminal tape that was sold to the public has the statement *Smoking damages my lungs*. Imagine the possibilities if you continue smoking while your subconscious is programmed that smoking is damaging your lungs!

Be Here Now

Use the present tense. Replace future tense—*"I am going to be happy,"* which "futures" your outcomes and puts off being happy—with affirmations such as:

I am happy.
I am at peace.
I am spontaneous and free.
I am loving and loved.

This gives your mind/brain the directive to make it happen now!

Be as Simple and Clear as You Can

Writing clear and concise affirmations is not always easy. When I was making a career change and trying to write a "next appropriate job" script, my affirmations were running very long. I had statements such as *I now attract the most appropriate next career that provides me financial security and creative freedom for the highest good.* I was struggling to state what I wanted in a simple way. Then a friend gave me the lines:

I get the perfect job in the perfect way.
I do the perfect things for the perfect pay.

That said it all.

Be Mindful

Play devil's advocate with yourself when you write affirmations, and look at them from all sides. Close examination of some positive sentences can reveal hidden "possibilities," or what I call unintended consequences.

When I was serving the governor as director of Child Support Enforcement, I was in a significant power struggle with one of the highest-ranking elected officials. His son owed a huge amount of child support, and we were not in accord on how that case should be handled. I was "doing my job," and the case was being treated like all other cases and enforced equally. This led to some interesting "power politics," including a class action lawsuit against me, an extensive accounting audit, etc.

I wrote a clearing script to dissolve and neutralize the negativity, citing specific people and events and including general issues around passive-aggression, lack of integrity, dishonesty, and hidden agendas. For the filling-the-cup script, to bring closure to the situation, I cited the names of the persons opposing me in the following statements:

I cut all ties that bind me to _____ in this life and all others, past and future, in all appropriate ways.
I cut all ties that bind me to _____ in this life and all others, past and future, in all immediate ways.
I cut all ties that bind me to_____ in this life and all others, past and future, in all healthy ways.

I cut all ties that bind me to _____ in this life and all others, past and future, in freedom and grace.

After ten nights' SuperSleeping, I was asked to resign. I indeed cut all ties that bound me to those people! The fun ending to this story came when I called my dad to relay the news. In my honest, work-ethic family, being "fired" was an issue. My dad listened, was silent a moment, and then asked, "Kid, how long have you been working in politics now?" I answered, "Eighteen months, Dad." Hmmm, he mused. "If you'd lasted much longer, I would worry about you." Needless to say, that made me laugh and restored my perspective. I have done numerous tapes on work and career since then, and I have been self employed ever since (see Chapter 8, *Careers* and *Working*).

Practice

Like any skill, writing affirmations gets easier the more you do it. During the day, make a game out of recognizing negative, limiting, closed-ended statements. Notice newspaper stories and news broadcasts. Monitor conversations with friends for positive statements versus negative statements. Be alert to business communications. Listen to yourself—what you say to yourself and what you say to others. Once you recognize the negative, limiting, closed-ended statements, make a game out of converting them to positive, open, supportive ones.

To practice this concept, I developed a *good news/bad news* game with my daughter. Whenever she told me something negative, I would ask, *"So what is the good news about that?"* She quickly mastered the game. When she was sixteen, within six months of getting her birthday gift sports car, she got several speeding tickets and had two auto accidents. I had promised her dire consequences on her next driving infraction. A few days later, I was awakened by a late-night phone call. I answered it to hear my daughter say, *"Mom, I've got some good news. You never have to worry about me driving my sports car again. I just totaled it!"*

How to Use the A to Z Scripts in Chapter 8

Prepared scripts are listed alphabetically by subject in Chapter 8. Choose a subject that interests you, such as *Goals*, and read through that script with a pen in your hand. If you don't want to make notes in the book, make a copy of the script and work on the copy. If you prefer working on the computer, scan the script in.

Make notes on the script, changing sentences or words to fit your personal style and vocabulary. Personalize the script as much as possible.

Be aware of your "self talk" as you read each filling-the-cup statement.

Your self talk is important, because the statements you agree with have the *least* value for you. Conversely, the statements that make you the most uncomfortable or that your self talk disagrees with bring you *greatest* value. Those statements are "arguing" with your nonconscious messages, and those messages need to be changed!

As you read through a script, note the affirmations your self talk argues with and mark them. For instance, reading through the *Health: General* script in Chapter 8 might trigger this "self talk":

I take good care of myself every day; no, I don't take care of myself.
I give my body the rest it needs; yes, I go to bed at a set time and sleep well.
I sleep deeply, peacefully, and restfully; yes, I sleep well.
I awake invigorated and refreshed, ready to experience another day; no, I awake dreading going to work.
I eat what is best for my continuing health; no, I don't eat healthily.
I eat fresh, live, healthy food daily; no, I eat fast food and pizza nearly every meal.
I eat slowly and chew each bit thoroughly; no, I'm in the habit of eating fast because I'm always running late for work or am on a short lunch hour.
I schedule my exercise, and I stick to my schedule; yes, I walk every day.

In this example, you would mark the statements that you didn't agree with. You can do clearing statements on those issues—empty your cup—and then add personalized positive statements about them:

Taking good care of myself is my number one priority, and I do it in all appropriate ways.
I take good care of myself at the right time in the right way for the right reasons.
I consistently and persistently take good care of myself, and I enjoy it.

One script often leads to another. The statements on healthy eating could lead to a clearing script on working long hours and not taking time for yourself. For instance, you might realize you do not take time for yourself because you were taught work comes first, and that work is a drudgery that has to be endured for money. Clearing those issues could create changes in your working style and job/career as well as your eating habits.

How to Use the Self Talk Technique

To develop your filling-the-cup script, decide what you want to change in your mind and your life, and get a working goal statement. Perhaps you want to be free of consumer debt. Write or say out loud—*I am free of consumer debt*—and list each self talk thought, image, or feeling you have. Take your time, and let your mind float and wander freely, jotting down your reactions. Perhaps you think *I'll never get these credit cards paid off; I'm no good at budgeting.*

Begin with a clearing script (see Chapter 2), and follow it with the affirmations that rescript your negative self talk.

Rewriting Negative Self Talk

Self talk: I'll never get these credit cards paid off.

Rewrite:

> *I am committed to being free of consumer debt.*
> *I take positive action steps every day to achieve my goal.*
> *I focus on consumer debt elimination in all positive ways.*
> *I focus on accelerating my debt payments, and I do it easily.*
> *I reduce my credit card debt consistently.*
> *I pay cash for pleasure, comfort, and vanity.*
> *I live on less than I earn easily and effortlessly.*
> *I live on less than I earn and enjoy it.*
> *I make a game of saving money, and it is fun.*
> *I save money in the right way at the right time for the right reasons.*
> *My income now exceeds my expenses.*

Self talk: I'm no good at budgeting.

Rewrite:

> *I am in control of my finances and my financial state.*
> *I manage my money with professionalism.*
> *I manage my money effectively and efficiently.*
> *I am good at budgeting, and I enjoy doing it.*
> *I set my budgeting goals, and I am committed to them.*
> *I set reasonable, attainable goals, and I keep them.*
> *I read my budgeting goals every day and recommit to them.*
> *I track my daily expenses to determine how I spend my money.*
> *I find the money that slips through the cracks.*
> *It is fun to set a budget, keep a budget, and reap the rewards of a budget.*
> *Budgeting has all positive outcomes for me now.*

How to Use the So What? and Why? Technique

Another technique for writing affirmations is the so what? and why? technique. Identify what you want, and ask yourself a series of so what and why questions:

Perhaps you have a "want" in your professional life.

I want a better job.

Why?	*Because I don't like what I'm doing.*
Why?	*Because it is boring.*
So what?	*So I don't feel good when I'm at work.*
So what?	*So I don't feel as if I'm doing anything important.*
So what?	*So I don't feel like I'm important.*

Affirmations could be:

I have the most appropriate job now.
My job is appropriate for my style of thinking.
My job is appropriate for my style of living.
My job is appropriate for my abilities, talents, and gifts.
My job is one of my greatest pleasures.
I enjoy my job.
I like going to work every day.
I am enthusiastic about what I do.
I provide value with what I do.
I feel good about what I do.
I am appreciated for what I do, and I feel it.
I appreciate myself.
I see the importance of what I do.
I see the benefits of doing my job well.

This script may be very different from your old messages. It can *change your mind* about your present job or lead you to seek another one, so don't be surprised with the results. (And don't be disappointed if it takes a few months for all of this to materialize in your life.)

Perhaps you have a "want" in your personal life.

I want to have a good relationship.

Why?	*So I won't be lonely.*
So what?	*Then I'll feel good.*
So what?	*Then I'll be happy.*
Why?	*Because I'll have a purpose for my life.*

Write positive affirmations for each of the whys and so whats:

I have love in my life at all times.
I am loving, and I am loved.
I am open to give love.
I am open to receive love.
I give and receive love equally.
I am happy with myself at all times.

I am happy with the people in my life.
I am attracting positive healthy relationships.
I am attracting fulfilling nurturing relationships.
I am at peace with who I am and what I do.
I am happy with who I am and who I am becoming.
I am now willing to accept my life's purpose.
I have a purpose, and I know it.
I am on my path now.

How to Use Filling-the-Cup Stems

When you are working with a core level issue, thinking and writing positive statements about it can be the most challenging part of the script to write. I ask my clients to write twenty positive statements for each issue they clear. One of my steadfast clients collected the positive statements I wrote for her over the years and created "stems" from them. The stems made it easier to write her affirmations, as it became a fill-in-the-blank exercise. She shared her stems with me for this book. Thanks, Judy.

I stand firmly in _____ .
I believe completely in _____ .
I feel deeply _____ .
I move forward with _____ as appropriate.
I open myself to _____ as appropriate.
I am totally comfortable and at peace with/when _____ .
I give myself permission to _____.
I take pleasure in _____.
I have positive reactions to _____.
I feel wonderful receiving _____ .
I find emotional satisfaction and fulfillment in _____.
I find mental satisfaction and fulfillment in _____.
I find physical satisfaction and fulfillment in _____.
I find spiritual satisfaction and fulfillment in _____.
I replace _____ with _____ in my life moment to moment.
I stand in my power and _____.
I trust myself completely when _____.
I place great value upon _____.
I have the wisdom to handle _____ .
I recognize the natural perfection within _____.
Love's power protects me in the face of _____.
The power of _____ protects me at all times and places.
I abide in _____ continuously and effortlessly.
I accept, allow, and integrate _____ into my life now.

I open to and embrace _____ into my life now.
I accept myself as _____ .
I act on _____ as appropriate.
I allow, invite, and create _____ in my life moment to moment.
I allow full balance and harmony into _____ .
I balance _____ with _____ in all appropriate ways.
I carry forward the positive aspects of _____ .
I now create and embody _____ .
I stay fully conscious and responsible around _____ .
It is easy and natural for me to _____ .
I have a perfectly developed ability to discern _____ at all times and places.
I deserve to have/be/do _____ .
I express _____ in all appropriate ways.
I honor the _____ .
I give myself the gift of _____ moment to moment.
I have the wisdom and ability to create _____ , and I do so in grace.
It is easy and fun for me to _____ .
I am always deeply centered and relaxed about _____ .
I am clear on _____ .
I am in control of _____ in every way.
I am in control of _____ at all times and places.
I am divinely guided to _____ .
I am divinely protected when _____ .
I am filled with _____ .
I am a magnet for _____ .
I _____ at the right time in the right way for the right reasons.

Questions and Answers

I'm ready to make a tape. Which script should I write first?

Good! Start wherever it feels best for you. If you want to begin by clearing the past, start with a clearing script. If you want to start with an easy project to get comfortable with the method (relaxation intro, music, cadencing), consider starting with a *Change* script (see Chapter 8, *Change*). It can ease your future changes.

Each script is personal to you, and the sequence of scripts is personal to you. The program is designed to be changed, altered, modified, combined, adjusted, and mixed. It's your puzzle to play with. Assemble it your way.

I'm new at this. What if I write the wrong thing and give my mind/brain the wrong message?

Over the years, I've had to correct some of my own scripting mistakes, so

I developed ways to prevent or neutralize them. Here are strategies that worked for me:

1. Sprinkle *as appropriate* liberally throughout your script.
2. Record a protection statement onto the beginning of your script such as

   I am divinely protected as I listen to this tape.
   I integrate affirmations that are for my highest good, dissolving all else.
   My mind/brain increases in health daily, accepting the messages that promote that health, and dissolving all else.
   My mind/brain/body/spirit is surrounded by healing love, and only healing messages get through.
   I am at peace with the healing messages I receive, and I dissolve all others.
   Every message I accept into my mind/brain is for my highest good.
   I trust _____ to protect me as I listen to this tape.

   Just as you would rewrite any prepared script, rewrite this protection to blend with your belief system and vocabulary. (Note: I add a protection script to the beginning of every prerecorded tape I create for you as well.)
3. Listen to your self talk about writing a script. Convert your negative statements and fears into positive affirmations, and record them as part of your next tape. Some possible affirmations are

   I know what to say and how to say it.
   I am clear about my desired outcomes.
   I make the right tape at the right time for myself.
   I say the right things in the right way to get the results I want.
   I use appropriate words in my scripts.
   I deal with appropriate issues in my scripts.
   I identify the issues easily and effortlessly.
   I move through the issues to the appropriate solutions.
   I phrase my script statements perfectly.
   I feel good about writing my own scripts.
   I am at peace being in control of my own process.
   I trust myself completely to take care of myself in perfect ways.
   I know what's best for me, and I act on what I know as appropriate.

What if I don't know what I want?

Let the program do the work for you. Write a script about it.

I easily identify my wants.
I easily identify my needs.
I easily distinguish between my wants and needs.
I easily distinguish between my real wants and the wants of others.
I easily distinguish between what I want and what others want for me.
I easily distinguish between my real wants and my past programming.

How long does it take for my tape to work . . . for me to see results in my life?

Most situations in your life today are in process—they were set in motion in the past. Changing your mind today will set new situations in process for your future. Some people experience these changes in one day, while others experience change over weeks, and months. For me, the scripts on time management, writing, and personal power worked the fastest. However, getting results from my scripts on financial security and career satisfaction have taken longer and have shifted several times.

When I feel I'm not making progress on an issue, I inventory the events around that issue. If the events causing me dissatisfaction are results of past actions that occurred *before* I changed my mind—such as credit card debt from old charges, time crunches from old commitments, unequal relationships with old friends—I label them "paying for past mistakes." I separate them from the events more recently initiated that reflect my new way of thinking and being.

Where can I learn more about writing affirmations?

Courses are offered in many areas on writing affirmations and creative visualization. You can check your area for those, or you might want to read the following books: *Creative Visualization* by Shakti Gawain, *The Only Diet There Is* by Sondra Ray, and *What to Say When You Talk to Yourself* by Shad Helmstetter.

How many topics can I cover in one tape? Can I mix up scripts?

As many as you want. Your conscious mind may be worried about how much your subconscious can take, but your subconscious is fine! Some people limit each script to a few topics and structure each script in an orderly progression from one topic to another (left-brain processors). Others throw in various topics as they come to mind and mix up the scripts (right-brain processors). Subliminal research indicates you process best in your own brain-processing style (see Chapter 5), so do what is comfortable for you.

I've always been told to be specific with my goals. Does that work with these scripts?

Personally, I am not specific with my scripts. I do not use specific dollar amounts, dates, locations, jobs, etc. My standard money affirmation is *My income now exceeds my expenses.* When I want to bring something into my life, I use *I am now attracting the most appropriate next _____ (home, career, relationship, etc.).* I add *for the highest good* to many affirmations as well.

Several of my clients have written scripts with specific goals, however, with surprising results.

Renee wanted a pleasant, inexpensive office space for her personal counseling. She listed her specific "I wants" on her tape: the part of town, amount of rent, size of building, color of carpet, size and shape of office, kinds of people working in the building, etc. Within thirty days of SuperSleeping to that script, she found an office that matched her script.

Sarah wanted to lose ten pounds in fourteen days so she could wear a particular dress to a fancy party. She wrote a script with that specific weight and the specific date. A few SuperSleep™ days later, she lost a crown off a tooth. Her dentist was on vacation, and she wouldn't use anyone else, so she endured ten days in pain without solid food. She lost exactly ten pounds in fourteen days.

Mary wanted to earn $50,000 a year as an independent consultant. She had earned that much in a previous job, but she was earning only half that in her own consulting business. She wrote a script saying she earned $50,000 by the end of the year. The week after SuperSleeping to that script, her consulting business decreased dramatically. After much consideration, she decided the only way to make that much money right away was to work for someone else, which she was not willing to do. She changed her script.

Evidently, using specific goals can have both advantages and disadvantages. If you decide to use specific goals, consider adding a disclaimer such as

> *I get what I ask for as appropriate.*
> *I get more than I ask for as appropriate.*
> *This or something better is brought to me now.*
> *I get what I ask for in all appropriate ways.*
> *I get what I ask for at the right time in the right way for the right reasons.*
> *I get what I ask for in natural and healthy ways.*
> *I get what I ask for in harmonious and loving ways.*

I don't feel good saying these affirmations. Aren't I just lying to myself?

Affirmations contradict the messages you've been given all your life, the "you're not okay" and "you don't deserve" and "you can't do" and "you can't have" messages. If you've been told you have to work hard, saying *My creative mind creates my wealth* probably sounds like "lying" to you. If you've been taught to believe that you're not very interesting or much fun, saying *I have a winning personality* probably sounds like "lying" to you. If you have anxiety making cold calls, saying *I make new friends and gather new information prospecting* probably sounds like "lying" to you.

This program allows you to determine *what you want to be true for you*, and to repattern your mind with that truth, easily and effortlessly.

Your past thoughts determined your present. If your past thoughts were negative, your present is negative. Your present thoughts determine your future. If you change your present thoughts to positive, then your future will be positive! This program gives you a simple method to create the future you want.

Can I make recordings for other people?

The program was designed for you to use for yourself. You can use it to make recordings for others, but I suggest you ask yourself why you want to, and be sure your intentions are very clear and very appropriate first.

Kim really wanted to help others. She made tapes for her daughter, her partner, her friends, her coworkers. After a year of making tapes for others, she realized each of those scripts related specifically to her issues. She began to face her own issues and began healing herself as she had healed others— a double win!

If you want to make recordings for others more than you want to make them for yourself, try the following affirmations: *I put myself first as appropriate. I am loved and accepted when I take care of myself first. I recognize my issues and acknowledge them. I recognize when I project my issues onto others. I dissolve projection in all healthy ways. I have the emotional courage to face my issues openly and honestly. I heal myself and my issues first as appropriate.*

Interestingly, I have observed people affected by a recording that had statements about them, though they never heard the recording.

Kathy was returning to college and had math anxiety. She worked with me to make a tape which would change her mind about taking math tests. The more we talked, the more I felt she had an incident in her childhood that was blocking her natural memory, so we wrote a general clearing script. After ten days of Kathy's SuperSleeping to that script, her mother called from her home across the country to "confess" an incident from Kathy's childhood. Kathy's math anxiety dissolved and she got an A in her math class.

David listened to a "Healing Your Childhood" recording. He had been estranged from his father for twenty-seven years since coming out as a gay teen. They had no contact in those years, and David did not know his father's whereabouts. After twenty-one days of SuperSleep™, David received a phone call from his father who had located him. They talked for hours. His father flew out to visit for two weeks, and they reestablished their relationship.

Angela wrote and recorded a clearing script on conflict with her husband. She included a clearing on his emotionally demanding and abusive ex-wife and her stepdaughter who were a major reason for the ongoing conflict. After three days of SuperSleep™, the ex-wife stopped her daily phone calls and became conciliatory toward Angela. All the relationships improved.

Can I make recordings for my kids? How young can they be?

I struggled with this questions for years. While I was developing the program, my daughter was muddling through her teen years. I knew a tape would help her (and me) get through it faster. I tried persuading her to make tapes, but she refused for over a year. There were days—and weeks— when I was tempted to make a tape and put it on without her consent, but I wanted her to control her own process. I decided not to make a tape for her. When she faced a difficult situation, she asked my help in making a tape for herself, and it worked. She became an on-again, off-again tape user for five years. As she cleared her issues, she opened more to the ease of the process. Now, she is a regular tape user, and when she has an issue to clear, she often asks me to write a script for her.

So the answer is yes, you can make recordings for your kids. Spend time thinking about why you are doing it, and get clear on your intentions. If you are trying to control another person, do a clearing script for yourself on control. If you are trying to get a child to conform to your standards, do a clearing script for yourself on parenting.

If you feel you have clear and honorable intentions that are serving the highest good of the child, discuss it with the child and involve him or her in the process if possible.

For young children, simple self-esteem and school scripts are usually appropriate. Include *Mommy and I are one, Mommy loves me, Daddy and I are one, Daddy loves me.* and each of the family members and extended family members.

I've seen the program work for a child as young as two years old. Denise did a tape for her two-year-old son who did not sleep through the night because of severe eczema. By playing detective, we realized the eczema began when his younger brother, Bobby, was born. We wrote a simple script about being loved and cared for, sleeping well, and having smooth, soft, cool skin. We included *Mommy loves me as much as Bobby. Daddy loves me as much as Bobby.* By day two, the condition improved and he was sleeping through the night.

Single-issue scripts for older children work also. Dolores recorded the wrestling script for her high school son who was competing in wrestling, and he took the state championship!

What about couples? Can we do a couples script?

Absolutely. And I encourage it. You can cowrite a script and co-record it to improve your relationship, plan for your retirement, plan your social activities, or whatever.

Some couples co-record by alternating voices. One person says the first statement, and the other person follows with the next statement. Some couples speak at the same time, layering one voice over the other. Find what works for you.

Cowriting the script is probably half the work! Agreeing on the messages takes time; the recording is easy. Use the word *cocreate. We cocreate a loving environment. We cocreate an equal partnership. We cocreate equal sharing. We cocreate open communication.*

Sharon and Steve were changing careers and relocating. They used the following script, and everything went effortlessly!

We creatively brainstorm each issue as appropriate.
We determine the best approach to our transportation issues.
We determine the best approach to our house issue.
We determine the best approach to our relocation issue.
We find ways to dispose of our physical property that benefit everyone.
We find it easy to bring closure to our move-related issues.
We are now attracting mutually beneficial outcomes for all of our issues.
We recognize the best outcomes when they present themselves.
We release all outcomes to the highest good.
We release the move to the highest good.
We have a similar sense of our activities.
We have the same view of our priorities.
We share our vision of the future.
We are at peace with our future vision.
We translate our vision into action effortlessly.
We codevelop a plan of action with ease.
We honor each other's viewpoint in the process.
We creatively brainstorm each issue as appropriate.
We see the process as fun.
We support each other throughout this process.
We recognize and accept each other's personal style and idiosyncrasies.
We are at peace with making plans and revising plans.
We are at peace with acting without a plan.
We are safe when we are flexible.
We function independently as appropriate.
We function dependently as appropriate.
We cocreate our relationship in all positive ways.
We blend our differences in all peaceful ways.
We honor ourselves and each other.
We stand alone in peace.
We stand together in peace.
We are comfortable asking for what we want and what we need.
We give and receive equally.
We nurture ourselves in all healthy ways.
We nurture each other in all healthy ways.
We lovingly cocreate a mentally healthy environment for ourselves.
We lovingly cocreate a physically healthy environment for ourselves.
We lovingly cocreate an emotionally healthy environment for ourselves.
We lovingly cocreate a spiritually healthy environment for ourselves.
We codevelop our interest in new age theories, skills, and knowledge.
We support each other in our continuing evolution and growth.
We support each other in our continuing change and personal development.

What about a family tape? Can we make one for the family?

Yes. For a family tape, consider playing it throughout the house at night. Find a relaxation introduction that works for everybody or put the tape on after the family has gone to sleep. *Self-love* is a great foundation script (see Chapter 8, *Self-love*).

I want to quit smoking or lose weight. Which script should I use?

These two issues usually require very personalized clearing scripts. About 50 percent of the time, the first recording works. About 50 percent of the time, it doesn't. If you are a moderate smoker or eater, one script may clear the issue for you. If not, you have to find *why* you do it, and take the *why* out. Determine when you started smoking, or when you became overweight the first time, and analyze what was going on in your life. Then create a clearing script for those issues.

For instance, if you started smoking at fourteen to be accepted by your peer group, you would do a clearing script on anyone who didn't make you feel accepted, etc. Personalize the scripts with statements such as *Smoking and being accepted are separate for me now. Smoking and having friends are separate for me now. Smoking and feeling liked are separate for me now. Smoking and being one of the gang are separate for me now. Smoking and being social are separate for me now.* Also, look at the *Self-love,* and *Healing* and *Health* scripts in Chapter 8.

If you became overweight right after you married, you might want to be less physically attractive so you'll be "safe" from sexual advances or temptations. Do a clearing script that includes the issue of seduction, and add affirmations such as *I am safe when I am attractive. I am safe when I am sensuous. I am safe when I am sexy. I trust myself when I am attractive, sensuous, and sexy. My behavior is appropriate at all times.* Also, look at the *Self-love, Personal Power, Intimacy,* and *Commitment* scripts (see Chapter 8).

Can I learn Spanish, math, or history this way?

Some people can sleep-learn, and some can't. You may be one of the people who can. If you're not, try the Superlearning® system awake to learn the facts, and the CYM system asleep to program yourself to learn easily and effortlessly.

For instance, if you want to learn Spanish, purchase the Superlearning® Spanish tapes (or other tapes of your choice) and listen to them according to the instructions. Do a SuperSleep™ recording with clearing statements such as *Learning Spanish and I are one. I release and forgive myself for learning Spanish easily. I release and forgive myself for not learning Spanish easily,* etc. Add affirmative statements such as *It is fun to learn Spanish. I learn Spanish easily and effortlessly. I feel comfortable learning Spanish. I enjoy listening to Spanish. I enjoy speaking Spanish. It is simple for me to think in Spanish at will. I can understand when Spanish is spoken to me. I hear the intonations of the language. I mimic the flow of the language. My accent is flawless. I speak Spanish fluidly.* etc.

I've used this approach effectively with people studying for the CPA exam, the Bar exam, the FAA exam, the Morse code exam, and various classes and subjects.

I have a favorite book with sayings that are really meaningful to me. Can I use them in my scripts?

Yes, using books as a foundation for scripts is great! I've done that with several scripts (*Conscious Evolution,* in Chapter 8, for instance). Using the work of experts to develop scripts leverages your ability to *change your mind* in any desired area.

Read through a book the same way you read through the workbook scripts—with a pen in your hand. Mark the ideas that appeal to you and convert them to clearing scripts and short, simple, be here now affirmations. You can convert anything to a script . . . how-to books on sports, crafts, and skill building; self-help books on winning in life, parenting, doing your own taxes; business books on managing change, leading, delegating . . . anything.

**There is no limit to how you can use the program
to improve yourself and your life.**

Experiment with it, and make it yours!

Recording Your Voice to Music:

Simple Technical Instructions

Your Tools

Assemble the following tools to make your *Change Your Mind SuperSleep*™ recording:

1. Recording equipment
2. A blank audiotape/CD
3. A *Change Your Mind* music tape/CD
4. A go-to-sleep introduction
5. A script of suggestion statements (clearing/affirmations)

1. Recording Equipment

It's easy to combine your voice with music to create a recording. You can use a sound-over-sound recording machine, or two cassette recorders, or your computer, or other recording equipment.

Using a Sound-over-Sound Machine

Sound-over-sound machines are dual cassette tape recorders that mix your voice (via a microphone) with music (via a music tape) onto a blank tape. You can also use a child's sing-along machine or karaoke recorder.

To identify a sound-over-sound machine easily, look at the microphone plug-in spot. If it says MIX MIC, that machine is a sound-over-sound model. *(Dubbing and sound-over-sound are not the same.)*

Once you have located a sound-over-sound machine, check the instructions with it. General instructions for most machines are

1. Place the function selector of the cassette recorder in the dubbing-normal position.
2. Place the *Change Your Mind* music tape/CD in the playing side.
3. Place the blank tape in the recording side.
4. Plug the earphones into the jack that says headphones (optional).
5. Plug the microphone into the jack on the recorder labeled mixing mike. Turn the microphone on.
6. Simultaneously push the play button on the music tape and the play and record buttons on the blank tape.
7. Both tapes should be turning. You will hear the music in the earphones. Begin speaking into the microphone.

Using Two Cassette Recorders
1. Put the *Change Your Mind* music tape/CD in one recorder (A) and place it close to the other machine (B).
2. Put the blank tape in B.
3. Plug the microphone into B (optional, if B has a built-in mike).
4. Push the play button on the A machine and the play and record buttons on the B machine.
5. Both tapes will be turning. You will hear the music. Begin speaking into the microphone.

Using Your Computer
If you have the computer equipment and expertise to create recordings, great. One of my clients is a computer programmer. He reads his script into his computer, which is programmed to repeat each sentence three times to an eight-second cadencing with a background music CD playing. He sets the entire program to start at 2:30 A.M., and his computer plays his script for him while he sleeps.

Using Other Recording Equipment
Use any equipment that works for you. The objective is to record a script and listen to it while you sleep. Any method that meets that objective is a good method.

2. A Blank Audiotape/CD

You need a blank as long as your script. For a single-issue script for a quick result (such as being relaxed in an interview), a shorter blank will work. For a standard script that clears several issues, you will need a longer blank.

To estimate how many statements you can get on a tape/CD, figure one affirmation every 24 seconds. Then determine the length of your go-to-sleep introduction. Also determine if you will listen to both sides of your recording each night.

For instance, if you have a six-minute go-to-sleep introduction and a ninety-minute tape you are playing on auto reverse, you have eighty-four minutes—or 5,040 seconds—of recording time remaining for your suggestion statements script. You can record 210 suggestion statements.

(90 minutes – 6 minutes of go-to-sleep intro = 84 minutes)

(84 minutes x 60 seconds = 5,040 seconds)

(5,040 seconds ÷ 24 seconds = 210 suggestion statements)

If you have a six-minute go-to-sleep introduction and a ninety-minute tape you are playing on a regular cassette recorder, you will want to have the go-to-sleep introduction on each side of the tape. Consequently, you have thirty-nine minutes—or 2,340 seconds—of recording time on each side of the tape. You can record 97 suggestion statements on each side of the tape.

(45 minutes – 6 minutes of go-to-sleep intro = 39 minutes)

(39 minutes x 60 seconds = 2,340 seconds)

(2,340 seconds ÷ 24 seconds = 97 suggestion statements)

3. A *Change Your Mind* Music Tape/CD

The music behind your script is very specific. You can purchase a *Change Your Mind* Music Tape or you can create your own background music using the music bibliography.

Create a master music recording and do not record over it.

Using the Change Your Mind *Music Tapes*

The *Change Your Mind* Music Tapes are orchestral largo (slow) music used for accelerated learning based on the Lozanov research (see Chapter 6, Music and Cadencing). Each tape is ninety-five minutes long and has a soft tone every eight seconds that signals you when to begin speaking.

Creating Your Own Music Tape

To make your own music tape, select the music pieces of your choice and record them onto a master tape/CD (honoring copyright laws). Design a timing device to alert you to an eight-second cadencing, as you will be saying one statement every eight seconds. You can record a tone onto the music tape, as I have done with the *Change Your Mind* Music Tapes; you can use a metronome; or you can create a timer clock.

After working with many people and techniques over the years, I believe having an eight-second timer tone on the music tape/CD itself is the simplest. That is why I had them created for my use and yours. Create what works best for you.

Sample music:

Vivaldi, A.

  Largo from "Winter" from *The Four Seasons*

  Largo from Concerto in D Major for Guitar and Strings

  Largo from Concerto in C Major for Mandolin, Strings, and Harpsichord

  Largo from Concerto in D Minor for Viola D'Amore, Two Oboes, Bassoon, Two Horns, and Figured Bass

  Largo from Flute Concerto no. 4 in G Major

Handel, G. F.

  Largo from Concerto no. 1 in F

  Largo from Concerto no. 3 in D

  Largo from Concerto no. 1 in B-flat Major, op. 3

Telemann, G.

  Largo from Double Fantasia in G Major for Harpsichord

  Largo from Concerto in G Major for Viola and Strings

Bach, J. S.

  Largo from Concerto in G Minor for Flute and Strings

  Aria (or Sarabande) to "The Goldberg Variations"

  Largo from Harpsichord Concerto in F Minor

  Largo from Solo Harpsichord Concerto in G Minor

  Largo from Solo Harpsichord Concerto in C Major

  Largo from Solo Harpsichord Concerto in F Major

4. A Go-to-Sleep Introduction

To assure that you use your powerful SuperSleep™ state for change, you play your recording while you sleep. So you begin the recording with a go-to-sleep introduction.

Your go-to-sleep introduction is personal; it is anything that puts you to sleep when you hear it. Use any background music you like. If you fall asleep easily, it can be a few minutes of restful music. If you don't, use a relaxation introduction. You may already have a relaxation tape or technique that you use. You can buy a commercially prepared relaxation tape/CD (try health food stores, bookstores, new age catalogs). You can write and record your own relaxation introduction. Or you can use one of the prepared scripts in Chapter 7. Anything that puts you to sleep works.

Create a master go-to-sleep recording and do not record over it.

After you have chosen your go-to-sleep introduction and recorded it, you are ready to record your suggestion statements script.

5. A Suggestion Statements Script

Scripts are provided in Chapters 8, and instructions for writing your personalized scripts are in Chapters 2 and 3.

You're Ready to Record

Begin by recording your go-to-sleep relaxation in a normal voice with a natural speaking rhythm. Use any background music that relaxes you. It is easiest to use the same music for the go-to-sleep relaxation and the script. If you have a master recording of your introduction, copy it onto the beginning of your tape/CD.

When you have completed recording your go-to-sleep introduction, record your suggestion statements script over your special music.

Repeat each sentence three times:

Mommy and I are one.
Mommy and I are one.
Mommy and I are one.

Repeat each statement to an eight-second cadencing.

If you are using a *Change Your Mind* music tape:

At the sound of the first tone, say statement A.
At the sound of the next tone, say statement A the second time.
At the sound of the next tone, say statement A the third time.
At the sound of the next tone, say statement B.
At the sound of the next tone, say statement B the second time.
At the sound of the next tone, say statement B the third time.
At the sound of the next tone, say statement C.

And continue this cadencing for the entire suggestion statement script.

If you are using your own music tape/CD, devise a system that tracks seconds so you begin saying your statements every eight seconds in the following rhythm:

Second 1–7—*Everything I do adds to my health.*
Second 8–15—*Everything I do adds to my health.*
Second 16–23—*Everything I do adds to my health.*
Second 24–31—*I increase in health daily.*
Second 32–39—*I increase in health daily.*
Second 40–47—*I increase in health daily.*
Second 48–55—*I am full of energy and vitality.*

And continue with this cadencing.

Some statements are short, lasting two to four seconds, and some are longer, lasting six to eight seconds. The length of the statement is not important, but beginning it on the eight-second beat is. If this feels awkward at first, don't worry. The rhythm becomes automatic very quickly.

SuperSleep™ to Your Tape

After you've recorded the script, your work is done. Turn your recording on each night when you go to bed. Your go-to-sleep relaxation will put you to sleep, and your suggestion statements will play while you are in the Super-Sleep™ state.

Listen to your recording at least twenty-one nights.

Don't put any effort into the changes you want—just flow with the process. Your mind/brain is already working for you, making the necessary changes.

After listening to the recording for twenty-one to thirty nights, you may continue or stop listening; it's your choice. If you are comfortable listening and the recording makes you feel good, continue listening. If you feel you are through, stop. You will know what to do next—make another recording, put a recording on that you haven't heard in a while for a refresher, stop listening, or whatever.

You will be changing automatically, so relax and enjoy it.

Questions and Answers

What if I can't go to sleep while the tape/CD is playing?

If you have trouble going to sleep the first or second night, relax and keep listening. On night three, you'll probably go right to sleep. I don't know the magic of *three,* but on the third night 98 percent of the people who have trouble getting to sleep on nights one and two go right to sleep. After you have heard your first recording for twenty-one or more nights, your mind/brain is trained to the method and automatically responds to subsequent tapes.

How many times a night should I play my recording?

Once is enough. I haven't seen any differences in effectiveness or immediacy of results based on repetitive listening. Some people listen only once. Some people use auto-reverse tape machines that play all night.

One engineer hooked up three machines to each other—so one machine triggered the next. He played three ninety-minutes tapes each night, all night long. However, we couldn't identify any added benefits with his system.

How long should I listen?

Listen at least twenty-one to thirty nights. If you want to listen longer, do so. If you want to stop listening, stop. Your mind/brain will give you the signals. If you forget to start your recording, fine. If you are regular in listening to it, fine. Just be sure you have heard it twenty-one to thirty nights. (If you skip a night or more, add a few nights longer.)

A clearing script can create tiredness, irritability, anger, grief, and other emotions. This is a sign you are clearing the negative; it is a natural part of the process. Don't stop listening to your recording if you experience these emotions. Know they will be over soon, and the issue you are clearing will be over for good.

What if I can't listen twenty-one or thirty nights in a row?

That's okay. Just listen to the recording a few extra nights for each night you skip. If you skip one night, add two. If you skip two nights, then add three or so. You will know when to stop listening, so listen until you think it's time to stop. There are no hard rules with this system. It just flows with you.

Can I play the recording during the day? In the car?

You can, but playing your SuperSleep™ recording while you're in the beta brainwave state doesn't create long-term core level change. Playing it during your SuperSleep™ state bypasses the conscious defense mechanisms, reaches a different processing part of your brain, and locks in your messages automatically (see Chapter 6, SuperSleep™ and Changing Your Mind).

If you're listening to a clearing script, you probably won't want to hear it awake. A clearing script deals with your past issues, and your goal is to neutralize and change those messages easily and effortlessly. There is no reason to relive the unpleasant parts of your past while you're awake when you can simply SuperSleep™ through them.

What if I can't hear my voice clearly, or can't hear it over the music?

It doesn't matter. Your SuperSleep™ recording is supraliminal because you write and record it "consciously." It is subliminal because you "listen" to it while you sleep. Even if your voice is inaudible, you "hear" it subconsciously. Most people want to hear their voices clearly and be able to understand what they are saying, but this is not necessary for the tapes to work.

Why should I make my own recording when I can buy one for $20?

If it is easier, purchase a prerecorded SuperSleep™ tape on a related subject. There are dozens of tapes with 180 statements on each tape, so there is a good chance you will get the change you want.

If you try a prerecorded tape and do not get the change you want, you know your issue requires more personal clearing. Then it is important to work with the clearing script (Chapter 2) and your personal language, people, and events.

Whose voice works best for me on a subliminal message?

Research indicates your mother's voice works best, but few people want their mothers to make their recordings. Your voice is next in effectiveness. And any other woman's voice is probably third.

How can I make a real subliminal recording—so I can't hear the voice?

The only difference between a SuperSleep™ recording and a subliminal recording is the loudness of the spoken voice. Turn down the microphone volume or speak more softly, and you will have a "real subliminal."

What quality of tape/CD should I use? What if my recording isn't very good quality?

The SuperSleep™ method changes the brain through words and messages, so the quality of the recording isn't critical. A good-quality recording is much more pleasant to hear, but not necessary. It is possible, however, that a better-quality recording—with clear music—may help the brain stay in theta longer (some research indicates this).

Note: If you are using specific frequencies for brain change, the quality of the recording is critical. Tapes designed to do that are very specific about equipment (a minimum of hertz) and have a left-ear earphone and a right-ear earphone so different frequencies can be sent to different parts of the brain. This program can be combined with those programs (such as hemi-sync), but it is not required for your changes.

What if a suggestion statement lasts longer than eight seconds?

Eight seconds is longer than you think, and most statements will fit into that time frame. Speak at your normal pace, and if a statement exceeds eight seconds, wait for the next tone and talk again. You will have a sixteen-second cadencing for that statement which appears to work also.

How long does it take to make a recording?

Generally, a 90-minute tape takes about two hours to record. Take the length of your recording (30, 60, 72, 90, or 120 minutes) and add 20 to 30 minutes for setting up and testing equipment.

Your first recording may take longer because you are learning the equipment and method. Hook everything up and do a few "testing, testing . . ." statements to gauge the volume of your music and your voice. Record a few statements to get used to the eight-second cadencing system. Then relax and read along easily.

You can make your recording in one sitting with a large block of time, or you can do several shorter sessions. If you're a light sleeper, consider making the recording in one sitting. Turning the recording equipment on and off can produce clicks that may awaken a light sleeper.

What kinds of problems can I have making a recording?

I've seen many "weird" things happen with *Change Your Mind SuperSleep*™ recordings that can't be logically explained. Personally, I've had music tapes go blank when I was working on a script I was resisting, though the same tape had music on it when I tried another script. I've made supraliminal tapes that became inaudible halfway through, though my recording style stayed the same. I've had tapes that recorded to a certain sentence, and then stopped recording. And I've had many clients experience similar incidents.

Linda, a physician who didn't believe in subliminals, couldn't get her machine to work. The machine worked perfectly for me. We stood side by side with the machine playing continuously and passed the microphone between us, talking sequentially. My voice recorded; hers didn't. When she asked my opinion, I told her I thought her disbelief was creating an electrical block. She thought that was preposterous but agreed to approach the machine with a different attitude, and her next sentence recorded perfectly, as did her subsequent tapes.

John agreed to be a guinea pig for the first test tape I made for public sale. He had never used a tape, but Carol, his therapist wife, used them regularly. The tape had a brief health section on it, and John was a sugar and junk food addict. I was interested in John's response, but I was especially interested in Carol's observations of John's eating habits. Carol set John up with a recorder, new batteries, and the tape, and he went to the guest bedroom for the first night. The next morning, they found the tape had only played halfway through. Carol replaced the batteries, thinking they must have been defective, and started the tape where it had stopped—which was exactly where the health affirmations began.

I've experienced dozens of these mechanical incidents, and there is no logical explanation for them.

What if someone else can hear my recording?

If someone else can hear your recording, great! Check with that person to see of s/he minds being "changed," and share a copy of the written script to be sure.

If the person objects to hearing your recording, use earphones or a pillow speaker. Earphones work if you can sleep with them. If you can't sleep in earphones, try a pillow speaker—an ear-sized speaker that plugs into the earphone outlet on your machine and fits into your pillow case just under your ear. Pillow speakers are available in many electronic shops and are reasonably priced (about $10.00).

Also, once people see your changes, they may want to hear your recordings. One woman was asked by her office friends what had happened to her, as she had made so many positive changes so fast. When she told them, they wanted to try it. After that, each time she made a tape for herself, she made copies for her entire office and passed them around!

**May your tapes work so well for you
that your friends want to borrow them!**

— 5 —

What Can I Expect?

You can expect changes! The exact form the changes will take and the time frame for those changes are unpredictable, however. There are as many change profiles as there are individuals using the *Change Your Mind SuperSleep*™ program.

Adventurous people usually find this unpredictability and uncertainty exciting. More conservative people frequently find it uncomfortable or unsettling. People who fear the unknown often find it alarming and frightening. All of these responses are normal based upon individual characteristics and reaction patterns. After working with hundreds of people and observing their responses, I have developed some general guidelines for what you can expect.

I assure you that anything and everything that happens as a result of listening to a SuperSleep™ recording is normal. Every form of reaction and response is normal for the person, the situation, and the pattern that is being cleared, changed, healed, and transformed!

Clearing and Processing

Clearing and *processing* are terms I use to name what you experience while you are listening to the suggestion statements on a SuperSleep™ recording. They are your mind/brain/body's personal and unique way of working through the issues on those statements. They are what is happening while you release and transform your core level thoughts, feelings, and patterns. You are "clearing" the past from your long-term memories, and your "process" to do this can occur on all levels—mental, emotional, physical, and spiritual. This can be intense and is usually over in a few days.

Mentally, you may have long-forgotten memories surface. You may be "cotton-headed," foggy, confused, or unclear for a short time. For instance, if you have issues with overspending and are clearing money, you may think of the times you spent foolishly or extravagantly. You may think nothing in your financial life is working, especially the way you spend money.

Emotionally, you may feel grief, anger, sadness, irritation, remorse—or any unexpressed or unhealed emotion around the issues you are addressing. For instance, if you have trouble saying no and you are clearing assertiveness, you may feel fear of speaking up for yourself. You may reexperience your anger about being ignored, denied, or ridiculed when you spoke up in the past.

Physically, you may become tired, experience flulike symptoms, or have discomfort in areas of your body in which memories/experiences/patterns are stored. For instance, if you had chronic stomachaches during childhood, and you are clearing childhood or family dysfunction, you may experience a stomachache.

Processing is normal and usually over within a few days. When the clearing process is complete, you will have neutral or no feelings about the issues that were on your recording. They will no longer control you, and you will be free to create your future without their influence or effect.

Your processing experiences, while significant, will be minor in comparison with your new freedom from the past, comfort with the present, and faith in the future.

Processing by Past Experiences

It seems logical that your processing is in direct proportion to the significance of the issues you are clearing and neutralizing. If you were raised in a wonderful, loving, stable, open environment and had a peaceful, harmonious life, your processing will probably go unnoticed (and your personalized clearing script will be very short).

To the degree your life experiences vary from that scenario, you will probably (1) have a longer clearing script, (2) not enjoy making your tape, (3) have resistance to releasing and/or forgiving some people or incidents in your life, and (4) have some form of mental, emotional, and physical release during your clearing process.

If you have abuse or abandonment in your past, you can expect significant processing. You may have a few intense days! Once you have completed the clearing process, *you are through with that issue.* It is well worth a few days of discomfort to empty that cup so you can refill it with positive loving experiences and living.

Processing Time Frames

Different people process differently and in different time frames. Those working with the level one clearing (see Chapter 2) have the least significant processing. About half of the people I have worked with on level one scripts process in their sleep and never consciously notice their changes. They often report awakening tired for a few days, as if they had worked all night (which they have, of course). They often clear in three to ten days.

People clearing deeper core level issues often take longer and have more noticeable processing that can involve intense emotions, visual flashbacks, nightmares, and physical discomfort. Most people at this level complete their processing within the twenty-one- to thirty-day "listening" period. A few feel a need to listen longer, and their process may go longer. For instance, one woman with a fifty-year history of severe physical ailments, accidents, and surgeries listened to the recorded tape *Opening to Healing* for six months before feeling physically ready to move on. For her, that was normal.

In contrast, a man who had been physically healthy all his life listened to the same tape for ten days and felt physically fine the entire time. However, in response to the section on emotional healing, he went into significant processing on a past relationship that had ended against his will. He promptly moved on to *Releasing Past Relationships* and his processing on that tape lasted several weeks.

Most people find a pattern in their processing.

Dick did three SuperSleep™ tapes before he recognized his processing time frame. He reported being tired on day one, and on day two he "wanted nails for breakfast." About 3:00 P.M. on day two, everything smoothed out. His process was consistent: each tape he did after that, he experienced his breakthrough around 3:00 P.M. on day two.

Marilyn kept a journal while listening to her *Self-love* clearing tape. Day 1: Made tape. Felt myself rebelling against some of the statements. Day 2: Did not use tape. Day 3: Used tape. Had trouble going to sleep. Day 4: Restless night. Was tired all day and didn't feel good. Day 5: Again a restless night and tired all day. Did not feel good about myself. Played tape and couldn't fall asleep. Day 6: Unorganized day but felt all right about myself. Dinner out with friends whose lifestyle I admire, but I didn't envy them. Day 7: Fell asleep right away. Day 8: Felt confident. Well-balanced day. Listened to tape. Good feeling. Day 9: Feel better. Another well-balanced day. Day 10: Good day for accomplishing things, taking charge of life. Did not listen to tape. Day 11: Feel good and now I'm in control.

The first level of attitude and behavior change is usually immediate. This can begin a chain reaction in other areas of your life that may take a year or more to fully integrate. When I am working with core level issues that I have named soul imbalances and transgenerational patterns, I sometimes take two years for full integration and complete lifestyle change, redirection, and transformation. Of course, without this process, I would probably never get those transformational changes at all!

Processing by Emotional Style

Your emotional style of processing SuperSleep™ recordings will follow your emotional norm, whatever that is. If you respond to emotional situations with fear or anger, you'll probably get scared or angry. If you respond to emotional situations with hurt and tears, you'll probably feel hurt or cry. If you respond to emotional situations by withdrawing, you'll probably withdraw.

Mary, a thirty-year-old office manager, had coped with difficult situations in her teen years by running away. She did a combination clearing and success-for-women script. On day three listening to her tape, she impulsively walked out of her office, got in her car, and drove more than two hundred miles. She called me long-distance from a pay phone to report her actions. Laughing, she said she saw her patterns clearly now. As an abused teen, she had run away from home, and she had been running away from bad situations ever since. As she drove the two hundred miles back home, the whole issue and her need to escape were dissolved. She has not run away from a situation since.

People who have ignored or denied their emotions for a long time often experience a release of those emotions. They get angry (if they have ignored or denied their anger) or grief-stricken (if they have ignored or denied their grief).

Bob, a southern gentleman stockbroker/manager, did a combination clearing and success-for-men script. On day four listening to his tape, he called a meeting of his staff and climbed on the conference table, yelling. He said he knew what the staff had been doing for six months and he wasn't going to let them get away with it anymore. Everyone was surprised with his outburst, including him. When he recovered from his embarrassment, he reported he was glad he did it. He reestablished his leadership, and his staff "got back in line."

Grace had a kidney disease and recorded the *Healing: Christian* script (see Chapter 8, *Healing: Christian*). She became exhausted and sad and cried for three days. Upon review, she told me her husband had died a year before. She had not accepted his death and had never grieved. The healing tape for her kidney disease triggered that buried grieving for her husband. She experienced seven tumultuous grief-filled days and then moved on with her life in peace.

Processing by Hemispheric Dominance

The left-brain processors (logical, sequential thinkers; verbal expressers) often process verbally. They talk about each issue as it comes up for clearing. In most cases, that verbal release completes the clearing process.

A left-brained couple, Mark and Mary, did their clearing tapes the same week. At dinner on the fifth night, they talked for hours about the issues on their tapes. Then they looked at each other and said, "Why are we talking about this? Who cares about this old stuff?" They've been clear and neutral about each of those issues ever since.

The right-brain processors (visual, emotive, creative) often process in images. They see pictures float up from the past, see old scenes, dream about the people and issues involved. In most cases, that visualization completes the clearing process.

The more extreme right brainers (about 5 percent of the people I have observed) seem to process in bad dreams or nightmares. Often, one person or issue clears per nightmare, which can mean several nights of bad dreams.

Jane was clearing incest issues with three male family members. For three nights, she had nightmares. In each nightmare, she killed an offender—one per night. The nightmares disturbed her logical waking mind, but she kept listening to her tape until she felt neutral and complete with the issue. At the next family gathering, she saw all three of the abusers and was comfortable in their presence—not intimidated or frightened or shamed as she had been in the past. Jane is confident and self-determined now, and rebuilding her personal and professional life in healthy ways.

Processing by Gender

There appears to be gender-based processing patterns as well. For instance, the connection between the left and right hemispheres, the corpus callosum, is larger in women than men. Women process information more holistically, sharing it between the hemispheres. Men's brains are more separate or divided, and they focus on one side or the other more readily.

This could result in women and men responding differently to the SuperSleep™ recordings. About half of the men I have observed go into denial about the tape working.

John came in because he did nothing but "veg out." He was receiving workers' compensation which just paid for his subsistence lifestyle. Supposedly, John worked as a real estate agent, but he admitted he really spent his days going from the TV to the refrigerator and back. He had no direction, no motivation, and no joy. We did some scripts for him. On the tenth day, he told me the tape wasn't working. He was very angry about wasting money on a tape that wasn't working because he needed the money for his house payment. I asked him how much TV he was watching each day now, and he exploded, "Watch TV! Why would I watch TV? There's nothing worth watching on TV. I've got too much to do to watch TV." John made one tape every ten days, and by the thirtieth day he was expressing impatience that he didn't have everything in place yet—he had so many plans.

About 10 percent of the men I've observed deny ever hearing the recording, much less having it work. Joseph made a tape for himself and called me every day to report he was not able to sleep. He was angry, and according to him, he was exhausted after being up all night every night struggling with his tape. After three weeks, I suggested he simply abandon the program, as it obviously wasn't working for him. The following day, Joseph's wife called me. We had never met, but she told me they were good Christians (Joseph was a minister), and she could not listen to her husband telling me untruths any longer. She said she was the one not sleeping, as her husband's deep and loud snoring was keeping her awake. Clearly, he had been asleep every night, and she just wanted me to know he really was sleeping. I don't know if one, both, or neither of them were sleeping, but they both made the desired life changes addressed on the tape.

Questions and Answers

Why can't I tell when it's working?

Some people can tell right away, but most of us go through a denial stage. The five stages of change are denial, anger, bargaining, depression, and acceptance. If you're lucky, you go through all five stages in your sleep. Most people I have observed go into denial on the conscious level and don't think the recordings are working, even though their behavior is changing daily.

When I reviewed my very first scripts on goal setting and time management, I decided I must have made them to experiment with the system, as I certainly never needed them! I had already made the changes and integrated them so completely that I couldn't remember my pretape behavior.

Will I become dependent on these recordings?

Because SuperSleep™ works so quickly and so well, you might use it a lot. But I haven't observed anyone becoming dependent on it. Remember, the more recordings you SuperSleep™ to, the healthier you get, which means the less dependent upon external sources you become.

If you are concerned about becoming dependent on this approach, simply write a clearing script/affirmation script to dissolve the issue. Use a format like this:

Being dependent on SuperSleep™ and I are one.
I release and forgive myself for being dependent on SuperSleep™.

I release and forgive myself for not being dependent on SuperSleep™.

I dissolve all imbalances on the soul level around being dependent on SuperSleep™.

I dissolve all imbalances on the soul level around fearing being dependent on SuperSleep™.

I transcend being dependent on SuperSleep™ .

Being dependent on and using SuperSleep™ are separate for me now.

I am fully conscious of how and when I use SuperSleep™.

I recognize my true reasons for using SuperSleep™.

I use SuperSleep™ at all appropriate times and in all appropriate ways.

I use SuperSleep™ for the right reasons.

I use SuperSleep™ to increase my health.

I use SuperSleep™ to increase my personal power and strength.

I use SuperSleep™ to _____.

Can a SuperSleep™ recording hurt me?

I have no experience of a SuperSleep™ recording hurting anyone. However, in the early days of experimentation, we wrote some loosely worded statements that led us to actions we didn't intend to take.

For instance, when I first realized the method really worked, I got very excited. I decided to write a script to get everything I wanted. Struggling to write that script, I realized I didn't know what I wanted. I had spent my life focusing on my have to's, ought to's, shoulds, and musts, without much thought for my "wants." Unable to determine what I really wanted, I simply recorded *I know what I want and I do it.*

At the time, I was a full-time college teacher and was building a management consulting/training company. I wanted to do the consulting/training full-time, but my teaching salary was still my primary income. After three days of SuperSleep™, I resigned from my teaching position. Fortunately, the dean refused my resignation and urged me to rethink it. Of course, it was much wiser to stay in that job until my consulting/training income exceeded my teaching income. In addition, I was positioned to vest in the teacher retirement program in another three years of employment. So I wrote and recorded a new statement for myself, *I know what I want, and I do it as appropriate.* I stayed in the teaching position three more years, and I am enjoying the benefits of that decision every month.

Since then, I have uncovered a core issue around my doing and having. I was taught I could do anything I was "big enough" to do, but there would always be things I couldn't have. Consequently, I wrote the statement "I know what I want and I *DO* it. My mind did not allow me to *HAVE* it." Before I developed my comprehensive scripting formulas, my scripts simply mirrored my existing limitations. As Albert Einstein said, "Our present problems cannot be solved at the level of thinking at which they were created."

If I had originally written the statement, *I know what I want and I have it,* I might have focused on *having* the financial aspects (instead of *doing* the consulting/training) and not resigned. Subtle refinements in scripting like this have taken years to discover, uncover, rework, and revise. And the results have been well worth the effort!

Most important, I have expanded my "play detective" approach in two specific areas: (1) ways the wording/phrasing of a script statement can be limiting, and (2) ways our minds can act and react to a suggestion statement that created different results than we intended. This deep level of investigation and analysis brings a self-awareness that is a mind-changing activity on its own.

Will I hurt anyone while I'm clearing and processing?

I have no experience of anyone hurting any living thing using Super-Sleep™. I do have one case of a person acting out violence against an object.

Roy made a tape and called me on mornings one, two, and three to say he hadn't heard his tape yet. We decided he had so much resistance he was "sabotaging" putting the tape on at night, though the recorder was right beside his bed. On the fourth morning, he reported he had still not heard his tape—at least as far as he knew. But he wanted me to know that he found his tape recorder in pieces on the floor across the room from his bed that morning, where it had apparently been smashed against the wall. He was a former CIA agent who had spent years controlling his emotions—primarily fear and anger. An interesting side note about Roy: he had worked extensively with hypnosis. His intellectual understanding of the brain and how to program it did not change the intensity of his emotional processing or the need for his clearing and healing.

You may say things while you are clearing and processing that you would not *normally* say. These are things you have been thinking/feeling and not saying. I often become brutally blunt when I am clearing and processing, so I avoid teaching, training and meeting with clients during those times.

For instance, while I was processing one of my most intense scripts, I mistakenly took a phone call from a management consulting client. I had been doing team building for one of her groups for two years and had just completed a *no-holds-barred* session to bring the dysfunctional group back into productivity. The manager calling me was most of the teams' problem, as she was always "stirring the pot" and keeping everyone off center to maintain control. That day, in response to her drama, I *unloaded*. I told her she reminded me of a child playing in a sandpile, hoarding the shovel and pail, and she was the problem. Needless to say, I lost that consulting contract.

How will I know if it is working?

Because you are interacting with your unconscious mind, the conscious mind may or may not recognize the changes. I have observed many people who vehemently deny the program is working, though they are changing daily. I have observed others who recognize subtle changes in themselves and their habits and patterns. I believe this is determined by the person's level of self-awareness and ability to see himself or herself objectively.

Consider keeping a journal. Date each script and note your behavior and feelings for three or four weeks. In three months, review your notes. And listen to feedback from family and friends. They'll probably notice your changes before you do.

For me, the ability to recognize my changes increased after I made a tape to see myself objectively and recognize the effect of the tapes on my everyday life. If you are interested in tracking your changes, you can try this approach.

It is easier to determine if a script is working that directs you to change your behavior. For instance, if you listen to a recording stating you drink at least eight glasses of water each day, you can monitor that behavior. You either do or do not drink the water. It is a yes or no answer.

Monitoring results with emotional clearing scripts is more subtle. The script has worked when you no longer react emotionally to a situation that would have triggered an emotional response from you before. You may continue the mental habit of thinking about that issue for a while, but you will not have any emotional reactions or responses to it.

Charlotte wrote me about her first clearing script dealing with childhood abuse: "I have not listened to my tape except in my sleep. Today as I sat down to write you and write another script, I picked up my clearing script to go over it. I couldn't do it. As I started to read it, it became boring, and I threw it away." Clearly, she no longer reacted emotionally to those past experiences. Consequently, they no longer controlled her or had power over her.

May all of your negative past
become just too boring for you to read or go over again!

What Is SuperSleep™ and How Does It Work?

Understanding the Research

There's a revolution going on . . . The present era in neuroscience is compara-
ble to the time when Louis Pasteur first found that germs cause disease.
Neurochemist Candace Pert

Brainwave States

Brainwaves are the rhythm of the brain. They are electrical signals or pat-terns generated by brain cells (neurons) and other brain structures. When a large number of neurons beat together in synchrony, they create a strong rhythm/pattern/signal/wave that can be detected on the scalp sur-face by electrical monitoring equipment (electroencephalograph—EEG). This equipment measures the vibrations in cycles per second (cps) called hertz (Hz) and graphically charts them—EEG brain mapping. A thin line on the graph means faster brainwaves, and a curving/spiking line on the graph means slower brainwaves.

Currently, brainwave states are generally categorized as follows:

High Beta, which ranges from 29 to 100+ Hz: the research on these higher frequencies is relatively new and there is much to be learned. Up to 35–40 Hz is anxiety and stress. Yet the higher frequencies are higher states of functioning.

Beta, which ranges from 14 to 28 Hz: the brainwave state of normal wak-ing consciousness—of logical thought, analysis, concentration, alertness, problem solving, and action. You are in beta most of your waking hours—when you are thinking, speaking, and doing, and when you are reading this book. In beta, you discern, compare, judge, and criticize.

Alpha, which ranges from 8 to 14 Hz: the brainwave state of relaxation—of pleasant feeling states, automatic and routine activities (nonthinking ac-

68

tivities such as brushing your teeth), freedom from pain, and physical healing. You are in alpha when you are feeling soothed and calm—relaxing, letting your mind wander, daydreaming, bathing or showering, meditating, praying, letting go, dissolving into the environment, drifting off to sleep, being in a twilight state.

In alpha, you have rapid learning with heightened memory. You may experience an altered sense of time, free association (nonlogical), and extrasensory perception. Alpha is the doorway to the nonconscious. It is conducive to creative imagery and personal psychotherapeutic insights—the "awakened mind."

Theta, which ranges between 4 and 8 Hz: the brainwave state of deep meditation, sleep and sleeplike states, and dreaming sleep. You are in theta when you are in deep reverie. When you are awake, it brings quietness of body, emotions, and mind and builds a bridge between the conscious and nonconscious. This waking state is associated with creative people and hypnotic susceptibility.

Delta, which is below 4 Hz: the brainwave state of deep dreamless sleep—a deep trancelike nonphysical state.

The process of learning to identify and control your brainwave states is called brainwave training, biofeedback, neurofeedback, and neurotherapy. Using EEG instruments, you learn to identify your brainwave states and to change or produce them at will. Depending on the condition or change desired, treatments last from several to fifty sessions. Do-it-yourselfers can work with brainwave states through simple electroencephalography computer programs and light and sound machines (available through wellness catalogs and internet sites).

Biofeedback is best known for its stress reduction origins, but it is emerging as a tool to treat attention-deficit disorder, migraines, epilepsy, anxiety, learning disabilities, depression, head injuries, seizures, sleep disorders, chronic fatigue, headaches, posttraumatic stress disorder, mood swings, alcohol abuse, and addiction.

For instance, many individuals with attention problems produce more slow brainwaves (theta) and fewer fast brainwaves (beta). Slower brainwaves indicate daydreaming, reverie, and other forms of mental drifting, while faster brainwaves indicate concentration. Individuals trained to reduce their amount of slow brainwaves and produce larger amounts of beta increase their attention and concentration time.

I encourage you to work with your brainwave states in any healthy positive way that works for you. To get a list of brainwave training practitioners, send a stamped, self-addressed envelope to The Association of Applied Psychophysiology and Biofeedback, 10200 W. 44 Avenue, Suite 304, Wheat Ridge, CO 80033.

Of course, changing while I sleep is the easiest method for me!

SuperSleep™ and Changing Your Mind

I believe REM sleep (functions) are in fact the Freudian unconscious.
—Jonathan Winson, psychiatrist and brain researcher

I believe REM is where the action is for transformation.
—Teri Mahaney, creator of the Change Your Mind method

The theta REM sleep state is your SuperSleep™ state. Sleep states are divided into two main types: Rapid Eye Movement (REM) dreaming sleep and non–Rapid Eye Movement (NREM) sleep. Mammals (except spiny anteaters) and birds have REM, while reptiles do not. About 25 percent of total sleep is spent in REM and 75 percent is spent in NREM. Adults experience four or five REM cycles per night, and infants are in REM about eight hours a day.

REM sleep is a puzzling state because it appears paradoxical and self-contradictory. While your heart rate and breathing are higher during REM sleep (which means light sleep), your muscles are more relaxed and it is harder to awaken from this state (which means deep sleep). Your eyes dart and flit, your pulse surges, your breathing is rapid and irregular, and you have fine finger movement. To observe this, watch a cat sleep. During REM sleep, a cat's whiskers, tail, ears, and paws twitch.

Neuroscientists are learning what areas of the brain and what combinations of brain cells are essential for specific tasks such as learning and encoding memory. Jonathon Winson, noted brain researcher, had found that theta rhythm hits the memory center when an animal is learning things essential to survival. For instance, cats display theta in their memory centers when stalking prey: rabbits display theta in their memory centers when they are afraid of a predator. Winson has shown that the very same "memory" brain cells that register animals' learning during wakefulness are reactivated when the animals go into REM sleep. He believes information processing occurs during REM sleep, which merges the new information with the old memories. He states REM is the neural process whereby, from early childhood on, strategies for behavior are being set down, consulted, or modified.

Other researchers, psychiatrists, and scientists agree the theta brainwave state is the key to changing your mind:

Thomas Budzynski, a biofeedback researcher, describes the theta state as "a zone . . . in which one can absorb new information in an uncritical, non-analytical fashion." He speculated that this allows new information to bypass the critical filters of the left hemisphere and be "learned" by the right hemisphere. Therefore, information leading to a change in self-concept, change in belief system, and change of habitual behaviors would occur more easily in theta. "In theta, behavior and belief systems change more easily, as we bypass the critical and logical beta state. We absorb new information in an uncritical, non-analytical fashion." (Dixon, *Subliminal Perception*)

Norman Dixon states that emotionally determined memories are more affected by subliminal messages, making this brainwave state the most appropriate for changing emotional memories or emotional patterns subliminally. (Dixon, *Subliminal Perception*)

Gary Lynch states for memories to form, long-term potentiation (LT) must take place. The LT process involves electrical and chemical changes in the neurons associated with memory, and the key to LT is the theta brainwave pattern. "We have found the magic rhythm that makes LT is the theta brainwave pattern." (Lynch, "The Biochemistry of Memory")

James Chalet states the theta brainwave state has specific mental-processing functions, and "it seems reasonable to assume that sleep is a particularly favorable time for strengthening and consolidating memories."

Gene Brockopp states that we may facilitate an individual's ability to allow more variations in functioning through breaking up patterns at the neural level. This moves the individual away from habit patterns of behavior to develop elegant strategies of functioning.

By listening to your *Change Your Mind* SuperSleep™ recordings while you sleep, you bridge the conscious and nonconscious. Working in your Super-Sleep™ state, you mix the new learning (the statements on your recording) with your long-term memories. The old is dissolved and integrated, and you create new ways of thinking, feeling, and acting.

Mommy and I Are One

Dr. Lloyd Silverman of New York University blazed the trail for psychologically sound subliminal "therapy." Working with the idea that conflicting wishes in the subconscious often underlie mental problems, he began using subliminal messages with schizophrenics. He found he could increase or decrease their symptoms dramatically by using different subliminal messages. He eventually discovered one simple five-word sentence that had universal effects when given subliminally, yet lost its effectiveness when given supraliminally. This sentence became the subject of hundreds of subliminal research projects and has proven effective with programs for weight loss, smoking cessation, alcoholism, and academic achievement.

The sentence—*Mommy and I are one.*

Dr. Silverman believes *Mommy and I are one* is a symbiotic fantasy or fantasy of merging, and that merging with the "good mother of infancy" is a sort of archetypal experience that paradoxically allows us to become self-sustaining individuals.

Mommy and I are one seems to fulfill a number of psychological needs, but its strength may lie beyond psychology. Fantasies of oneness have been interpreted psychologically as an unconscious desire to return to the womb—the prebirth state of safety and comfort—when we were one with the mother. This state of preexistence (before the pain of birth and the agony of a separate existence) is considered the unconscious source of religious myths about a lost paradise. Conditions such as alcoholism, drug addiction, violence, and suicide are viewed psychoanalytically as stemming from the unresolved desire to return to this "oneness."

Spiritually, mystics maintain that meditation creates oneness with a cosmic consciousness, and the merging or reconnecting with spirit (God) is at the heart of all major religions. Perhaps *Mommy and I are one* sparks this oneness as well. Clearly, including this statement in a *Change Your Mind* SuperSleep™ recording meets many needs.

Another way to spark this oneness is with music.

Music and Cadencing

Ancient cultures used the natural power of sound and music to influence states of consciousness both for religious ceremonies and to increase psychological and physical health. Today, the idea that sound can affect consciousness is widely accepted.

Several researchers found that seventeenth- and eighteenth-century composers encoded certain harmonics, tones that resonate high above the audible music, into their pieces. Leading-edge brain research suggests the neurons of the brain resonate to these harmonics, leading to a state of health, healing, and greater personal awareness.

Georgi Lozanov, a Bulgarian physician and psychologist, incorporated this music into his system of learning called Suggestopedia or Suggestology in Europe and Superlearning® in the United States. Lozanov found that people performing supernormal feats of memory had a relaxed state of body during their heightened state of mind. Their brain waves were at alpha and their heartbeat was slowed. He experimented with classical music to induce that relaxed state (which was much easier than having his subjects practice years of mental yoga, meditation, and mind control to get the same results).

Lozanov studied the baroque composers—Vivaldi, Telemann, Corelli, Handel—and found that the slower (largo) sections of their music induce a meditative state. Each of these sections of music has sixty beats to the minute, which slows the heartbeat and relaxes the body while leaving the mind alert.

Lozanov's next step was to study rhythm and learning. Material presented at one second intervals was retained at a rate of 20 percent. With five-second intervals, the retention rate jumped to 30 percent. At ten-seconds intervals, the retention rate rose to 40 percent. Americans using the Lozanov system found that the eight-second cadencing was most effective. To learn more about the Lozanov method, read *Superlearning*® by Sheila Ostrander and Lynn Schroeder.

Your *Change Your Mind* SuperSleep™ recordings are based on this research. The music is created from the largo sections of baroque symphonies, and the suggestion statements are repeated three times to an eight-second cadencing. This assures their effectiveness.

Subliminals and Supraliminals

Subliminal perception, or the concept of discrimination by the brain without conscious awareness by the person, is a scientific fact. Your brain takes in messages below your level of conscious awareness, and it responds to those messages. "Subliminal perception is not just a 'watered down' version of normal perception . . . but different in kind" as well. (Somekh, "Perception Without Awareness") Laboratory research projects have repeatedly demonstrated that subliminal messages affect your dreams, memory, verbal behavior, emotional responses, drive-related behavior, conscious perception, and perceptual thresholds.

In everyday language, the words *subliminal* and *supraliminal* are commonly used for subthreshold (below the threshold) and supra-threshold (above the threshold). Your threshold is your point of conscious awareness. For instance, if you are listening to a recording with a spoken message on it, and you can consciously hear the words and understand them, you are receiving a message above your threshold. This is called a supraliminal message. If you can't hear the words, you are receiving a message below your threshold, called a subliminal message.

Most laboratory subliminal research is based on visual experiments that are conducted using a tachistocope, a device that flashes words or pictures onto a screen at intervals of four milliseconds or less. Very little research has been done on verbal subliminal messages (subaudible messages) in which a voice is embedded under music, ocean waves, or nature sounds so that it cannot be heard.

Some research has been done on the effectiveness of subliminal versus supraliminal messages, however, and on the effectiveness of using the two together. Howard Shevrin presents words both above and below conscious detection levels—supraliminally and subliminally—and analyzes the response of brainwaves recorded at the moment each stimulus is delivered. Both supraliminal and subliminal messages cause brainwave activity, but this does not mean behavior change will follow. One study showed perception could be altered with subliminal messages, but supraliminal messages were necessary to change physical performance such as learning a new sport. To change a sensory task required a combination of subliminal and supraliminal messages. (Zenhausern and Hansen, "Differential Effect of Subliminal and Supraliminal Accessory Stimulation")

In addition, research shows that "emotionally laden messages must be shown longer than neutral messages before a subject will respond to them." (Garner) In addition, each of us has a unique subconscious that gives different affective and motivational meaning to the same messages. (Dixon, *Subliminal Perception*) While this can be strikingly demonstrated in individuals, it has been difficult to repeat in experimental settings. (Westerlundh, "Subliminal Influence on Imagery")

Simply stated, each person responds differently to the same subliminal message, making it difficult to generalize about results from any research model that looks for similarities. Each of us has a different and unique set of experiences, beliefs, feelings, and thoughts in our brains (mental patterns) that interact with new messages, whether they are supraliminal or subliminal, and create responses unique for us.

The *Change Your Mind* SuperSleep™ program incorporates all these factors to create an effective program that works for you. When you create a personal recording, it is both subliminal and supraliminal. You know consciously what is on the recording, and you listen to it subliminally. The script is written about your unique issues in your words, so the subject and language are personally meaningful for you. You get to direct your changes.

Questions and Answers

Do all brain researchers agree theta is the subconscious?

I've never found any cutting-edge area in which all researchers agree! I've summarized some of the research that supports this belief. My beliefs are based on seventeen years of observation of myself and hundreds of others using the program.

REM sleep doesn't last that long. How can I stay in the SuperSleep™ state while my recording plays?

The background music can stabilize your brainwave state so you remain in the SuperSleep™ state throughout the recording. See the section on music and cadencing.

Is SuperSleep™ like hypnosis?

Yes and no. The yes is that both SuperSleep™ and hypnosis involve working with a person in a lower brainwave state to deliver new messages that will make a positive difference. The no is that hypnosis occurs in low alpha to high theta brainwave states, while SuperSleep™ is the REM theta state.

An interesting note about hypnosis is that highly hypnotizable people generate more theta activity than low-susceptible (difficult to hypnotize) people.

I've used subliminal tapes before and they didn't work. Why not?

Subliminal suggestions work, but getting the right message to your mind/brain in the right way is the key to your personal success. There are many possible reasons the commercial tapes don't work for you:

1. Most commercial subliminal tapes have ten to twelve messages embedded under the music. If one of those messages doesn't click for you, that tape won't work for you.
2. More than 95 percent of the commercial subliminal tapes are recorded in the male voice (a few are now co-recorded male/female voices). My observations indicate many women don't accept subliminal messages in a male voice. So, if you're female, most commercial tapes may not work for you.
3. Some commercial subliminals are well written, but some are poorly written and are totally ineffective, and some are so inferior they actually worsen the conditions they are meant to correct.
4. Some tapes claim to be subliminal that are really music only. There is no recorded message under the music.

Sometimes you can't find the answers to what works and what doesn't, as a 1989 University of Northern Colorado study shows. A weight loss tape from one of the major tape producers was studied for sixteen weeks. Sixty people were divided into three groups:

Group A listened to a tape with music only.
Group B listened to a tape with music and a subliminal message on weight loss in both male and female voice.
Group C listened to a tape with the same message as Group B, both supraliminally in a male voice, and subliminally in a male and female voice.

At the end of six weeks

Group A, the music only group, lost more weight than Group B.
Group B, the music and subliminal message group, had no visible trends of weight loss, and some actually gained weight.
Group C, the music and supraliminal and subliminal message group, lost the most weight.

The researcher is still trying to find some explanation for this one! (Herman, interview)

How long have subliminals been around?

Subliminals are not new. For centuries, they have been used in physical and emotional healing and education. For instance, practitioners of ancient disciplines used a "whispering technique" to help students memorize lessons. The teacher whispered behind other sounds (strong winds, ocean waves, musical instruments) so students couldn't consciously hear the whispered lesson. We are not using subliminal learning today, though it is becoming more widely accepted for self-help.

What is subliminal advertising?

It is something very different in advertising than in the research laboratory. In advertising, it originally meant triggering a pleasant thought or association with an ad so the consumer would buy the product. One study involved Chivas Regal and Marlboro. An ad photo of Chivas Regal scotch whiskey was manipulated to include a "subliminal" naked woman image. The ad with the image got higher ratings for credibility, attractiveness, sensuality, and the likelihood the viewers might buy the product than the ad without the woman image. A similar study with a male sexual image in a Marlboro ad did not score higher ratings, however.

Subliminal advertising has a more subtle side today. One form it has taken is "cinematic product placement" and "plugging" in motion pictures. Movies advertise products "subliminally" by prominently placing them on the screen or by mentioning specific brand names in the dialogue. For this placement and plugging, the movie producers receive large sponsorship fees to help finance making the film. (Miller, "Hollywood: The Ad")

I heard about a movie theater that flashed messages on the screen to get people to buy popcorn. Did it work?

James M. Vicary, a motivational researcher and amateur psychologist serving as Vice President of the Subliminal Projection Company, supposedly tried this. On September 12, 1957, Vicary held a press conference to announce a six-week ad campaign at a New Jersey movie theater to sell popcorn and cokes. Using special equipment, his company flashed messages on the movie screen for 1/3,000 of a second saying "Hungry? Eat popcorn." And "Drink Coca-Cola." Vicary announced sales rose dramatically, but he never produced sales figures to prove his claims. Evidently, the entire thing was a sales gimmick to promote the Subliminal Projection Company. Vicary coined the term *subliminal advertising* to describe this form of advertising.

I've heard some stores use subliminals to stop shoplifting. Is that true?

Yes. Subliminals are being used in various business settings. One New Orleans supermarket buried honesty and productivity messages under background music and reversed cash register shortages and stealing, while two others reduced employee turnover. The McDonagh Medical Center used relaxation messages subliminally in the clinic which reduced patient anxiety 60 percent and eliminated patient fainting during treatment. Two surprising side effects were the development of more harmonious working relationships and the reduction of smoking among the medical staff members. (Schroeder and Ostrander, "Subliminal Report")

I want to know more about why SuperSleep™ works. What else can I study?

You can do a literature search and find thousands of references to follow up. Before you start that, I suggest you do a clearing script on the "knowing" being more important than the "doing," and the "doing" being more important than the "being." I include the research chapter to provide foundation and credibility to the program. Understanding the research is not the goal. Living a better life is the goal. While I enjoy understanding my brainwave states, I find it much more pleasurable to *experience* alpha than to read about it!

May your understanding of your brain serve as support for you to *experience* a clear, calm, highly functioning mind!

What is the best way to use SuperSleep™?

The best way to use SuperSleep™ is the way that it works for you. My purpose is to empower you to heal and lead a clear, purposeful, joyful life. My experience has proven to me that working with the REM brainwave state is the easiest, fastest, most direct way to transform the core level issues that block healing.

I believe the *Change Your Mind* SuperSleep™ program is the most comprehensive self-help method developed. It can go into any area of your life. You can't outgrow it. You can use it alone or in combination with other brainwave trainings and therapies. I used biofeedback and sound therapy while I was developing the program. Now I SuperSleep™ for my "brain changes," and get body work for the physical integration of those changes.

I believe the inner journey is a private journey. With guidance, we can be our own experts. My intention is for this book to provide some of that guidance for you—to become your own self-directed expert at changing your life . . . your way.

Good luck, and go for it!

— 7 —

Go-to-Sleep Introduction Scripts

To reach your powerful SuperSleep™ state, you must be asleep while your suggestion statements play. So you begin each recording with something that puts you to sleep easily.

Your go-to-sleep introduction can be any length—as short as four minutes and as long as twenty-five minutes—and you can use any background music you like. Use music only, use a prerecorded relaxation, or create your own. Your SuperSleep™ recording is tailored to your style and your needs, so enjoy the process.

When selecting a go-to-sleep introduction, use the relaxation technique that fits you. There are two kinds of relaxation techniques:

Progressive (body) relaxation: an actual tensing-relaxing of specific muscle groups that leads to physical relaxation

Meditation (mind) relaxation: imagination exercises that lead you somewhere in your mind, often taking you down an escalator or on a walk in nature.

While both of these techniques may work for you, research indicates that many people respond to only one type of relaxation. If your body is usually tense but your mind is clear, try a progressive (body) relaxation technique. Conversely, if your mind is usually anxious, try a meditation (mind) relaxation technique. Research indicates that "low suggestibility" people—those who don't take suggestion easily—respond better to progressive relaxation, while people who are suggestible respond better to meditation relaxation.

If you haven't used relaxation techniques before, experiment and discover your own style. Purchase relaxation recordings and try them, or work with these relaxation scripts. Often, you can tell which relaxation works best for you by reading the script and noticing your response. If reading the script relaxes you, it will probably put you to sleep. You can have someone read the script to you, or you can record it and feel your response while you are listening.

When I started using the program, my introduction started with "As I listen to the music, I begin to relax. I release the tiredness, the tension, the frustrations of my day." I added a progressive relaxation that included deep breathing and relaxing my shoulders (which are routinely tight). Then I visualized a rubber band stretched tight as it went loose and limp on a table-top. After hearing a few tapes, my mind/brain became "trained" to the relaxation process and responded easily. As a bonus, I was able to relax at will during the day by simply visualizing a rubber band stretched tight as it went loose and limp.

You might receive the bonus of biofeedback or antistress relaxation from your go-to-sleep introduction also. Many people do. Once your mind/brain has repeatedly heard the statements, they can lock in as a relaxation trigger. Then, whenever you hear those words or see those images, you automatically relax. Try it. After you have heard your go-to-sleep introduction three or more nights, try it during the day for relaxation. When you are feeling tired, tense, or irritable, repeat a few lines of your introduction to yourself in your mind or out loud (or visualize a scene from it). You may automatically take a deep breath and relax.

When you have selected your go-to-sleep introduction, create a master of it. Then copy it onto the beginning of each of your recordings.

Progressive Relaxation: Muscle Relaxer

(Read each sentence once in a normal voice with natural rhythm.)

As I listen to the music, I begin to relax. I release the tiredness, the tension, the frustrations of my day.

I begin to breathe deeply as I relax and release . . . release . . . release.

I feel myself release the tension from my face . . . from my neck . . . from my shoulders . . . from my entire body.

I tense my toes as tightly as I can. I curl my toes as tightly as I can. I hold that tenseness. I relax my toes. I relax my toes completely. Ahhhh.

I tense my toes, feet, ankles, and legs. I make those muscles tense while I relax the rest of my body. I hold that tenseness. I relax and enjoy that feeling. Ahhhh.

I tense my thighs and buttocks. I make those muscles tense while I relax the rest of my body. I hold that tenseness. I relax and enjoy that feeling. Ahhhh.

I tense the muscles in my lower back and abdomen. I make those muscles tense

*while I relax the rest of my body. I hold that tenseness. I relax and enjoy that
feeling. Ahhhh.*

*I relax, unwind, let go, and relax more. I let the tension drain out of every mus-
cle. I let go of all my weight. I enjoy feeling free and weightless.*

*I tense the upper part of my torso. I tense the muscles in my back and chest. I make
those muscles tense while I relax the rest of my body. I hold that tenseness. I exhale as I let go of all the tenseness in those muscles. I let the tension drain out
of every muscle. I let go. I feel those muscles unwinding, relaxing, and letting
go. I feel all the tightness disappear. Ahhhh. I am clear.*

*I tense both arms and clench both fists. I hold the tenseness. I relax my arms, I
relax my hands. I enjoy the release from the tension. Ahhhh.*

*I tense the muscles in my face . . . my jaw, my mouth, my eyes, my forehead. I hold
the tenseness. I relax, smoothing out the wrinkles in my forehead, relaxing my
scalp, my eyes, my mouth, my tongue, my throat. I remove all tension and
tightness. I feel the difference. Ahhhh.*

*I let go completely. I relax completely. I unwind completely. I feel the pleasure of
peace and calm spread over my body. I feel the warmth spread throughout my
body. I scan my body in its relaxed state, and I know it is free and clear. Waves
of relaxation wash back and forth from my head to my toes. I am relaxed. I am
completely relaxed.*

*With this relaxation, I can easily connect with areas of my subconscious mind.
And now, in a state of perfect readiness, I listen to the messages on this recording. I know I am divinely protected as I accept and embrace the messages that
are for my highest good and perfect healing, dissolving all else.*

Progressive Relaxation: Back and Neck

(Read each sentence once in a normal voice with natural rhythm.)

*As I listen to the music, I begin to relax. I release the tiredness, the tension, the
frustrations of my day. I begin to breathe deeply as I relax and release . . . release . . . release.*

*I feel myself release the tension from my face . . . from my neck . . . from my shoul-
ders . . . from my entire body.*

*I am lying on a beach. I feel warm sand under my back and I sink into it. The
warm sand under me supports every joint, every muscle, every bone. A warm
breeze brushes over me and I smell the clean salt air of the ocean. I see the blue
sky, the green palms, the white frothy water. I hear the gulls overhead.*

*I relax completely and totally. My muscles are loose like a rubber band that has
been stretched, then loosened. My muscles have been stretched and now they
relax.*

*I visualize my spinal cord. I see it in my mind. Starting with the very tip of the
coccyx, I move up my back vertebra by vertebra. Each vertebra is sitting neatly*

on top of the other in perfect alignment. Each disc is in place. I travel up my vertebrae, one at a time. Each one is in perfect harmony with the next.

I reach my waist in the middle of my back. The nerves coming from the lumbar vertebrae are whole and healthy. They spread out from the right side and the left side. They're fat and full and have total freedom. They are free of pressure, free of pain. They are healthy. My muscles relax throughout my whole lumbar area. My pelvis is relaxed.

I travel upward to my lower thoracic vertebrae. They lie in perfect alignment, one gently floating over the other. All my nerves are streaming out from the right and the left, feeding my body with electrical impulses. All those nerves are fully rounded and whole. They come out from each vertebrae, totally free and unencumbered. They feel good. They are healthy. Each disc is in its proper place and is full and whole and cushiony.

I move up into the upper thoracic area, and each vertebrae is in perfect alignment. The nerves running from them are full and have total freedom. Muscles crisscross my back and run up and down my spinal cord. They are relaxed and loose.

I move up into my shoulders and my neck. My cervical vertebrae begin to curve and are in perfect alignment, perfectly balancing one on the other. The nucleus pulposa is full and pink and free. Cushions rest between my vertebrae.

On my left side, the nerves that come from my cervical vertebrae are full and healthy. They move out in appropriate ways into my body. Muscles surrounding my left shoulder are like rubber bands that have been pulled tight and then relaxed totally.

On my right side, the nerves that come from my cervical vertebrae are full and healthy. They move out in appropriate ways into my body. Muscles surrounding my left shoulder are like rubber bands that have been pulled tight and then relaxed totally.

My muscles are loose around the nerves that come from my cervical spine. They untighten, they unwind. They allow those nerves to have total freedom and to relax. My right shoulder is relaxed. Nerves on that side are floating in perfect alignment to the very base of my skull. My left shoulder is relaxed. Nerves on that side are floating in perfect alignment to the very base of my skull.

My skull rests comfortably on top of my spinal column. It rotates with perfect ease, from side to side. My neck muscles are loose and they allow free movement. They feel so good, and they are completely relaxed and well. The muscles are warm and loose and comfortable. My head is lying totally supported, totally rested. My scalp is loose and the capillaries are open and allowing blood to feed my scalp freely.

I move down my arms and the blood vessels open and dilate freely. They allow blood into my hands and fingers. My fingers are totally open to the blood supply. The temperature around them is warm and comfortable, as if I am lying on the beach with warm sunshine all over my body.

My body is at peace. My neck, my shoulders, and my back are relaxed. My hips are totally relaxed. I am at peace, and I am sleeping peacefully.

My spinal cord, my nerves, my body, and my spirit are whole and healthy and at peace.

And now, in a state of perfect readiness, I listen to the messages on this recording. I know I am divinely protected as I accept and embrace the messages that are for my highest good and perfect healing, dissolving all else.

(One of my clients developed this script for a chronic stiff neck and got good results using it. The name is withheld by request.)

Meditation Relaxation: The Escalator

(Read each sentence once in a normal voice with natural rhythm.)

As I listen to the music, I begin to relax. I release the tiredness, the tension, the frustrations of my day. I begin to breathe deeply as I relax and release . . . release . . . release.

I feel myself release the tension from my face . . . from my neck . . . from my shoulders . . . from my entire body.

I am on the fifth floor of a building. I am in a lobby area, and the walls all around me are painted a warm orange. I am standing at the top of an escalator. The escalator is silver colored, and it is working smoothly and noiselessly. It is completely secure and dependable. I see my feet in front of the escalator steps as they rhythmically roll down.

Feeling completely safe, I take hold of the railing and step on the descending steps. I begin to glide down without any sound . . . slowly, safely. I am on a relaxing journey to the inner level. I feel myself unwinding and relaxing . . . unwinding and relaxing . . . as I watch the warm orange walls glide past me. I see the large number 5 on the orange walls of the fifth floor. I take a deep breath and exhale slowly. I mentally repeat 5 several times. It is the end of the ride, and I step off.

I see the 4 on the wall of the next floor, and I walk to the escalator and step on. The walls of the fourth floor are painted a yellow-gold. I see the large number 4 standing out against the yellow-gold wall. I mentally repeat the number 4 several times as I glide effortlessly down the escalator. It is the end of this level, and I step off.

I see the 3 on the wall of the next floor, and I walk over to the escalator and step on. The walls gliding past me are a beautiful green, and I enjoy this beautiful joyous color as I glide silently down. I mentally repeat the number 3 several times as I continue to descend. I reach a more pleasant and relaxing area, and I step off.

I see the 2 on the wall of the next floor. The walls of this floor are a beautiful blue, and I feel saturated with the peace of this color. I pause several seconds in this peace before continuing. I feel a sense of harmony and deep inner peace. I mentally repeat the number 2 several times. I walk to the escalator and I step on to descend. Lower . . . lower . . . lower . . . I continue to glide down.

I see the 1 on the wall of the first floor. The walls are a deep purple, and I float in the protection of this color. I mentally repeat the number 1 several times, knowing that I am completely safe and protected at this level. I enjoy the color that surrounds me. I step off the escalator into this restful place. I feel very very peaceful, relaxed, rested, and healthy.

I am now at my main inner level. I am completely relaxed. At this level, I can easily connect with areas of my subconscious mind.

And now, in a state of perfect readiness, I listen to the messages on this recording. I know I am divinely protected as I accept and embrace the messages that are for my highest good and perfect healing, dissolving all else.

Meditation Relaxation: Releasing

(Read each sentence once in a normal voice with natural rhythm.)

As I listen to the music, I begin to relax. I begin to breathe deeply and evenly, releasing any tiredness, any tension, any frustrations from my day.

I feel my body rhythms relax and slow . . . and I begin to experience a calm and peaceful feeling. And I release.

And now, in my mind's eye, I see a beautiful violet flame shaped like a teardrop, and I see myself inside the teardrop flame.

I feel the warmth and glow from the flame, and I see myself open to receive this warmth. I see the violet color deepen and build in intensity as I open to it.

I see myself as a delicate rosebud inside the flame, tightly closed. Though the rosebud is closed, I have a sense of knowing about its beauty when it opens to its full blossoming potential.

I know it will open in its own time . . . gently . . . as it is warmed and protected by the violet flame. I know I am completely safe and secure in my unfolding. I see the rosebud open more and more, and I feel myself open more and more.

And now, I see the violet flame begin a clockwise spiral motion around me, spinning things away from me.

I gently release and let go of all shields . . . all blocks . . . all limitations . . . barriers . . . and see them spinning with the violet flame . . . spinning upward.

I know these shields, blocks, limitations, and barriers are being transformed into openness and trust and emotional courage.

I feel emotional courage and peace flowing into my openness to fill it.

I feel unconditional love flowing into my openness to fill it.

And now, in a state of perfect readiness, I listen to the messages on this recording. I know I am divinely protected as I accept and embrace the messages that are for my highest good and perfect healing, dissolving all else.

Meditation Relaxation: Forgiving

(Read each sentence once in a normal voice with natural rhythm.)

As I listen to the music, I begin to relax. I begin to breathe deeply and evenly, releasing any tiredness, any tension, any frustrations from my day. I feel my body rhythms relax and slow . . . and I begin to experience a calm and peaceful feeling. And I release.

I am in a lush tropical forest . . . in a clearing, surrounded by beautiful trees, plants, and wildflowers. I feel the humidity on my skin. I hear the birds chattering in the trees overhead. I smell the fragrant scent of many flowers.

A shaft of sunlight is beaming through the forest into the clearing. I feel the warm sun on my skin, and I sink deeper and deeper into relaxation.

I see a beautiful clear pool of water with a small waterfall pouring into it. I see myself walking into the shallow pool, and I feel the cool water on my legs. I walk over to the waterfall, and I hear the gurgling sounds of running water.

The waterfall and pool are filled with the vibration of unconditional love and forgiveness. I walk under the waterfall and stand there with the water flowing gently over the crown of my head. I allow the energy of love and forgiveness to wash over me, clearing me.

I step back out of the waterfall, feeling clear and radiant. I luxuriate in this feeling, and sink deeper and deeper into relaxation.

I see and feel the bright sunshine shining directly on the crown of my head. It passes through the crown of my head, and down into my heart.

The bright warm sun becomes a spark in my heart which kindles into a flame. I focus on the flame and see it glowing brightly in my heart. The flame becomes violet and expands until it fills my chest area. The violet flame is a pure radiant form of unconditional love. I feel its unconditional love and sink deeper and deeper into relaxation.

I feel the violet flame consume any feelings of anger, grief, remorse, sorrow, guilt, pain, or loss from my past.

I feel the violet flame transmute all heaviness and hardness in my heart.

I feel unconditional love fill my heart.

I feel unconditional love expanding throughout every atom and cell in my body.

I feel every atom and cell in my body glowing with pure radiant love.

I allow my body to glow with the pure radiant force of love coming from my higher presence, through my crown, into my heart, into my body, and out into my personal space.

The intensity of this flame increases, and as the flame increases, I sink deeper and deeper into relaxation.

The flame increases until my body is a glowing sheath of light. Every emotion I have ever had is radiating with the pure violet flame of unconditional love. Every feeling I have ever felt is radiating with the pure violet flame of unconditional love.

I am vibrating with the pure frequency of unconditional love, as I sink deeper and deeper into my own personal process.

The love in my heart is my own I Am Presence. I merge with my I Am Presence, meeting Self at the level of pure Spirit.

And now, in a state of perfect readiness, I listen to the messages on this recording. I know I am divinely protected as I accept and embrace the messages that are for my highest good and perfect healing, dissolving all else.

Meditation Relaxation: Emotional Healing

(Read each sentence once in a normal voice with natural rhythm.)

As I listen to the music, I begin to relax. I begin to breathe deeply and evenly, releasing any tiredness, any tension, any frustrations from my day.

I feel my body rhythms relax and slow . . . and I begin to experience a calm and peaceful feeling. And I release.

And now, in my mind's eye, I see myself sitting in an outdoor scene that is beautiful and serene . . . (at the ocean, in the woods, in front of a waterfall) . . . and it creates a feeling of peace and security.

I notice the colors all around me; I smell the fresh clear air; I hear the subtle sounds of nature all around me.

Sitting comfortably in this serene outdoor scene, I see small figures like toy soldiers or dolls all around me. As I look closely at these figures, I see they are all figures of me . . . as a child, an adolescent, a teenager, and an adult.

Some of these little figures represent times I was being criticized or punished, or times I was made to feel bad about myself and my actions. Some of these little figures represent times I was unhappy with myself, or nonaccepting of myself. Some represent times I was not treating myself well.

I realize that they are all from the past.

And now, I see a large crystal bowl before me. I notice its beautiful design. I see bright white light from the sun filling the crystal bowl with fluid light. It sparkles and shines with luminescent liquid light.

I gather up all of the little figures now and all the times in my life they represent— the times in my life in which I was feeling unloved or unloving toward myself—and I place them in this large beautiful luminescent crystal bowl.

I see the little figures floating in the crystal white liquid light, like children sunbathing on a silver pond.

I know that these little figures—and the times in my past they represent—are being cleansed and healed in the liquid light. I know that my unloving past is being cleansed and healed. I know that I am now entering a peaceful, loving state with myself.

And now, in a state of perfect readiness, I listen to the messages on this recording. I know I am divinely protected as I accept and embrace the messages that are for my highest good and perfect healing, dissolving all else.

Meditation Relaxation: Physical Healing

(Read each sentence once in a normal voice with natural rhythm.)

*As I listen to the music, I begin to relax. I begin to breathe deeply and evenly, re-
leasing any tiredness, any tension, any frustrations from my day.*

*I feel my body rhythms relax and slow . . . and I begin to experience a calm and
peaceful feeling. And I release.*

*And now, in my mind's eye, I picture my physical body . . . and realize it is made
up of parts . . . bones, muscles, lungs, glands, arteries, veins, nerves—lots of
parts—connected together and covered with skin.*

*I see that each part of my body is made up of even smaller parts—cells—billions
and billions of cells.*

*I pick one cell in my body—on the tip of my nose, or on my hand, or anywhere in
my body—and I focus on this one microscopic cell.*

*And I see that this cell is expanding and becoming gigantic, and I see myself go
inside that cell. I take time to look around. It is vast inside.*

*I feel like I have gone into the sky . . . into space . . . because there are no limits,
no boundaries. I feel the vastness and spaciousness in this single cell, and I see
that it is beautiful.*

My cell is full of light . . . and warmth . . . and harmony. I feel the warmth.

My cell is filled with peace and joy. I feel the balance and health.

*And now, I see a large pair of loving compassionate eyes inside this cell . . . look-
ing at me . . . sending love and compassion to me.*

*I see these loving eyes multiply and become millions of eyes inside this cell. I feel
waves of love and compassion and healing emanating from this cell . . . and
these waves of love and compassion and healing are being shared with all
other cells. I feel all the cells in my body moving in rhythm with these waves of
love and compassion.*

*And I know that all the cells of my body are connected in harmony. And all my
cells are being restored in perfect health.*

I know my body is being restored in perfect health on the cellular level.

*And now, in a state of perfect readiness, I listen to the messages on this recording.
I know I am divinely protected as I accept and embrace the messages that are
for my highest good and perfect healing, dissolving all else.*

Meditation Relaxation: Inner Peace

(Read each sentence once in a normal voice with natural rhythm.)

*As I listen to the music, I begin to relax. I begin to breathe deeply and evenly, re-
leasing any tiredness, any tension, any frustrations from my day.*

*I feel my body rhythms relax and slow . . . and I begin to experience a calm and
peaceful feeling. And I release.*

And now, in my mind's eye, I see a laserlike ray of violet light tinged with gold. I see this light come down through the top of my head, down through my neck, down through my body, down my legs, and into the earth.

I see this concentrated beam of violet light expand to fill my head, and I know it brings harmony and calm to my thoughts.

I see this concentrated beam of violet light expand to fill my chest, and I know it brings harmony and serenity to my emotions.

I see this concentrated beam of violet light expand to fill my entire body, and I know it brings serenity and calm to every cell in my body.

I see the light expand into a broad column of lovely violet light that fills and surrounds me, and I know it brings a vibration of peace and calm and serenity and harmony to my mind, body, and emotions.

I know it supports my field becoming congruent and coherent.

I know it assists my peaceful thoughts, feelings, and actions.

And I carry this peacefulness with me throughout my day, my week, and my life . . .

And now, in a state of perfect readiness, I listen to the messages on this recording. I know I am divinely protected as I accept and embrace the messages that are for my highest good and perfect healing, dissolving all else.

Meditation Relaxation: Manifesting

(Read each sentence once in a normal voice with natural rhythm.)

As I listen to the music, I begin to relax. I begin to breathe deeply and evenly, releasing any tiredness, any tension, any frustrations from my day.

I feel my body rhythms relax and slow . . . and I begin to experience a calm and peaceful feeling. And I release.

And now, in my mind's eye, I see a clear, sunny, summer day. I am in the middle of a beautiful field of flowers. I feel the warm sunshine . . . hear the birds singing . . . see the colors of the flowers in the field. I lie down in the field and feel that I am a part of the landscape itself.

From this perspective, I see a green layer under the flowers. I look closer and see that the green is a lush carpet of four leaf clovers. There are millions of four leaf clovers . . . bright and green and perfectly shaped.

I shrink down very small and become the center of one of those four leaf clovers. I am completely dressed in gold, in the middle of a four leaf clover.

The clear vibrant green petals extend from my center, fanning out around me. There is a petal above me . . . a petal below me . . . a petal on the left side of me . . . a petal on the right side of me . . .

From this perspective, I see the movement inside each of the petals. The movement is life and energy moving in each petal.

The life energy is a rainbow-colored liquid, circulating around the inside of the petals. I see the life force circulating inside each petal.

The rainbow-colored energy circulates like a figure eight . . . crisscrossing through me as it moves from one petal to another.

I feel the magic and miracle of the life energy in the rainbow liquid.

I feel the automatic flow and natural ease of movement of the rainbow liquid.

I allow the rainbow liquid to expand throughout my body, filling every atom.

I feel nourished by the rainbow liquid.

I feel the rainbow liquid move from the petal above me . . . through me . . . to the petal below me . . . and back through me . . . to the petal on the left of me . . . and back through me . . . to the petal on the right of me . . . and back through me.

I see this liquid moving continuously through the petals and through me. I know that all life energy is passing through me now, manifesting my heart's desires in ease and grace.

I know that the world before me is restored in divine order.

I know that the world behind me is restored in divine order.

I know that the world below me is restored in divine order.

I know that the world above me is restored in divine order.

I know that all things around me are restored in divine order.

I know that my powers of manifestation are restored in divine order.

And now, in a state of perfect readiness, I listen to the messages on this recording. I know I am divinely protected as I accept and embrace the messages that are for my highest good and perfect healing, dissolving all else.

A to Z Scripts:

Clearing and Affirmation Suggestion Statements

These scripts are in draft form for you to reword, modify, change and rewrite.

To use the scripts effectively, read each statement, monitoring your reactions. If you feel an emotion or response to the statement, it means it has power over you in some way. Include it in your script.

When you come to a _____, try to fill in the blank. Take time to play detective and find a person, event, situation, feeling, or something else from your life that is significant in relation to that statement.

Mix and match the scripts in any order.

Remember, your processing will be in direct proportion to the significance of the suggestion statements you write, record, and listen to during your SuperSleep™ state.

You may experience deep emotions such as anger, grief, or depression while processing. You may develop temporary physical reactions such as body pains, rashes, stomach upsets, etc. These responses can be intense and usually pass quickly (see Chapter 5).

While listening to your tape, get plenty of rest, drink lots of healthy liquids, have a support system in place. Consider getting a massage or other form of body treatment. Soaking in a hot Epsom salts bath or a hot tub is great. Soothing aromatherapy such as lavender and homeopathic remedies for trauma can also ease the process for you.

Most important, take the action to create a recording for yourself.
The process is simple; the results can be dramatic.

Best of luck changing your mind . . . and your life!

Action

I get asked for help with procrastination regularly. I have the opposite issue—I take action too easily and quickly. So this script addresses both too much and too little action. The Concentration, Performing Well, and Time Management scripts work with this one nicely. (Written for the recording "Being Proactive"—the *Success* series.)

The Emptying-the-Cup Script

Taking action and I are one.
I release and forgive myself for taking action.
I release and forgive myself for not taking action.
I release and forgive myself for _____.

Do you still feel bad about something you did or did not do?

I release and forgive _____ for not taking action.

Who modeled not taking action to you?

I release and forgive _____ for _____.

Who didn't take action or took inappropriate action when you needed it?

I release, forgive, and dissolve my family model of taking action.
I release, forgive, and dissolve all false models of taking action.

Whom did you observe who did things differently than you do? Who influenced you who didn't take action?

I dissolve all imbalances on the soul level around fearing taking action.
I dissolve all imbalances on the soul level around fearing not taking action.
I dissolve all imbalances on the soul level around _____.

What happened in childhood if you didn't do your "chores"—if you didn't do them "right?"

I dissolve all imbalances on the soul level around judging myself for taking action.
I dissolve all imbalances on the soul level around judging myself for not taking action.
I dissolve all imbalances on the soul level around others judging me for taking action.
I dissolve all imbalances on the soul level around others judging me for not taking action.
I dissolve all imbalances on the soul level around being told my actions are wrong.
I dissolve all imbalances on the soul level around _____.

What messages did you get about your actions/inactions?

I dissolve all imbalances on the soul level around believing my actions are wrong.

Who told you your actions weren't good enough? What made you think or feel you were always doing things wrong?

I dissolve my field of experience around procrastinating.
I dissolve my field of experience around taking timely right action.
I transform my vibrational patterns around procrastinating.
I transform my vibrational patterns around taking timely right action.
I transcend taking action, and I am at peace with it.
I surrender to taking action, and I allow it in my life as appropriate.
I bring all past issues around taking action to an elegant completion in total grace.
I take total and complete responsibility for my actions as appropriate.
I allow and assign others total and complete responsibility for their actions as appropriate.
Taking action and _____ are separate for me now.

What worries you about taking action?

The Filling-the-Cup Script

Taking timely right action has all positive outcomes for me now.
I am safe and protected when I take timely right action.
I am loved and accepted when I take timely right action.
I am supported and nurtured when I take timely right action.
I am acknowledged and recognized when I take timely right action.
I am well rewarded on all levels when I take timely right action.
I direct my attention toward taking the right action at the right time for the right reasons.
I direct my energy toward taking the right action at the right time for the right reasons.
I direct my resources toward taking the right action at the right time for the right reasons.
I control and channel my energy into timely right action.
I transform thoughts and feelings into timely right action.
I recognize effective action, and I take it as appropriate.
I recognize when to move to action, and I do it.
I am sensible and practical when I take action as appropriate.
I am spontaneous and free when I take action as appropriate.
I am willing to try new actions and learn from them.
I focus on my actions that have worked.
I learn from my actions that have not worked.
It is natural and effortless for me to direct my energy to actions that work.

It is natural and effortless for me to take each action to its best outcome and conclusion.
I know when to take action and when to delay, postpone, or cancel.
I automatically respond to each situation in the right way at the right time for the right reasons.

Aging

For me, aging is positive, for I was taught it means gaining wisdom and earning respect. If that is not your heritage, consider this script to establish an honoring for your natural process.

The Emptying-the-Cup Script

Aging and I are one.
I release and forgive myself for aging.
I release and forgive myself for not aging.
I release and forgive myself for feeling _____ about aging.

sad, bitter, angry, confused, hopeless, frightened, rebellious, resigned

I dissolve all imbalances on the soul level around aging.
I dissolve all imbalances on the soul level around fearing aging.
I dissolve all imbalances on the soul level around judging aging.
I dissolve all imbalances on the soul level around all fantasies and illusions about aging.
I dissolve all imbalances on the soul level around false concepts and models of aging.
I dissolve all imbalances on the soul level around all stereotypes of aging.
I dissolve all imbalances on the soul level around the dangers of aging.
I dissolve all imbalances on the soul level around the possibilities of aging.
I dissolve all imbalances on the soul level around dysfunctional responses to aging.
I dissolve all imbalances on the soul level around denying aging.
I dissolve all imbalances on the soul level around hiding aging.
I dissolve all imbalances on the soul level around becoming rigid and inflexible.
I dissolve all imbalances on the soul level around settling into patterns of having, doing, and being.
I dissolve all imbalances on the soul level around immortality.
I dissolve my field of experience around aging.
I transform my vibrational patterns around aging.
I transcend aging, and I am at peace with it.
I surrender to aging, and I allow it in my life as appropriate.
I bring all past issues around aging to an elegant completion in total grace.

I dissolve all future issues around aging before they materialize.
I take total and complete responsibility for my aging.
I allow and assign others total and complete responsibility for their aging.
Aging and _____ are separate for me now.

What concerns you about your aging? Illness, poverty, being ignored, being forgotten, being mistreated, disability, being segregated, being rejected, loneliness, isolation, senility, physical appearance?

The Filling-the-Cup Script

Aging has all positive outcomes for me now.
I am safe and protected as I age.
I am loved and accepted as I age.
I am nurtured and supported as I age.
I understand aging is the most common experience of all living things.
I accept and allow my aging as fulfilling the cycle of my life.
I understand and affirm aging as a growth process which reveals the mystery of life to me.
The characteristics of aging are well worth the wisdom, peace, and understanding I have.
I retain my mental openness and elasticity of youth.
I am able to enjoy the rewards of my life experience every day.
I prevent what is preventable in aging, and I accept and allow what isn't preventable.
I change my habits and attitude to remain youthful at any age.
I take good care of myself mentally, physically, emotionally, and spiritually.
I continue to learn and have new and challenging experiences.
I continue to take an interest in others and their lives as appropriate.
I continue to take an interest in world events as appropriate.
I am conscientious about my eating and exercising habits.
I am conscientious about my medical care.
I am active and vigorous as appropriate.
I use my aging time to help restore the broken connections between the generations.
I use my aging time to _____.

paint, read, sculpt, reflect, meditate, plan, volunteer for global causes, care for children, realize my life's dreams, do what I've always wanted to do

Anger

We all feel anger at some time. How we handle it determines in some measure our mental, emotional, physical, and spiritual health. I invite you to play detective with your own anger issues and dissolve them—for increased longevity, health, and love in your life. (Written for the recording "Loving Conflict"—the *Loving Relationship* series.)

The Emptying-the-Cup Script

Anger and I are one.
I release and forgive myself for feeling anger.
I release and forgive myself for not feeling anger.
I release and forgive myself for expressing anger.
I release and forgive myself for not expressing anger.
I release and forgive everyone with whom I have been angry.
I release everyone who has been angry with me.
I release and forgive _____ for _____.

What happened when others were angry with you? What did they say or do?

I dissolve all false models of being angry.
I dissolve all imbalances on the soul level around feeling anger.
I dissolve all imbalances on the soul level around fearing feeling anger.
I dissolve all imbalances on the soul level around judging feeling anger.
I dissolve all imbalances on the soul level around denying my anger.
I dissolve all imbalances on the soul level around expressing anger.
I dissolve all imbalances on the soul level around fearing expressing anger.
I dissolve all imbalances on the soul level around judging expressing anger.
I dissolve all imbalances on the soul level around feeling powerless.
I dissolve all imbalances on the soul level around feeling used or put down.
I dissolve all imbalances on the soul level around _____.

What makes you angry, triggers your anger, how do you react?

I dissolve all imbalances on the soul level around my family's anger.
I dissolve all imbalances on the soul level around my family's anger with me.
I dissolve all imbalances on the soul level around my _____'s anger with me.

What were some significant events around others' anger with you?

I dissolve all imbalances on the soul level around my anger with _____.

What were some significant events around your anger with others?

I dissolve all imbalances on the soul level around being controlled by my anger.
I dissolve all imbalances on the soul level around being controlled by others' anger.
I dissolve all imbalances on the soul level around controlling others with my anger.
I dissolve all imbalances on the soul level around societal and cultural anger.

I dissolve all imbalances on the soul level around religious and philosophical anger.

I dissolve all imbalances on the soul level around _____ anger.

I dissolve all imbalances on the soul level around traditions and social customs of anger.

I dissolve all imbalances on the soul level around rituals and taboos of anger.

I dissolve all imbalances on the soul level around stereotypes and social roles of anger.

I dissolve all imbalances on the soul level around anger leading to violence.

I dissolve all imbalances on the soul level around anger leading to _____.

screaming, yelling, revenge, back biting, temper tantrums, overapologizing, guilt

I dissolve all imbalances on the soul level around externalizing or projecting my anger.

I dissolve all imbalances on the soul level around substituting _____ for expressing my anger appropriately.

withdrawing, stonewalling, complaining, annoyance, irritation, disappointment, depression, self criticism, guilt

I dissolve my field of experience around feeling and expressing anger.

I transform my vibrational patterns around feeling and expressing anger.

I transcend feeling and expressing anger, and I am at peace with it.

I surrender to feeling and expressing anger, and I allow it in my life as appropriate.

I bring all past issues around feeling and expressing anger to an elegant completion in total grace.

I dissolve all future issues around feeling and expressing anger before they materialize.

I take total and complete responsibility for my anger and how I express it.

I allow and assign others total and complete responsibility for their anger and how they express it.

Being angry and _____ are separate for me now.

losing control, hurting others, yelling, blaming

The Filling-the-Cup Script

I recognize and understand my anger.

I recognize and understand the true source of my anger.

I am safe and protected when I accept my anger.

I am loved and accepted when I accept my anger.

I am nurtured and supported when I accept my anger.

I acknowledge my anger in all appropriate ways.

I am at peace with having and expressing anger as appropriate.
I express my anger appropriately and realistically.
I express my anger at the right times in the right ways.
I express my anger for the right reasons to the right people.
I am in control of myself and my anger.

Assertiveness

I have always been considered assertive, so I was quite surprised when the "Speaking Up for Yourself" recording (from the *Empowerment* series) triggered significant process for me. That led me to expand the assertiveness script.

The Emptying-the-Cup Script

Being assertive and I are one.
I release and forgive myself for being assertive.
I release and forgive myself for not being assertive.
I release and forgive myself for _____.

What do you do in place of being assertive? What times do you regret not being assertive?

I release and forgive my family for not teaching me to be assertive.
I release and forgive my family for _____.

What did you family do when you tried to speak up for yourself?

I release and forgive every person and situation that denied my assertiveness.
I release, forgive and dissolve all false models of assertiveness.
I dissolve all imbalances on the soul level around fearing being assertive.
I dissolve all imbalances on the soul level around judging being assertive.
I dissolve all imbalances on the soul level around feeling guilty when I am assertive.
I dissolve all imbalances on the soul level around feeling _____ when I am assertive.

defensive, anxious, selfish, out of control, impolite, bossy, aggressive, arrogant

I dissolve all imbalances on the soul level around being feared and judged for being assertive.
I dissolve all imbalances on the soul level around being criticized and punished for being assertive.
I dissolve all imbalances on the soul level around being _____ when I am assertive.

ignored, discounted, shamed, humiliated, punished, scared

I dissolve all imbalances on the soul level around being trapped in my patterns.

I dissolve all imbalances on the soul level around associating assertiveness with anger and control.

I dissolve all imbalances on the soul level around associating assertiveness with _____.

anger, domination, oppression, manipulation, aggression, control, power

I dissolve all imbalances on the soul level around believing, feeling, or acting powerless.

I dissolve all imbalances on the soul level around believing, feeling, or acting submissive and indecisive.

I dissolve all imbalances on the soul level around being passive or giving in.

I dissolve all imbalances on the soul level around being aggressive or vicious.

I dissolve all imbalances on the soul level around overreacting or attacking.

I dissolve all imbalances on the soul level around being passive-aggressive and tricking and manipulating.

I dissolve all imbalances on the soul level around attitudes that trigger and support nonassertive behavior.

I dissolve all imbalances on the soul level around emotions that trigger and support nonassertive behavior.

I dissolve all imbalances on the soul level around situations that trigger and support nonassertive behavior.

I dissolve all imbalances on the soul level around people that trigger and support nonassertive behavior.

I dissolve all imbalances on the soul level around expressing my feelings directly and spontaneously.

I dissolve all imbalances on the soul level around asking for what I want and need.

I dissolve all imbalances on the soul level around traditional standards and stereotypes.

I dissolve all imbalances on the soul level around culturally imposed customs.

I dissolve all imbalances on the soul level around conforming to others' standards and role definitions.

I dissolve all imbalances on the soul level around taking care of others.

I dissolve all imbalances on the soul level around being taken care of.

I dissolve my field of experience around being assertive.

I transform my vibrational patterns around being assertive.

I transcend being assertive, and I am at peace with it.

I surrender to being assertive, and I allow it in my life as appropriate.

I bring all past issues around being assertive to an elegant completion in total grace.

I dissolve all future issues around being assertive before they materialize.

I take total and complete responsibility for my assertiveness.
I allow and assign others total and complete responsibility for their assertiveness.
I allow and assign others total and complete responsibility for their reaction and response to my assertiveness.
Being assertive and being _____ are separate for me now.

right, wrong, guilty, defensive, angry: losing acceptance, approval, love, security, safety

The Filling-the-Cup Script

Being assertive has all positive outcomes for me now.
I am safe and protected when I am assertive.
I am loved and accepted when I am assertive.
I am supported and nurtured when I am assertive.
I believe in my own worth, honesty, and equality.
I respect myself, and I respect others.
I believe in my right to say what I mean and mean what I say, and I do so in all appropriate ways.
I believe in my right to say no, and I do so in all appropriate ways.
I choose for myself, and I allow others to choose for themselves.
I understand the difference between being assertive and being aggressive.
I understand being assertive means stating my truth without blame or judgment.
I understand being assertive means asking for what I want and need.
I understand being assertive means stating my thoughts and feelings honestly, without subterfuge or manipulation.
I understand being assertive means stating my thoughts and feelings directly without putting others down.
I understand being assertive means stating my thoughts and feelings spontaneously without overreaction or attack.
I understand being assertive means allowing others to state their thoughts and feelings.
I understand assertiveness is a skill to be learned.
I do what is necessary to learn assertive skills through awareness, practice, and reinforcement.
I am increasingly aware of my attitudes, actions, reactions, and support systems.
I recognize the attitudes, people, and situations that support being assertive.
I recognize the attitudes, people, and situations that inhibit being assertive, and I change them as appropriate.
I express honest feelings comfortably.
I am direct and straightforward as appropriate.
I exercise my personal rights without denying the rights of others.
I exercise my personal rights without feeling fear, anxiety, or guilty.

I exercise my personal rights without feeling _____.

I state my thoughts and feelings simply, clearly, and objectively as appropriate.

I state my thoughts and feelings simply, clearly, and without anger as appropriate.

I state my thoughts and feelings simply, clearly, and without blame or judgment as appropriate.

I enjoy being honest and asking for what I want and need.

I ask for what I want and need simply and clearly.

I ask for what I want and need firmly and smoothly.

I ask for what I want and need with ease and grace.

I ask for what I want and need in harmony and peace.

I bring discussions about what I want and need to completion with ease.

I monitor what I receive in relation to what I ask for.

I give appropriate feedback when I get what I ask for.

I give appropriate feedback when I don't get what I ask for.

I ask questions in the right way at the right time for the right reasons.

I ask the right questions of the right people.

I listen to others openly and nonjudgmentally.

I am assertive in the right way at the right time for the right reasons.

I maintain open, honest, assertive communication moment to moment.

I increase in assertiveness daily.

I maintain an assertive body image with posture, facial expression, and tone of voice.

I maintain eye contact, keep my head upright, and lean forward during conversations as appropriate.

I achieve independent assertiveness easily and automatically.

It is natural and normal for me to be assertive.

It is easy and effortless for me to be assertive.

It is _____ for me to be assertive.

I am assertive in all times, places and situations with all kinds of people.

I understand my assertiveness is central to the liberation of all around me.

Betrayal

Most of us have been betrayed or betrayed another or both. Betrayals can be as major as infidelity or as seemingly minor as being late. For me, the worst betrayals have been around people saying they will be there for me, and then not "showing up" when I need them. Of course, I was able to trace that back to an unhealed childhood issue, and when I healed that, the betrayals stopped. (Written for the recording "Loving Commitment"—the *Loving Partnership* series.)

The Emptying-the-Cup Script

Betrayal and I are one.
I release and forgive myself for _____ .

What have you done to others you feel bad about?

I release and forgive _____ for _____ .

Who betrayed you and what did that person do that made you feel betrayed?

I release and forgive everyone who betrayed me in all times and places.
I release and forgive myself for every betrayal I have made in all times and places.
I dissolve all imbalances on the soul level around betrayal.
I dissolve all imbalances on the soul level around fearing and judging betrayal.
I dissolve all imbalances on the soul level around fearing and judging dishonesty
*   and deceit.*
I dissolve all imbalances on the soul level around fearing and judging unfaith-
*   fulness and infidelity.*
I dissolve all imbalances on the soul level around fearing and judging _____ .

What makes you feel betrayed? What do you not want to happen to you again?

I dissolve all imbalances on the soul level around the guilt, shame, and self-doubt
*   of betrayal.*
I dissolve all imbalances on the soul level around using betrayal to punish myself
*   and others.*
I dissolve my field of experience and transform my vibrational patterns around
*   betrayal.*
I transcend betrayal, and I am at peace with it.
I transcend betrayal for openness, honesty, dependability, and integrity in grace.
I transcend suspicion and distrust for consciousness and discernment in har-
*   mony.*
I transcend bitterness, pain, scapegoating, and blame in compassion and peace.
I bring all my past issues around betrayal to an elegant completion in total grace.
I dissolve all future issues around betrayal before they materialize.
I take total and complete responsibility for my betrayals as appropriate.
I allow and assign others total and complete responsibility for their betrayals as
*   appropriate.*

The Filling-the-Cup Script

I move beyond betrayal to satisfaction and fulfillment.
I recognize the signs of recovery and healing from betrayal and acknowledge them
*   accordingly.*

As a betrayer, I recognize and understand the reason for my betrayal.
As a betrayer, I show empathy for the pain I caused another with my actions.
As a betrayer, I take responsibility for my actions without excuse, rationalization, or blame.
As the betrayed, I refuse to tolerate continuing betrayals.
As the betrayed, I give myself permission to end the relationship as appropriate.
As the betrayed, I recognize signs of betrayal and act accordingly.
As the betrayed, I recognize when a person may be lying or betraying.
As the betrayed, I refuse to give unequally or abandon myself.

Boundaries

One of my women friends calls me "the queen of boundaries." Because this is an automatic part of my life, her statement surprised me. I dedicate this script to her and others who are working to develop healthy boundaries. (Written for the recording "Claiming Your Personal Power"—the *Empowerment* series.)

The Emptying-the-Cup Script

Having boundaries and I are one.
I release and forgive myself for having boundaries.
I release and forgive myself for setting limits.
I release and forgive myself for not having boundaries.
I release and forgive myself for not setting limits.
I release and forgive everyone who did not teach me how to have boundaries.
I release and forgive everyone who did not teach me how to set limits.
I release and forgive everyone who taught me I couldn't have boundaries.
I release and forgive everyone who crossed my boundaries.
I release and forgive _____ for _____.

Who crossed your boundaries? How? What was the result?

I release and forgive myself for crossing others' boundaries.
I release and forgive myself for _____.

Have you crossed others' boundaries, ignored their limits?

I dissolve all imbalances on the soul level around boundaries.
I dissolve all imbalances on the soul level around fearing boundaries.
I dissolve all imbalances on the soul level around judging boundaries.
I dissolve all imbalances on the soul level around understanding the nature of boundaries.
I dissolve all imbalances on the soul level around setting limits.
I dissolve all imbalances on the soul level around fearing setting limits.

I dissolve all imbalances on the soul level around judging setting limits.
I dissolve all imbalances on the soul level around maintaining boundaries.
I dissolve all imbalances on the soul level around maintaining my boundaries with firm assertiveness.
I dissolve all imbalances on the soul level around saying no when my boundaries are crossed.
I dissolve my field of experience around setting limits.
I dissolve my field of experience around having boundaries.
I dissolve my field of experience around maintaining boundaries.
I transform my vibrational patterns around setting limits.
I transform my vibrational patterns around having boundaries.
I transform my vibrational patterns around maintaining boundaries.
I transcend setting limits, and I am at peace with it.
I transcend boundaries, and I am at peace with them.
I surrender to setting limits, and I allow it in my life as appropriate.
I surrender to boundaries, and I allow them in my life as appropriate.
I bring all my past issues around setting limits to an elegant completion in total grace.
I bring all my past issues around boundaries to an elegant completion in total grace.
I take total and complete responsibility for setting limits and having boundaries for myself.
I allow and assign others total and complete responsibility for setting limits for themselves.
I allow and assign others total and complete responsibility for having boundaries for themselves.
Setting limits and _____ are separate for me now.

feeling selfish, defensive, guilty

Having boundaries and _____ are separate for me now.

What are your negative experiences around having boundaries?

The Filling-the-Cup Script

Having boundaries has all positive outcomes for me now.
Setting limits has all positive outcomes for me now.
I am safe and protected when I have boundaries and set limits.
I am loved and accepted when I have boundaries and set limits.
I am nurtured and supported when I have boundaries and set limits.
I understand setting limits is a form of self-love, self-nurturing, and self-care.
I understand having boundaries is a form of self-love, self-nurturing, and self-care.

I understand maintaining boundaries is a form of self-love, self-nurturing, and self-care.

I understand setting limits and maintaining boundaries is a skill to be learned.

I learn to set limits and maintain boundaries in harmony and grace.

I set limits for the right things in the right way.

I set limits at the right times for the right reasons.

I feel good when I set limits and keep them.

I feel good when I develop boundaries and maintain them.

I allow myself and others to have boundaries without blame or judgment.

I allow myself and others to have boundaries without _____.

conflict, pain, anger, rejection

Budgeting

I don't know many people who enjoy budgeting, and that includes me! This script got me on track. Use it with the *Debt* and *Prosperity* Scripts. (Written for the recording "Managing Money Flow"—the *Money* series.)

The Emptying-the-Cup Script

Budgeting and I are one.

I release and forgive myself for having a budget and spending plan.

I release and forgive myself for not having a budget and spending plan.

I release and forgive myself for _____ .

I release, forgive, and dissolve all false messages and models around budgeting.

I dissolve all imbalances on the soul level around budgeting.

I dissolve all imbalances on the soul level around family and generational patterns of budgeting.

I dissolve all imbalances on the soul level around societal and cultural patterns of budgeting.

I dissolve all imbalances on the soul level around gender and age patterns of budgeting.

I dissolve all imbalances on the soul level around fearing and judging budgeting.

I dissolve all imbalances on the soul level around associating budgeting with pain, loss, and limitation.

I dissolve all imbalances on the soul level around underbudgeting and overbudgeting.

I dissolve all imbalances on the soul level around not following my budget.

I dissolve all imbalances on the soul level around not meeting my financial obligations.

I dissolve my field of experience and transform my vibrational patterns around budgeting.

I transcend budgeting, and I am at peace with it.

I surrender to budgeting, and I allow it in my life.

I bring all my past issues around budgeting to an elegant completion in total grace.

I dissolve all future issues around budgeting before they materialize.

I take total and complete responsibility for my budgeting as appropriate.

I allow and assign others total and complete responsibility for their budgeting as appropriate.

The Filling-the-Cup Script

I understand and accept the role budgeting plays in my life and my financial success.

I develop and maintain a budget and spending plan that support my value based goals.

I budget in the right way at the right time for the right reasons.

I have the self-discipline to maintain my budget, and I do so effortlessly.

I maintain my budget in the right way at the right time for the right reasons.

I review, revise, and modify my budget as appropriate.

My budget and budgeting process are simple, efficient, and effective.

My budget and budgeting process are satisfying, gratifying, and successful.

I use my budget to record how much money is coming in and going out.

I use a simple method of tracking my income and spending that fits me and my lifestyle.

I establish categories of spending tailored to my lifestyle and goals.

I enjoy the record-keeping functions of my budget and spending plan.

I feel safe when I estimate the amount of money coming in objectively and realistically.

I feel secure when I track my spending, and I do so at appropriate times in appropriate ways.

I feel fulfilled and gratified when I eliminate my inappropriate spending.

I feel powerful taking control and redirecting my spending to achieve my goals.

I stay in the flow of effective budgeting moment to moment, and I prosper.

Careers

I have had a rich and varied professional life with over a dozen different careers. I have been everything from an artist's model to white-water guide to college professor. I have "dropped out" periodically to raise my daughter, return to school, and revitalize myself. I traded having financial security for following my heart. May this script support your having both. (Written for the recording "Achieving Right Livelihood"—the *Money* series.)

The Emptying-the-Cup Script

Having a career and I are one.
I release and forgive myself for having a career.
I release and forgive myself for not having a career.
I release and forgive myself for choosing my career.
I release and forgive myself for not choosing my career.
I release and forgive myself for changing careers.
I release and forgive myself for not changing careers.
I release and forgive myself for being in the right career.
I release and forgive myself for being in the wrong career.
I release and forgive everyone who _____.

told me to be a doctor/nurse, told me I couldn't be a poet/artist, etc.

I dissolve all false models and messages around choosing and changing careers.
I dissolve all imbalances on the soul level around having a career.
I dissolve all imbalances on the soul level around my career and career path.
I dissolve all imbalances on the soul level around family and generational patterns of careers and career paths.
I dissolve all imbalances on the soul level around societal and cultural patterns of careers and careers paths.
I dissolve all imbalances on the soul level around gender and age patterns of careers and careers paths.
I dissolve all imbalances on the soul level around choosing and changing careers.
I dissolve all imbalances on the soul level around family and generational patterns of choosing and changing careers.
I dissolve all imbalances on the soul level around societal and cultural patterns of choosing and changing careers.
I dissolve all imbalances on the soul level around gender and age patterns of choosing and changing careers.
I dissolve all imbalances on the soul level around fearing and judging choosing and changing careers.
I dissolve all imbalances on the soul level around gaining my identity through what I do and earn.
I dissolve all imbalances on the soul level around myths, fantasies, and illusions about careers and career paths.
I dissolve all imbalances on the soul level around myths, fantasies, and illusions about professionalism.
I dissolve all imbalances on the soul level around myths, fantasies, and illusions about success and failure.
I dissolve my field of experience and transform my vibrational patterns around choosing and changing careers.
I transcend choosing and changing careers, and I am at peace with them.

I surrender to choosing and changing careers, and I allow them in my life as appropriate.

I bring all past issues around choosing and changing careers to an elegant completion in total grace.

I dissolve all future issues around choosing and changing careers before they materialize.

I take total and complete responsibility for choosing and changing careers as appropriate.

I allow and assign others total and complete responsibility for choosing and changing careers as appropriate.

The Filling-the-Cup Script

I have the courage to examine my life and work honestly and objectively.

I determine what makes my heart glad—working with people, things, or ideas—and in what combination.

I open to being surprised by my self-assessment, and I reimagine and reinvent my career accordingly.

I open to the possibility of a new ideal career, and I proceed with right timing and right action.

I choose the ideal career for my values, knowledge, skills, abilities, and desired lifestyle.

My ideal career can be the same, the same with modifications, or completely new and different.

My ideal career can be part-time, full-time, or a composite of part-time or full-time careers.

My ideal career can be a new business, a new direction, and a new lifestyle.

I have the wisdom to recognize my windows of opportunity and the courage to go through them.

I am at peace leaving the secure and familiar, and I move boldly forward choosing and changing careers as appropriate.

I open to and embrace meaningful coincidences, guidances, and synchronicities to choose and change careers.

I give myself permission to experiment and fail along the way, knowing it is part of the process.

My career provides value regardless of its irritations, frustrations, obstacles, and hardships.

My career provides fulfillment regardless of its time demands, pressures, complications, and conflicts.

I open to and embrace my career as a way to use the special and unique talents and gifts I came to use.

I embrace my career as a way to live my highest values through my work.

I embrace my career as a way to express my authentic self through my work.

I embrace my career as a way to express my positive, caring, compassionate self.

I embrace my career as a way to live my greatest joy through my work.

I embrace my career as a way to express my energized, joyful, playful self.

I embrace my career as a way to be a functioning contributing member of humanity.

I embrace my career as a way to support the well-being of people and the environment.

I move beyond the work paradigm to a work life of heart and meaning.

I move beyond the career paradigm to a work life of authenticity and sovereignty.

I move beyond the productivity paradigm to a work life of feeling and fulfillment.

I move beyond the materialistic paradigm to a work life of exuberance and vitality.

I move beyond the "get ahead" paradigm to a work life of contribution and making a difference.

My career supports my turning to deeper more truthful parts of myself.

My career brings the conflicting and controversial aspects of my own nature into harmony and peace.

I engage in my career willingly and enthusiastically.

I engage in my career with full awareness and mindfulness.

Change

As a change agent, I get the "opportunity" to process change continually. I am aware of my reactions and stages, but that doesn't make them less intense. I keep a change recording by my bed for "refresher" listening! (Written for the recording "Accepting Changes & Facing Your Future"—the *Empowerment* series.)

The Emptying-the-Cup Script

Change and I are one.

I release and forgive myself for changing.

I release and forgive myself for not changing.

I release and forgive _____ for changing.

What upsets you the most about change—certain people, rules, social conventions, beliefs, values?

I release and forgive _____ for not changing.

Who frustrates you for not changing, being stubborn, obstinate? What system/belief/pattern do you believe must change?

I release and forgive everyone who taught me it was better not to change.

I release and forgive everyone who taught me _____.

the old ways were better, the good old days were the best

I dissolve all imbalances on the soul level around change and changing.
I dissolve all imbalances on the soul level around fearing change and changing.
I dissolve all imbalances on the soul level around judging change and changing.
I dissolve all imbalances on the soul level around associating change with being out of control.
I dissolve all imbalances on the soul level around associating change with _____.

I dissolve all imbalances on the soul level around denying or resisting change.
I dissolve all imbalances on the soul level around _____ change.

What are your reactions to change when you didn't initiate it?

I dissolve my field of experience around change and changing.
I transform my vibrational patterns around change and changing.
I transcend change and changing, and I am at peace with them.
I surrender to change and changing, and I allow them in my life as appropriate.
I bring all past issues around change and changing to an elegant completion in total grace.
I take total and complete responsibility for my changes.
I allow and assign others total and complete responsibility for their changes as appropriate.
Changing and _____ are separate for me now.

What do you fear about change—growth, the unknown, loss of control?

The Filling-the-Cup Script

Change is natural, and I accept and welcome it.
Change has all positive outcomes for me now.
I am safe and protected during changes.
I am safe and protected when I change.
I am loved and accepted during changes.
I am loved and accepted when I change.
I am nurtured and supported during changes.
I am nurtured and supported when I change.
I understand the change process, and I flow with it in grace.
I choose to change, and I make positive changes daily.
I change easily and effortlessly.
I move to the new with ease and joy.
I accept the paradox of being the same while I change.
I accept the paradox of being constant while I am changing.

Childhood

The more I learn about the SuperSleep™ state, the more I recognize my childhood programming in my adult patterns. Fortunately, most of mine were life-affirming and empowering. I feel clearing childhood and adding self-love are the most powerful tools for personal growth. Use this script to address your personal events and issues. (Written for the recording "Healing Your Childhood"—the *Empowerment* series.)

The Emptying-the-Cup Script

My childhood and I are one.
I release and forgive my childhood.
I release and forgive myself for having a _____ childhood.
I release and forgive everyone who created my _____ childhood.
I release and forgive _____ for _____.

specific types of abuse such as beating, molestation, incest, etc. and the people who did it: specific events that still hold power over your mind, emotions, body, and spirit

I release and forgive _____ for _____.

letting it happen, for allowing it, for not protecting me, for ignoring it, for not being strong enough to stop it, supporting it, facilitating it

I dissolve all imbalances on the soul level around my childhood.
I dissolve all imbalances on the soul level around fearing my childhood.
I dissolve all imbalances on the soul level around denying my childhood.
I dissolve all imbalances on the soul level around everyone who denied me a childhood.
I dissolve all imbalances on the soul level around judging my childhood.
I dissolve all imbalances on the soul level around accepting my childhood.
I dissolve all imbalances on the soul level around _____.
I transcend my childhood, and I am at peace with it.
I surrender to my childhood, and I allow it in my life as appropriate.
I bring all my past issues around my childhood to an elegant completion in total grace.
I take total and complete responsibility for my part in my childhood.
I allow and assign others total and complete responsibility for their part in my childhood.

The Filling-the-Cup Script

I am safe and protected when I acknowledge my true childhood.
I am loved and accepted when I acknowledge my true childhood.

I am nurtured and supported when I acknowledge my true childhood.
I am safe and protected when I let go of the past and heal my injured inner child.
I am loved and protected when I let go of the past and heal my injured inner child.
I am supported and nurtured when I let go of the past and heal my injured inner child.
I move beyond my childhood to an adult life of mental and emotional health.
I move beyond my childhood to an adult life of physical and spiritual health.
I move beyond my childhood to an adult life of compassion, peace, and harmony.
I move beyond my childhood to an adult life of love, happiness, and fulfillment.
I move beyond my childhood to an adult life of _____.

Commitment

Several men I dated insisted I had a problem with commitment when I wouldn't marry them. I always felt I was deeply committed—to principles, values, and behaviors. This script helped me get clarity about the nature of commitment and my personal approach to it (the bonus was being very clear that not marrying them was appropriate for me!). (Written for the recording "Loving Commitment"—the *Loving Partnership* series.)

The Emptying-the-Cup Script

Commitment and I are one.
I release and forgive myself for making commitments.
I release and forgive myself for not making commitments.
I release and forgive myself for making commitments and keeping them.
I release and forgive myself for making commitments and not keeping them.
I release and forgive everyone who would not make a commitment to me.
I release and forgive everyone who made a commitment to me and did not keep it.
I release and forgive Mom and Dad for not keeping their commitments to me.
I release and forgive _____ for _____.

Who made a commitment to you he or she did not keep?

I dissolve all false models and messages around commitment.
I dissolve all imbalances on the soul level around commitment.
I dissolve all imbalances on the soul level around fearing and judging commitment.
I dissolve all imbalances on the soul level around avoiding, undermining, and sabotaging commitment.
I dissolve all imbalances on the soul level around craving and needing commitment.

I dissolve all imbalances on the soul level around fearing and judging not being in a committed relationship.

I dissolve all imbalances on the soul level around seeking, rushing into, and freely giving commitment.

I dissolve all imbalances on the soul level around fearing and judging rejection and abandonment.

I dissolve all imbalances on the soul level around fearing and judging acceptance and engulfment.

I dissolve all imbalances on the soul level around getting equal excitement from acceptance and rejection.

I dissolve all imbalances on the soul level around making and keeping a commitment to the wrong ideas, values, and principles.

I dissolve all imbalances on the soul level around making and keeping a commitment to the wrong causes, organizations and actions.

I dissolve all imbalances on the soul level around making and keeping a commitment to the wrong people.

I dissolve all imbalances on the soul level around making and keeping a commitment to _____.

What have you been committed to that did not serve you? That was false? A career, a lifestyle, a belief?

I dissolve all imbalances on the soul level around making and keeping a commitment for the wrong reasons.

I dissolve all imbalances on the soul level around using commitment to control others.

I dissolve all imbalances on the soul level around allowing others to use commitment to control me.

I dissolve all imbalances on the soul level around associating commitment with protection, safety, and status.

I dissolve all imbalances on the soul level around associating commitment with security, stability, and certainty.

I dissolve all imbalances on the soul level around associating commitment with weakness, restriction, and limitation.

I dissolve all imbalances on the soul level around associating commitment with submission, obligation, and duty.

I dissolve all imbalances on the soul level around associating commitment with _____.

What were you told commitment stood for? Being strong or good or right?

I dissolve all imbalances on the soul level around believing everything can or will be fixed by making a commitment.

I dissolve my field of experience and transform my vibrational patterns around commitment.

I transcend commitment, and I am at peace with it.

I surrender to commitment, and I allow it in my life as appropriate.

I bring all my past issues around commitment to an elegant completion in total grace.

I dissolve all future issues around commitment before they materialize.

I take total and complete responsibility for my commitments as appropriate.

I allow and assign others total and complete responsibility for their commitments as appropriate.

The Filling-the-Cup Script

I recognize the sign of authenticity is the willingness to take a stand and declare it.

I am committed to my own true nature and authenticity first and foremost.

I am loved and accepted when I make commitments.

I am safe and protected when I make commitments.

I am nurtured and supported when I make commitments.

I make the right commitments for me in all times and places.

I am committed to the values, principles, and ethics that serve my highest good.

I am committed to the ideas, concepts, and beliefs that serve my highest good.

I am committed to the actions, behaviors, and conduct that serve my highest good.

I take my commitments seriously, and I speak and behave accordingly.

I make commitments honestly and earnestly, and I maintain them as appropriate.

I make commitments to the right things at the right times for the right reasons.

I make commitments to the right people for the right things at the right times for the right reasons.

Communication

This script deals with the speaking part of communicating. For the more important aspect of listening, refer to the *Listening* script. (Written for the recording "Loving Communication"—the *Loving Relationships* series.)

The Emptying-the-Cup Script

Communicating and I are one.

I release and forgive myself for communicating.

I release and forgive myself for not communicating.

I release and forgive myself for _____.

being abrupt, indirect, nonverbal, dominating

I release and forgive everyone who did not communicate with me.

I release and forgive Mom and Dad for their communication patterns with each other.

I release and forgive Mom and Dad for their communication patterns with me.

I release, forgive, and dissolve all false models of communication.

I dissolve all imbalances on the soul level around communication.

I dissolve all imbalances on the soul level around fearing and judging communication.

I dissolve all imbalances on the soul level around fearing and judging what others will say.

I dissolve all imbalances on the soul level around any and all nonloving communication models and patterns.

I dissolve all imbalances on the soul level around aggressive, abusive, and hostile communication.

I dissolve all imbalances on the soul level around dominating and competing communication.

I dissolve all imbalances on the soul level around insulting, belittling, and ridiculing communication.

I dissolve all imbalances on the soul level around interrupting and finishing the speaker's sentences.

I dissolve all imbalances on the soul level around passive-aggressive communication and hostile humor.

I dissolve all imbalances on the soul level around passive, defensive, and justifying communication.

I dissolve all imbalances on the soul level around indirect, triangulating, and secret communication.

I dissolve all imbalances on the soul level around superficial and misleading communication.

I dissolve all imbalances on the soul level around critical, complaining, and whining communication.

I dissolve all imbalances on the soul level around judgmental, blaming communication.

I dissolve all imbalances on the soul level around generalized, global, fault-finding communication.

I dissolve all imbalances on the soul level around mechanical, habitual communication.

I dissolve all imbalances on the soul level around substituting advice and problem solving for communication.

I dissolve all imbalances on the soul level around assertive and honest communication.

I dissolve all imbalances on the soul level around clear, simple, and transparent communication.

I dissolve all imbalances on the soul level around nurturing and supportive communication.

I dissolve my field of experience and transform my vibrational patterns around my transgenerational patterns of communication.

I dissolve my field of experience and transform my vibrational patterns around loving communication.

I dissolve my field of experience and transform my vibrational patterns around my communication style and patterns.

I transcend communication, and I am at peace with it.

I surrender to communication, and I allow it in my life as appropriate.

I take total and complete responsibility for my part in communication.

I allow and assign others total and complete responsibility for their part in communication.

The Filling-the-Cup Script

I understand communication is the foundation of my relationships.

I recognize communication is an essential tool for living well.

I recognize the immediate benefits of listening and speaking effectively.

I am willing to dedicate the time and energy to earn those benefits and do so in grace.

I recognize and assess my conditioned and habitual communication patterns.

I open to, allow, and embrace changing all facets of my communication patterns to achieve effective communication.

I have the persistence and patience to increase my communication skills daily.

I have the desire and emotional courage to communicate openly and honestly.

I have the motivation and commitment to listen actively.

I have the objectivity, clarity, and confidence to receive communication nondefensively and nonreactively.

I give and receive the human respect, dignity, and honor inherent in communication.

I know my purpose for speaking and match my content and delivery style to my purpose.

I ask for attention and create interest in my listener in appropriate ways.

I present my message simply, clearly, and speak in common language.

I present one concept or issue at a time and assure it is understood before proceeding.

I match my speaking style to the listener's needs, style, and ability.

I feel how my listener is responding and adjust my speaking style accordingly.

I use the body language and tone of voice that support my loving communication.

I restate my message in different ways until it is received as appropriate.

I tell the truth simply and consistently without blame or judgment.

I say the right thing to the right person at the right time for the right reasons.

Completing: Projects/Tasks

I'm always intrigued by what I complete and what I don't. It took a lot of experience to learn my incompletions were often time-savers—not procrastinators. This script helps get clear on when and what to complete.

The Emptying-the-Cup Script

Completing tasks and projects and I are one.

I release and forgive myself for completing tasks and projects.

I release and forgive myself for not completing tasks and projects.

I dissolve all imbalances on the soul level around fearing completing tasks and projects.

I dissolve all imbalances on the soul level around fearing my work won't be good enough.

I dissolve all imbalances on the soul level around judging my work won't be good enough.

I dissolve all imbalances on the soul level around fearing criticism of my work.

I dissolve all imbalances on the soul level around expecting perfection from myself.

I dissolve all imbalances on the soul level around others expecting perfection from me.

I dissolve all imbalances on the soul level around fearing I won't have anything else to do.

I dissolve all imbalances on the soul level around fearing boredom when I complete.

I dissolve all imbalances on the soul level around substituting a task I like for a task I need to complete.

I dissolve all imbalances on the soul level around substituting a project I like for a project I need to complete.

I dissolve my field of experience around completing my tasks and projects.

I transform my vibrational patterns around completing my tasks and projects.

I transcend completing tasks and projects, and I am at peace with them.

I surrender to completing tasks and projects, and I allow them in my life as appropriate.

I bring all past issues around completing tasks and projects to an elegant completion in total grace.

I take total and complete responsibility for completing my tasks and projects as appropriate.

I allow and assign others total and complete responsibility for completing their tasks and projects as appropriate.

Completion and _____ are separate for me now.

being evaluated negatively, being criticized, feeling let down, feeling lonely, being punished, being wrong

The Filling-the-Cup Script

Completing tasks and projects has all positive outcomes for me now.
I am safe and protected when I complete tasks and projects.
I am loved and accepted when I complete tasks and projects.
I am nurtured and supported when I complete tasks and projects.
I feel good about myself when I complete my tasks and projects.
I feel good about my work when I complete it as appropriate.
I have the ability to focus and concentrate, and I do so as appropriate.
I focus on the task and project at hand.
I pace myself appropriately as I complete tasks and projects.
I stay on track to complete the task and project as appropriate.
I know what to complete, and I do so.
I know when to complete, and I do so.
I know how to complete, and I do so.

Concentration

This script has been very helpful for my time management. When I focus completely, I am able to complete tasks in much less time. When I am unable to focus and concentrate, I have learned to delay working on the task or project.

The Emptying-the-Cup Script

Concentrating and I are one.
I release and forgive myself for concentrating.
I release and forgive myself for not concentrating.
I release and forgive myself for _____.

What have you lost because of not concentrating? How do you feel about yourself when you don't concentrate or focus?

I release and forgive everyone who told me I wasn't concentrating.
I release and forgive everyone who told me I couldn't concentrate.
I release, forgive, and dissolve any person, thing, event, or situation that interferes with my concentrating.
I release, forgive and dissolve _____.

What experiences have you had around concentrating, being focused?

I dissolve all imbalances on the soul level around concentrating.
I dissolve all imbalances on the soul level around fearing concentrating.
I dissolve all imbalances on the soul level around judging concentrating.
I dissolve all imbalances on the soul level around believing I'm not good at con-
centrating.
I dissolve all imbalances on the soul level around any and all blocks to my ability
to concentrate.
I dissolve all imbalances on the soul level around any and all blocks to my ability
to focus and stay focused.
I dissolve all imbalances on the soul level around having a lazy mind.
I dissolve all imbalances on the soul level around having an undisciplined mind.
I dissolve all imbalances on the soul level around allowing my mind to wander.
I dissolve all imbalances on the soul level around _____.

What are some reasons you don't concentrate—scattered mind, too much on your mind, not committed to what you are doing, resistance to the task, inability to do the task, lack of focus, lack of steady attention or energy?

I dissolve my field of experience around concentrating.
I transform my vibrational patterns around concentrating.
I transcend concentrating, and I am at peace with it.
I surrender to concentrating, and I allow it in my life as appropriate.
I bring all past issues around concentrating to an elegant completion in total
grace.
I dissolve all future issues around concentrating before they materialize.
I take total and complete responsibility for concentrating and being focused.
I allow and assign others total and complete responsibility for their concentration
and focus.
Concentrating and _____ are separate for me now.

What are your negative feelings/experiences around concentrating?

The Filling-the-Cup Script

Concentrating and being focused have all positive outcomes for me now.
I am safe and protected when I concentrate.
I am safe and protected when I control my own process and focus.
I am loved and accepted when I concentrate.
I am loved and accepted when I control my own process and focus.
I am nurtured and supported when I concentrate.
I am nurtured and supported when I control my own process and focus.
I am in control of my mind and my concentrating ability.
I manage my mind and concentration in the right ways at the right times for the
right reasons.
I have the ability and discipline to concentrate.

I choose when to concentrate and when to allow my mind to wander.
I automatically know when to concentrate, how to concentrate, and on what to concentrate.
I concentrate with peaceful intensity.
My random thought process stills for me to concentrate completely as appropriate.
I focus with single-minded calmness.
I balance concentration with mental relaxation in perfect ways.
I embrace everything that comes from my ability to concentrate.
I effortlessly move through the concentrating process with ease.
My mind allows me to focus effectively.
My emotions allow me to focus effectively.
I trust my body to have the wisdom for concentrating.
I trust my mind, body, and emotions to work with me for effective concentrating.
I welcome everything that comes from concentrating and being focused.
I focus at the right time in the right way for the right reasons.
I know when to begin and when to stop focusing and concentrating.
I begin and end concentrating at will.
I continue through completion as appropriate.
I prepare appropriately.
I provide for my physical comfort and begin by getting comfortable as appropriate.
I arrange my physical space to my liking and for effectiveness and efficiency.
I mentally and physically relax.
I let my body feel whole and sound.
I clear a mental space for concentrating.
I select the most appropriate issue or task for my focus.
I know what to pay attention to and what to release, and I do so.
I reject familiar patterns, habits, and behaviors to focus as appropriate.
I expect positive changes, and I get them.
I create positive changes, and I feel it in all positive ways.
I feel good when I focus and concentrate.
I focus and concentrate with ease and grace.

Confidentiality

I wrote this script when I began working with clients. I wanted to handle information with integrity. Several years later, when I was working as a political appointee, people continually commented on my excellent handling of sensitive information. Of course, it was a result of my confidentiality tape. I often get these positive unintended results. I make a tape with one thing in mind, and I get benefits in another area of my life. It's a nice bonus!

The Emptying-the-Cup Script

Confidentiality and I are one.
I release and forgive myself for keeping confidentiality.
I release and forgive myself for not keeping confidentiality.
I release and forgive everyone who did not keep my confidentiality.
I release and forgive _____ for _____.

Who betrayed your confidences, told your secrets? What was the result?

I dissolve all imbalances on the soul level around confidentiality.
I dissolve all imbalances on the soul level around fearing confidentiality.
I dissolve all imbalances on the soul level around fearing secrets.
I dissolve all imbalances on the soul level around judging confidentiality.
I dissolve all imbalances on the soul level around judging secrets.
I dissolve all imbalances on the soul level around keeping secrets.
I dissolve all imbalances on the soul level around understanding the nature of confidentiality.
I dissolve all imbalances on the soul level around sacrificing confidentiality for _____.

a feeling of power, revenge, a sense of belonging, the higher good

I dissolve my field of experience around confidentiality.
I transform my vibrational patterns around confidentiality.
I transcend confidentiality, and I am at peace with it.
I surrender to confidentiality, and I allow it in my life as appropriate.
I bring all past issues around confidentiality to an elegant completion in total grace.
I dissolve all future issues around confidentiality before they materialize.
I take total and complete responsibility for maintaining confidentiality as appropriate.
I allow and assign others total and complete responsibility for maintaining confidentiality as appropriate.
Maintaining confidentiality and _____ are separate for me now.

What triggers you to talk when you should maintain silence—power, recognition, need for attention, need for approval?

The Filling-the-Cup Script

Being discreet has all positive outcomes for me now.
I am safe and protected when I am discreet.
I am loved and accepted when I am discreet.
I am nurtured and supported when I am discreet.
I feel powerful when I am discreet.
I understand the power of information.

I am safe and secure with my power.
I am safe and secure with information.
I maintain clarity around information issues.
I give and receive information in all appropriate ways.
I know what to express and what to suppress, and I do so.
I pass on information at the right time in the right way.
I pass on information to the right people for the right reasons.
I balance my need to express with the need for confidentiality perfectly.
All of my expression needs are met in appropriate ways.

Conflict Resolution

One of the great joys creating *Change Your Mind* has been cocreating, co-listening and coprocessing recordings with a partner (a friend, family member, or intimate partner). Working together in this way accelerates growth and change exponentially. This is an example of a partner script. (Written for the recording "Loving Conflict"—the *Loving Relationships* series.)

The Filling-the-Cup Script

Together, we open to the power and potential of loving conflict resolution.
We have confidence in our ability to resolve the conflicts of our partnership.
We gracefully and graciously flow with the rupture, repair, and restoration phases of our partnership.
We transform our confrontation and negotiation styles to a positive, affirming process.
We transform our negotiation process to provide mutually satisfying outcomes.
We have the courage and strength to stay present and move through the stages of conflict.
We have the wisdom and skill to mutually engage in loving conflict resolution.
We have the commitment and persistence to cocreate a win-win outcome as appropriate.
We replace taking a position with sharing a goal and following a process.
We share the goal of improving our relationship and our understanding of ourselves and each other.
We cocreate a process we can trust and follow that process as appropriate.
We recognize and discuss our individual confrontation and conflict styles.
We recognize any incompatibility in our styles and discuss them openly.
We use our individual styles to create a workable conflict resolution process.
We suspend and control our reactions to create and maintain a loving atmosphere.
We cocreate and maintain fair guidelines, rules, and procedures for loving conflict resolution.

We cocreate and use methods to break stalemates and impasses.

We develop and practice relaxation methods and take time out as appropriate.

We cocreate and practice rituals and ceremonies for the process and its completion.

We evaluate the process and work to improve our methods and skills.

We select and use the best resources to improve our skills.

We open to coaching and professional help as appropriate.

We schedule our discussions for appropriate times and places.

We set our agenda and focus on one issue at a time as appropriate.

We approach confrontation and conflict with composure, clarity, security, and simplicity.

We approach confrontation and conflict calmly, objectively, and nondefensively.

We maintain steady, dignified, loving energy throughout the process.

We maintain mutual respect throughout the process as appropriate.

We thank each other for being willing to dialogue openly and negotiate fairly.

We affirm the value of each other and the relationship.

We recognize our masks and pretenses and dissolve them.

We speak and act in a perfect expression of our true and authentic selves.

We engage with sincerity, honesty, and integrity.

We take on specific problems, actions, and behaviors, not each other.

We are direct rather than devious, specific rather than general.

We recognize the merit of each other's thoughts and feelings.

We discuss and assess our perceptions and assumptions.

We recognize our own biases and subjective viewpoints.

We acknowledge and validate each other's viewpoints, positions, and feelings without abandoning our own.

We accept each other's emotions without assuming responsibility or blame.

We allow each others' expressions without feeling attacked or victimized as appropriate.

We work together to learn what is important to each other.

We identify and honor each other's needs and desires.

We identify each other's underlying motivations, fears, and concerns as appropriate.

We discover how our own and each other's needs and desires are being denied.

We look beyond the apparent problem for the true source of the conflict.

We are willing and able to understand the true source and do so with grace.

We see the true source of the conflict objectively and take action to resolve it.

We flow with the trivial and confront what is meaningful.

We confront chronic problems at the right time in the right way for the right reasons.

We negotiate from a place of clarity, equality, and personal power.

We replace argument with tact, diplomacy, dialogue, and inquiry.

We replace anger and hostility with natural compassion.

We ask ourselves and each other what we have at stake and we share it.

We prioritize concerns, interests, and needs.
We identify areas of mutual interest and areas of seeming contradictory interests.
We look for a basis of resolution consistent with each other's differing interests.
We understand our situation has many possible outcomes.
We agree having choices and alternatives is preferable, possible, and positive.
We create multiple approaches, choices, alternatives, and possibilities.
We explore different options for meeting both of our needs and interests.
We review and compare our choices and eliminate unworkable ones.
We choose the best workable choice from the variety of possibilities we have gathered.
We provide adequate time to play out the process fully to completion and closure.
We agree to mutual need-satisfying solutions.
We get enough of what we want without depriving each other.
We negotiate clear agreements with agreed-upon definitions and terms.
We lovingly share responsibility equally for keeping the agreement as appropriate.
We consistently reach a successful resolution that creates feelings of satisfaction and accomplishment.
We use loving conflict resolution as a transformative tool to deepen and expand our relationship.
We use loving conflict resolution for continued renewal of our relationship.
We celebrate the successful loving conflict resolution process and its outcomes.
We celebrate the healing nature of the loving conflict resolution process.
We celebrate our growth, reaffirm ourselves, and recommit to our relationship as appropriate.

Conscious Evolution

This is based by the book of the same name by Barbara Marx Hubbard, and I thank her for decades of transformative visionary thinking.

The Emptying-the-Cup Script

Conscious evolution and I are one.
I release and forgive myself for evolving consciously.
I release and forgive myself for not evolving consciously.
I release and forgive _____ for not evolving consciously.
I release and forgive _____ for not teaching me how to evolve consciously.

parents, school, religion, society, friends

I dissolve all imbalances on the soul level around conscious evolution.
I dissolve all imbalances on the soul level around _____ evolution.

personal, social, economic, scientific, educational, spiritual, biological

I dissolve all imbalances on the soul level around changing my self identify and image of the world.

I dissolve all imbalances on the soul level around fearing conscious evolution.

I dissolve all imbalances on the soul level around fearing _____.

changing conventions/cultures/mind-sets/beliefs/values, dramatic change, exponential change, revolution, political upheaval

I dissolve all imbalances on the soul level around judging conscious evolution.

I dissolve all imbalances on the soul level around the current power structure.

I dissolve all imbalances on the soul level around the current power structure fearing and judging conscious evolution.

I dissolve all imbalances on the soul level around everyone who has predicted violence, suffering, world war, self-destruction, and extinction.

I dissolve all imbalances on the soul level around everyone who has predicted _____.

I dissolve all imbalances on the soul level around evolving in response to _____.

a crisis, emergency, revolution, others' actions

I dissolve all imbalances on the soul level around living on a _____ planet.

wartorn, polluting, overpopulating, socially unjust

I dissolve all imbalances on the soul level around visionary thinkers of the past being ostracized, ridiculed, tortured, and killed.

I dissolve all imbalances on the soul level around being _____ for my visionary thinking.

I dissolve my field of experience around conscious evolution.

I transform my vibrational patterns around conscious evolution.

I transcend conscious evolution, and I am at peace with it.

I surrender to conscious evolution, and I allow it in my life.

I bring all past issues around conscious evolution to an elegant completion in total grace.

I dissolve all future issues around conscious evolution before they materialize.

I take total and complete responsibility for my part in conscious evolution.

I allow and assign others total and complete responsibility for their part in conscious evolution.

Conscious evolution and _____ are separate for me now.

isolation, losing friends, being too far out

The Filling-the-Cup Script

Conscious evolution has all positive outcomes for me now.

Participating in the evolution of humankind has all positive outcomes for me now.

I am safe and protected when I evolve consciously and participate in the evolution of humankind.

I am loved and accepted when I evolve consciously and participate in the evolution of humankind.

I am nurtured and supported when I evolve consciously and participate in the evolution of humankind.

I understand, embrace, and develop the world view of conscious evolution.

I understand the universe has a history, and the nature of nature is to transform.

I understand quantum transformations are nature's tradition.

I understand crises precede transformation.

I understand holism is inherent in nature.

I understand nature creates beauty, and beauty endures.

I understand evolution raises consciousness and freedom.

I believe in the possibility of a gentle, peaceful, graceful evolution.

I believe in the possibility of regeneration of individuality, liberty, community, and ethics.

I believe in the possibility of fulfilling the collective potential of the human race.

I believe in harmony with nature, one another, and divine intelligence.

I believe in _____.

I recognize the challenge of my time is filled with opportunity.

I operate from a spirit-motivated plan of action based on patterns of evolutionary success.

I make the shift from observer to participant and cocreator with the process of evolution in grace.

I support and participate in the ethical and creative use of power toward the next stage of human evolution.

I support and participate in accelerating the connections between innovating people and projects to shift humanity toward a more positive future.

I support and participate in a world-changing event to align our higher consciousnesses with our emerging capacities.

I carry a vision of a cocreative society filled with understanding and compassion.

I carry a vision of a cocreative society filled with _____.

peace, love, joy, harmony, tolerance, abundance, prosperity, health, support, mutuality, equality, justice

I find and fulfill my life purpose through organizations, activities, and teams already moving toward conscious evolution.

I join with a synergistic team and participate in the greater whole.

I join together with others in creative action and share in the grand adventure of world evolution.

I attract like-minded, -hearted, and -spirited people who share a universal, holistic, cosmic consciousness.

We enter into communion and community in all positive ways.

I open to an increase of synchronicities and to complexities self-organizing accordingly.

I open to increasing guidance and intuition, and I perform with spontaneous right action.

I open to joining my unique intelligence with others, and we converge to cocreate.

I align my thoughts and prayers with humanity's potential for goodness and creativity.

I take my rightful place in universal humanity and share my gifts lovingly.

I take my rightful place in the global culture and contribute my gifts to the evolution of the world.

Control

I have come to recognize my self-control is usually perceived as controlling, and my inability to be controlled by others is usually called controlling. This script helped me get clear on when and what I choose to control. It also helped me release the self-doubts others tried to create in me about my independent nature.

The Emptying-the-Cup Script

Control and I are one.
I release and forgive myself for being in control.
I release and forgive myself for not being in control.
I release and forgive myself for being controlling.
I release and forgive myself for not being controlling.
I release and forgive myself for controlling others.
I release and forgive myself for controlling _____.
I release and forgive myself for not controlling others.
I release and forgive everyone who controlled me.
I release and forgive _____ for controlling me.

mother, father, partner, children, boss, teacher, religious figure

I release and forgive myself for being controlled.
I release and forgive myself for not being controlled.
I release and forgive myself for allowing others to control me.
I release and forgive myself for not allowing others to control me.
I dissolve all imbalances on the soul level around control.

I dissolve all imbalances on the soul level around fearing control.

I dissolve all imbalances on the soul level around fearing what I will do if I am in control.

I dissolve all imbalances on the soul level around fearing what I will do if I am not in control.

I dissolve all imbalances on the soul level around fearing what will happen if I am not in control.

I dissolve all imbalances on the soul level around judging control.

I dissolve all imbalances on the soul level around judging what I will do if I am in control.

I dissolve all imbalances on the soul level around judging what I will do if I am not in control.

I dissolve all imbalances on the soul level around fearing being controlled.

I dissolve all imbalances on the soul level around judging being controlled.

I dissolve all imbalances on the soul level around _____.

What experiences do you have around control, loss of control, being controlled, authority figures, letting go?

I dissolve all imbalances on the soul level around controlling others in place of controlling myself.

I dissolve all imbalances on the soul level around controlling external factors when I feel out of control internally.

I dissolve my field of experience around control.

I dissolve my field of experience around being controlled.

I dissolve my field of experience around being controlling.

I transform my vibrational patterns around control.

I transform my vibrational patterns around being controlled.

I transform my vibrational patterns around being controlling.

I transcend control, being controlled, and being controlling, and I am at peace with them.

I surrender to control, being controlled, and being controlling, and I allow them in my life as appropriate.

I bring all past issues around control, being controlled, and being controlling to an elegant completion in total grace.

I dissolve all future issues around control, being controlled, and being controlling before they materialize.

I take total and complete responsibility for my control issues.

I allow and assign others total and complete responsibility for their control issues.

Control and _____ are separate for me now.

domination, abuse, unfairness, fear, pain

The Filling-the-Cup Script

I am in control of myself and my life as appropriate.
I am safe and protected whether or not I am in control.
I am loved and accepted whether or not I am in control.
I am nurtured and supported whether or not I am in control.
I am honored and acknowledged whether or not I am in control.
I am happy and free whether or not I am in control.
I am successful and productive whether or not I am in control.
I am taken care of and provided for whether or not I am in control.
I am _____ whether or not I am in control.
Control and power are separate for me now as appropriate.
Controlling others and feeling powerful are separate for me now.
I recognize my personal power comes from being in control of myself, not others.
I balance control and letting go perfectly.
I choose when to control and when to let go.
I control when appropriate: I let go when appropriate.
I control the right things at the right times for the right reasons.
I let go of the right things at the right times for the right reasons.
I am now willing to control _____.

habits, thoughts, responses, reactions, emotions

I am now willing to let go of _____.

situations, people, things, thoughts, illnesses, habits; domination, authority, governance

I am safe and protected when I let go.
I am loved and accepted when I let go.
I am nurtured and supported when I let go.
I am _____ when I let go.
I move beyond control to peace and harmony.
I move beyond control to allowing and accepting.
I move beyond control to _____.

faith, belief, flow, peace, acceptance

I move beyond control to _____.

observer, teacher, leader, role model, mentor, cocreator, equal partner, visionary

Creative Problem Solving

I've been teaching creative problem-solving classes for business and government for twenty years. This is an overview of the basic principles.

Remember to have fun and be outrageous while you generate ideas; be methodical, logical, and practical when you choose and implement them. (Written for the recording "Solving Problems Wisely"—the *Success* series.)

The Emptying-the-Cup Script

Creative problem solving and I are one.
I release and forgive myself for solving problems creatively.
I release and forgive myself for not solving problems creatively.
I release and forgive myself for _____.

How do you solve problems now—in routine ways, practically, with common sense?

I release and forgive everyone who did not teach me how to solve problems creatively.
I release and forgive _____ for _____.

How did your family solve problems, deal with your problems?

I release and forgive myself for creating problems.
I release and forgive everyone who created problems for me.
I release and forgive _____ for _____.

Who has created problems for you, who creates problems for you now? What are the results?

I dissolve all imbalances on the soul level around creative problem solving.
I dissolve all imbalances on the soul level around fearing creative problem solving.
I dissolve all imbalances on the soul level around judging creative problem solving.
I dissolve all imbalances on the soul level around the judgments that block creative thinking.
I dissolve all imbalances on the soul level around any and all blocks to creative problem solving.
I dissolve all imbalances on the soul level around creating problems.
I dissolve all imbalances on the soul level around confusing having problems with being important or powerful.
I dissolve all imbalances on the soul level around misunderstanding or misinterpreting the problem.
I dissolve all imbalances on the soul level around seeing the symptoms in place of the problem.
I dissolve all imbalances on the soul level around seeing constraints in place of possibilities.
I dissolve my field of experience around creative problem solving.
I transform my vibrational patterns around creative problem solving.

I transcend creative problem solving, and I am at peace with it.
I surrender to creative problem solving, and I allow it in my life as appropriate.
I bring all past issues around creative problem solving to an elegant completion in total grace.
I dissolve all future issues around creative problem solving before they materialize.
I take total and complete responsibility for my creative problem solving.
I allow and assign others total and complete responsibility for their creative problem solving as appropriate.
Solving problems creatively and _____ are separate for me now.

being weird, too far-out, unconventional, ignored, misunderstood

The Filling-the-Cup Script

Creative problem solving has all positive outcomes for me now.
I am safe and protected when I solve problems creatively.
I am loved and accepted when I solve problems creatively.
I am nurtured and supported when I solve problems creatively.

What other support would you like for your creative problem-solving process?

I understand there are infinite possibilities, and I have possibility thinking.
I see the positive side of problems.
I see problems as natural opportunities for change.
I see problems as lessons I can learn from as appropriate.
I turn problems into successes in creative ways.
I have a quick, creative mind, and I use it effectively.
I have an open, playful thought process, and I use it appropriately.
I give my mind permission to see things differently.
I accept random thoughts as part of the whole.
I recognize my own personal style of creative thinking.
I recognize my creative times, and I use them effectively.
I invite and welcome creative thoughts, and I shift into creative thinking at will.
I allow new ideas and approaches to spring into my mind.
I make new connections and reach new conclusions easily.
I reject familiar answers for new thoughts as appropriate.
I think holistically and synergistically when necessary.
I think _____ .

How else would you like your mind to work?

I clearly define the problem, free of misconceptions and distortions.
I give myself time to research the problem so I understand it.
I take time out to integrate my understanding and generate ideas.

I give myself sufficient time to generate an abundance of ideas.
I allow creative ideas and approaches to spring into my mind.
I am patient with myself while I formulate new ideas and approaches.
I am at peace with fragmented, half-baked ideas while I am being creative.
I easily generate several creative approaches to any situation.
I acknowledge each creative thought, no matter how outrageous.
I identify various possible creative solutions.
I identify the most probable creative solutions.
I gather and organize facts about the probable creative solutions.
I evaluate the probable creative solutions based on the facts.
I balance discernment and creativity in perfect ways.
I choose the best creative solution for the right reasons.
I allow myself to choose an alternative that doesn't seem practical if it will work.
I implement the best solution.
I evaluate the solution while it is in progress and modify it as appropriate.
I learn from the process and improve my creative problem-solving ability.
I _____.

What other outcomes would you like from the creative problem-solving process?

Creativity

I suppressed my creativity to be what my responsibilities required, as I was a single parent without support from my ex-spouse. I focused on careers that made money and provided flexible schedules. When my daughter was grown and my provider responsibilities fulfilled, I used this script to transition to living more creatively and artfully. Have fun with it!

The Emptying-the-Cup Script

Creativity and I are one.
I release and forgive myself for being creative.
I release and forgive myself for not being creative.
I release and forgive myself for believing I am not creative.
I release and forgive myself for hiding, repressing, or denying my creativity.
I release and forgive everyone who hid, repressed, or denied my creativity.
I release and forgive everyone who did not recognize my creativity for what it was.
I release and forgive _____ for _____.

What are your experiences around being creative, around your creative activities? What were the results?

I release, forgive, and dissolve all false models of creativity.
I dissolve all imbalances on the soul level around creativity.

I dissolve all imbalances on the soul level around fearing being creative.

I dissolve all imbalances on the soul level around judging being creative.

I dissolve all imbalances on the soul level around fearing being different.

I dissolve all imbalances on the soul level around fearing standing out.

I dissolve all imbalances on the soul level around any and all blocks to my creativity.

I dissolve all imbalances on the soul level around lacking the courage to express myself creatively.

I dissolve all imbalances on the soul level around my deepest creative power expressing itself.

I dissolve all imbalances on the soul level around limits on my capacity for self-expression.

I dissolve all imbalances on the soul level around limits on my capacity for self-awareness.

I dissolve my field of experience around creativity and being creative.

I dissolve my field of experience around myths of the creative personality and lifestyle.

I transform my vibrational patterns around creativity and being creative.

I transform my vibrational patterns around myths of the creative personality and lifestyle.

I transcend creativity and being creative, and I am at peace with it.

I surrender to creativity and being creative, and I allow it in my life.

I bring all past issues around being creative to an elegant completion in total grace.

I dissolve all future issues around being creative before they materialize.

I take total and complete responsibility for my creativity and its expression.

I allow and assign others total and complete responsibility for their creativity and its expression.

Being creative and _____ are separate for me now.

being eccentric, living in poverty

The Filling-the-Cup Script

Being creative has all positive outcomes for me now.

Being different has all positive outcomes for me now.

Expressing my creativity has all positive outcomes for me now.

I am safe and protected when I am creative and express it.

I am loved and accepted when I am creative and express it.

I am nurtured and supported when I am creative and express it.

I open to my own creativity in peace and grace.

I have the courage and discipline to bring my creative spirit into form.

I have the skill and ability to bring my creative spirit into form.

I express my creativity in my own unique form and style.

I express my creativity in the right way at the right time for the right reasons.
I accept there are infinite ways to express creativity, and I experiment as appropriate.
I find ways to express my creativity that suit me, my talents, and abilities.
I allow myself to be creative in all I do as appropriate.
I express my creativity within the routine of my daily living.
I express my creativity within the space and activities of my daily living.
I express my creativity in all positive, healthy, life-affirming ways.
I express my individuality in all positive, healthy, life-affirming ways.
I live my life as an art form, enjoying the process.
I trust my own natural creative rhythms and creative process.
I recognize my creative times, and I use them well.
I work with the right teachers in the right way at the right time for the right reasons.
I allow myself experimentation as appropriate.
I blend and balance focus and enjoyment with completion and flow.
I blend and balance usefulness and practicality with whimsy and fancy.
I blend and balance _____.
I take joy in creating.
The act and process of creating is its own end for me.
Creating is its own reward in my life.

Dating

I have been single most of my life, so dating has been an ongoing learning experience. I dedicate this script to all who are in the "dating game."

The Emptying-the-Cup Script

Dating and I are one.
I release and forgive myself for dating.
I release and forgive myself for not dating.
I release and forgive myself for not knowing how to date.
I release and forgive my partners for not knowing how to date.
I dissolve all false models and messages around dating from all sources.
I release and forgive myself for all my dating mistakes in all times and places.
I release and forgive myself for _____.

What do you regret doing in the dating game?

I release and forgive all disappointments and betrayals from dating.
I release and forgive _____ for _____.

Who and what do you regret around the dating game—someone who wouldn't go out with you, wouldn't take no for an answer, a friend who wanted to date your dates, someone who stood you up?

I release and forgive myself for dating the wrong person for the wrong reasons.

I dissolve all imbalances on the soul level around dating.

I dissolve all imbalances on the soul level around fearing and judging dating.

I dissolve all imbalances on the soul level around dysfunctional dating.

I dissolve all imbalances on the soul level around addicted or addictive dating.

I dissolve all imbalances on the soul level around fast, urgent, whirlwind dating.

I dissolve all imbalances on the soul level around risky, dramatic dating.

I dissolve all imbalances on the soul level around intense, passionate dating.

I dissolve all imbalances on the soul level around compelling, compulsive dating.

I dissolve all imbalances on the soul level around slow, methodical, deliberate dating.

I dissolve all imbalances on the soul level around inert, stagnant dating.

I dissolve all imbalances on the soul level around dating rituals and ceremonies.

I dissolve all imbalances on the soul level around dating archetypes and myths.

I dissolve all imbalances on the soul level around dating fantasies and fairy tales.

I dissolve all imbalances on the soul level around cultural, societal, and religious roles, rules, and models of dating.

I dissolve all imbalances on the soul level around gender and stereotyped roles in dating.

I dissolve all imbalances on the soul level around family models and pressures of dating.

I dissolve all imbalances on the soul level around creating a false image during dating.

I dissolve all imbalances on the soul level around my partner creating a false image during dating.

I dissolve all imbalances on the soul level around my partner and I projecting our true images during dating.

I dissolve all imbalances on the soul level around going unconscious during dating.

I dissolve all imbalances on the soul level around idealizing my partner and our compatibility.

I dissolve all imbalances on the soul level around idealizing the relationship and its possibilities.

I dissolve all imbalances on the soul level around facing the full truth of the emerging relationship.

I dissolve all imbalances on the soul level around seeing relationship strengths and possibilities objectively.

I dissolve all imbalances on the soul level around seeing relationship problems and incompatibilities objectively.

I dissolve all imbalances on the soul level around seeing relationship _____ objectively.

What parts of relationships do you not see clearly until it is over?

I dissolve all imbalances on the soul level around maintaining my power throughout dating in appropriate ways.

I dissolve all imbalances on the soul level around allowing inappropriate behavior during dating.

I dissolve all imbalances on the soul level around knowing my own heart and mind during dating.

I dissolve my field of experience and transform my vibrational patterns around dating.

I transcend dating, and I am at peace with it.

I surrender to dating, and I allow it in my life as appropriate.

I bring all my past issues around dating to an elegant completion in total grace.

I dissolve all future issues around dating before they materialize.

I take total and complete responsibility for my part in dating.

I allow and assign others total and complete responsibility for their part in dating me.

The Filling-the-Cup Script

I neither seek nor avoid dating: I open to it in grace.

I enjoy dating for the part it plays in my life.

I consciously choose when to date, how to date, and whom to date.

I go on dates to share experiences and enjoy others' company.

I go on dates to have varied experiences of companionship and communication.

I go on dates to learn about myself and my partnering style and preferences.

I go on dates to learn about others and their partnering style and preferences.

I go on dates to explore others' suitability for me.

I go on dates as one step toward establishing a loving relationship.

I use dating to determine compatibility and the possibility for a committed relationship.

I maintain my full powers of discernment throughout the excitement of dating.

I know and follow my own heart and mind throughout dating as appropriate.

I maintain balance and congruence between my head and my heart throughout dating.

I balance my feelings of love with my power of objective assessment in perfect ways.

I balance the fun and freedom of dating with the tasks and responsibilities of establishing intimacy.

I realize mutual and equal involvement in the tasks and goals of dating are an indication of a successful future relationship.

I allow dating to take its natural time for the healthy unfolding of the relationship.

I enter into dating to reveal my authentic self and learn my partner's authentic self.

I embrace dating as a time to deepen mutual love, appreciation, and trust.

I embrace dating as a time to deepen understanding and ways of relating.

I embrace dating as a time to develop open, honest communication.

I embrace dating as a time to explore similarities and differences.

I embrace dating as a time to explore values, beliefs, and moral codes.

I embrace dating as a time to explore habits, patterns, and lifestyles.

I embrace dating as a time to identify areas of potential conflict.

I embrace dating as a time to face issues and deal with them appropriately.

I embrace dating as a time to work through obstacles and resolve conflicts.

I embrace dating as a time to develop goals, priorities, and directions.

I embrace dating as a time to establish plans for work and finances.

I embrace dating as a time to explore attitudes toward children and child raising.

I embrace dating as a time to work out plans for family life.

I embrace dating as a time to explore relationships with future in-laws.

I embrace dating as a time to learn how to express affection and caring in mutually satisfying ways.

I embrace dating as a time to learn how to express disagreement in mutually satisfying ways.

I embrace dating as a time to learn how to vent frustration in mutually satisfying ways.

I embrace dating as a time to learn how to negotiate in mutually satisfying ways.

I embrace dating as a time to learn how to ask for what I want and need in mutually understood ways.

I embrace dating as a time to learn how to accept and refuse requests in mutually satisfying ways.

I embrace dating as a time to learn how to balance my needs and desires within the relationship.

I embrace dating as a time to learn how to balance the demands on my time, energy, and resources.

I embrace dating as a time to balance the I with the We.

My experiences and feelings during dating are a basis for my decision about the future of the relationship.

My perceptions and intuitions during dating are a basis for my decision about the future of the relationship.

I make my decisions about a future relationship based on all truthful and appropriate sources of information.

I am divinely guided to make the best decision about dating and its next step, and I follow that guidance.

Debt

Overspending and debt are common in our culture. This script addresses them and can be used with the *Budgeting* and *Prosperity* scripts. (Written for the recording "Managing Money Flow"—the *Money* series.)

The Emptying-the-Cup Script

Debt and I are one.

I release and forgive myself for overspending and being in debt.

I release and forgive myself for not overspending and not being in debt.

I release and forgive myself for _____.

I release, forgive, and dissolve all false messages and models of spending and debt.

I dissolve all imbalances on the soul level around spending, overspending, and debt.

I dissolve all imbalances on the soul level around family and generational patterns of spending and debt.

I dissolve all imbalances on the soul level around societal and cultural patterns of spending and debt.

I dissolve all imbalances on the soul level around gender and age patterns of spending and debt.

I dissolve all imbalances on the soul level around fearing and judging spending and debt.

I dissolve all imbalances on the soul level around going unconscious around spending and debt.

I dissolve all imbalances on the soul level around spending to make up for unhealed childhood issues.

I dissolve all imbalances on the soul level around addictive spending and shopping.

I dissolve all imbalances on the soul level around irresponsible spending and debt.

I dissolve all imbalances on the soul level around being seduced by advertising and marketing.

I dissolve all imbalances on the soul level around being seduced by consumerism and competition.

I dissolve all imbalances on the soul level around immediate gratification and impulse buying.

I dissolve all imbalances on the soul level around delayed gratification and long-range planning.

I dissolve all imbalances on the soul level around miserliness and penny-pinching.

I dissolve all imbalances on the soul level around hoarding and collecting.

I dissolve all imbalances on the soul level around spending too much and spending too little.

I dissolve all imbalances on the soul level around spending on myself and spending on others.

I dissolve all imbalances on the soul level around living beyond my means.

I dissolve all imbalances on the soul level around personal consumer debt.

I dissolve all imbalances on the soul level around credit, credit cards, and charging.

I dissolve my field of experience and transform my vibrational patterns around spending and debt.

I transcend spending and debt, and I am at peace with them.

I surrender to spending and debt, and I allow them in my life as appropriate.

I bring all past issues around spending and debt to an elegant completion in total grace.

I dissolve all future issues around spending and debt before they materialize.

I take total and complete responsibility for my spending and debt.

I allow and assign others total and complete responsibility for their spending and debt as appropriate.

The Filling-the-Cup Script

I am committed to being financially independent.

I am committed to being free of inappropriate debt.

I match my spending to my true goals, values, and priorities in all times and places.

My income exceeds my expenses, and I accelerate my payments to become debt-free.

I feel powerful planning how to spend my money and following my plan as appropriate.

I have fun deciding what to buy before I shop, and I buy only the planned items as appropriate.

I make it a fun game to compare prices and pick the best value.

I maintain sufficient cash on hand and pay cash for pleasure, comfort, and vanity.

I am a rational, disciplined, successful shopper and spender.

I put my time and energy into something more satisfying than shopping and spending.

Delegation

As an associate professor of business, I taught college supervision courses for eight years. I have been a management trainer since then. Business scripts such as this one are based on a combination of textbook theory and "real world" skills. Enjoy your new skills.

The Emptying-the-Cup Script

Delegation and I are one.

I release and forgive myself for delegating.

I release and forgive myself for not delegating.

I release and forgive everyone who delegated to me.

I release and forgive _____ for _____.

Who made you do things you didn't enjoy, weren't capable of? Who made you responsible for their jobs? Who shirked their responsibilities?

I release, forgive, and dissolve all false models of delegation.
I dissolve all imbalances on the soul level around delegation.
I dissolve all imbalances on the soul level around fearing delegation.
I dissolve all imbalances on the soul level around judging delegation.
I dissolve all imbalances on the soul level around giving others my responsibilities.
I dissolve all imbalances on the soul level around being given others' responsibilities.
I dissolve all imbalances on the soul level around allowing others to give me their responsibilities.
I dissolve my field of experience around delegation.
I transform my vibrational patterns around delegation.
I transcend delegation, and I am at peace with it.
I surrender to delegation, and I allow it in my life as appropriate.
I bring all past issues around delegation to an elegant completion in total grace.
I dissolve all future issues around delegation before they materialize.
I take total and complete responsibility for my responsibilities.
I allow and assign others total and complete responsibility for their responsibilities.
Delegating and _____ are separate for me now.

being irresponsible, losing control, losing quality, dumping on another

The Filling-the-Cup Script

Delegation has all positive outcomes for me now.
I am safe and protected when I delegate.
I am safe and protected when others delegate to me.
I am loved and accepted when I delegate.
I am loved and accepted when others delegate to me.
I am nurtured and supported when I delegate.
I am nurtured and supported when others delegate to me.
The art of delegation is natural for me.
I identify what work will be delegated.
I identify which person is appropriate to do the work.
I match the person's skills, abilities, and role to the task.
I delegate the right task to the right person.
I delegate at the right time in the right way for the right reasons.
I set guidelines for the delegated work as needed.
I provide the necessary tools for success when I delegate.
Before I delegate, I involve the person in the planning as much as possible.
I use more questions than statements to involve the person.

I earnestly seek and accept the person's ideas as appropriate.
I tell the person what to do, not how to do it as appropriate.
I let the person do it his/her way as appropriate.
I show the person how to do it as appropriate.
I explain the importance of and reason for the task clearly and simply.
I explain the objective and desired outcome of the task clearly and simply.
I describe my expected results, and what level of error is acceptable.
I give the person sufficient authority to do the task.
I give the person a clear picture of the role I will play in the task.
I provide sufficient time and resources for the task.
I create an obligation for the person to perform well.
I hold the person responsible for performing as appropriate.
We discuss the resources available and the deadline.
We set up a check-back system on the task, and I follow it.
I check on the person's progress at the right time in the right ways for the right reasons.
I monitor the person's progress as appropriate.
I monitor for acceptable performance, not perfection.
I know what to delegate, when to delegate, and how to delegate efficiently and effectively.

Deserving

I am continually intrigued with the difference clearing one word or one event can make in a person's life. One of my clients identified the feeling of "not deserving" as her core issue. This is an adaptation of her script. Thanks to her—and Go, Girl!

The Emptying-the-Cup Script

Being deserving and I are one.
I release and forgive myself for being deserving.
I release and forgive myself for not being deserving.
I release and forgive myself for believing I don't deserve _____.

health, wealth, happiness, love

I release and forgive myself for denying absolute fulfillment in every area of my life.
I release and forgive _____ for telling me I am not deserving.

mother, father, brothers, sisters, teachers, partner, myself, religious figures

I release and forgive _____ for telling me I don't deserve _____.

What specific events come to mind around what you deserve? What were
the results?

I dissolve all imbalances on the soul level around being deserving.
I dissolve all imbalances on the soul level around fearing being deserving.
I dissolve all imbalances on the soul level around judging being deserving.
*I dissolve all imbalances on the soul level around _____ messages about being
deserving.*

family, educational, societal, cultural, governmental, legal, religious

I dissolve all need to feel I am not deserving from my mental body in total grace.
I dissolve all need to feel I am not deserving from my physical body in total grace.
*I dissolve all need to feel I am not deserving from my emotional body in total
grace.*
I dissolve all need to feel I am not deserving from my spiritual body in total grace.
I dissolve my field of experience around being deserving.
I transform my vibrational patterns around being deserving.
I transcend being deserving, and I am at peace with it.
I surrender to being deserving, and I allow it in my life as appropriate.
*I bring all past issues around being deserving to an elegant completion in total
grace.*
I dissolve all future issues around being deserving before they materialize.
*I take total and complete responsibility for my thoughts and feelings about being
deserving.*
*I allow and assign others total and complete responsibility for their thoughts and
feelings about being deserving.*
Being deserving and _____ are separate for me now.

being selfish, greedy, unspiritual

The Filling-the-Cup Script

Being deserving has all positive outcomes for me now.
Getting what I want has all positive outcomes for me now.
I am safe and protected when I am deserving.
I am safe and protected when I get what I want.
I am loved and accepted when I am deserving.
I am loved and accepted when I get what I want.
I am nurtured and supported when I am deserving.
I am nurtured and supported when I get what I want.
I am _____ when I am deserving and get what I want.

happy, healthy, spontaneous, free, peaceful

I believe completely that I deserve _____ as appropriate.

all good, unlimited good, love, unconditional love, perfect health, happiness, financial stability, financial security, prosperity, abundance, personal wealth, to achieve my goals

I stand firmly in my entitlement to deserving.
I believe completely in my entitlement to deserving.
I feel deeply about my entitlement to deserving.
I hold steady mentally and emotionally in the process of getting what I want and deserve.
I hold steady physically and spiritually in the process of getting what I want and deserve.
I am at peace with deserving my highest good.
I carry forward the positive aspects of deserving.
I am deserving.
I am one with the prospering power of the universe.
I now prosper in a number of ways.
I deserve _____, and I attain it in grace.

good health, joy, happiness, freedom, pleasure, abundance

Divorce

This is the script I wish I had in 1974!

The Emptying-the-Cup Script

Divorce and I are one.
I release and forgive myself for being divorced.
I release and forgive myself for wanting the divorce.
I release and forgive myself for not wanting the divorce.
I release and forgive myself for causing the divorce.
I release and forgive myself for not causing the divorce.
I release and forgive myself for trying too hard.
I release and forgive myself for not trying hard enough.
I release and forgive myself for staying too long.
I release and forgive myself for not staying long enough.
I release and forgive myself for putting up with/allowing _____.

abuse, infidelity, control, irresponsibility

I release and forgive myself for being surprised by the divorce.
I release and forgive myself for not being surprised by the divorce.
I release and forgive everyone who did not support me through my divorce.
I release and forgive everyone who blamed or judged me for my divorce.
I release and forgive myself for recovering from my divorce.

I release and forgive myself for not recovering from my divorce.
I release and forgive myself for getting help through the divorce.
I release and forgive myself for not getting help through the divorce.
I release and forgive _____.
I dissolve all imbalances on the soul level around my marriage.
I dissolve all imbalances on the soul level around divorce.
I dissolve all imbalances on the soul level around fearing divorce.
I dissolve all imbalances on the soul level around fearing being single.
I dissolve all imbalances on the soul level around fearing being married.
I dissolve all imbalances on the soul level around judging divorce.
I dissolve all imbalances on the soul level around judging being single.
I dissolve all imbalances on the soul level around judging being married.
I dissolve all imbalances on the soul level around feeling _____ about my divorce.

ashamed, devastated, sad, resentful, shocked, scared, angry, wounded, like a failure, like a sinner, confused, abandoned, betrayed, victorious, vindicated, loss of faith, anger at God, disillusioned

I dissolve all imbalances on the soul level around playing the role of _____ through the divorce.

martyr, victim, wronged spouse, good mother/father

I dissolve all imbalances on the soul level around wanting revenge.
I dissolve all imbalances on the soul level around not grieving enough.
I dissolve all imbalances on the soul level around grieving too much.
I dissolve all imbalances on the soul level around unresolved grieving issues.
I dissolve all imbalances on the soul level around unresolved sources of stress.
I dissolve all imbalances on the soul level around emotional swings.
I dissolve all imbalances on the soul level around turning love into hate.
I dissolve all imbalances on the soul level around living in the past.
I dissolve all imbalances on the soul level around living in the future.
I dissolve all imbalances on the soul level around _____ my ex-spouse.

blaming, comparing, spouse bashing

I dissolve all imbalances on the soul level around maintaining an attachment to my ex-spouse.
I dissolve all imbalances on the soul level around my ex-spouse maintaining an attachment to me.
I dissolve all imbalances on the soul level around playing games with my ex-spouse.
I dissolve all imbalances on the soul level around _____ with my ex-spouse.

having power struggles, control issues, needing to be right/wrong

I dissolve all imbalances on the soul level around my ex-spouse playing games with me.

I dissolve all imbalances on the soul level around my ex-spouse having_____ with me.

power struggles, control issues, needing to be right/wrong

I dissolve all imbalances on the soul level around using things as a weapon against my ex-spouse.

I dissolve all imbalances on the soul level around using_____ as a weapon against my ex-spouse.

children, money, friends, property, religion

I dissolve all imbalances on the soul level around my ex-spouse using things as a weapon against me.

I dissolve all imbalances on the soul level around my ex-spouse using_____ as a weapon against me.

children, money, friends, property, religion

I dissolve all imbalances on the soul level around saying_____ about my ex-spouse.

negative things, rumors, lies, stories

I dissolve all imbalances on the soul level around my ex-spouse saying_____about me.

negative things, rumors, lies, stories

I dissolve all imbalances on the soul level around being hurt by what my ex-spouse says about me.

I dissolve all imbalances on the soul level around my relationship with_____.

my family, children, in-laws, friends, church, coworkers, baby-sitters, day care givers

I dissolve all imbalances on the soul level around putting my needs first.

I dissolve all imbalances on the soul level around putting my children's needs first.

I dissolve all imbalances on the soul level around telling my children the truth.

I dissolve my field of experience around divorce, being single, and being married.

I transform my vibrational patterns around divorce, being single, and being married.

I transcend my marriage, and I am at peace with it.

I transcend divorce and being single, and I am at peace with them.

I surrender to my marriage, and I allow it in my life as appropriate.

I surrender to divorce and being single, and I allow them in my life as appropriate.

I bring all past issues around my marriage to an elegant completion in total grace.

I bring all past issues around divorce and being single to an elegant completion in total grace.

I dissolve all future issues around my marriage before they materialize.

I dissolve all future issues around divorce and being single before they materialize.

I take total and complete responsibility for my part in the marriage.

I take total and complete responsibility for my part in the divorce.

I allow and assign my spouse total and complete responsibility for his or her part in the marriage.

I allow and assign _____ total and complete responsibility for his or her part in the marriage.

I allow and assign my spouse total and complete responsibility for his or her part in the divorce.

I allow and assign others total and complete responsibility for their part in the divorce.

I allow and assign _____ total and complete responsibility for his or her part in the divorce.

Being divorced and _____ are separate for me now.

being depressed, lonely, alone, poor

The Filling-the-Cup Script

I am safe and protected when I am divorced and single.
I am loved and accepted when I am divorced and single.
I am nurtured and supported when I am divorced and single.
I choose health mentally, emotionally, physically, and spiritually.
I choose to live a life of _____.

forgiveness, peace, harmony, ease, love

I realize grief is a normal reaction to divorce, and I grieve in appropriate ways.
I understand divorce changes my legal status: I must change my emotional status.
I choose honesty with myself and others, and I live accordingly.
I resolve the past, live in the present, and look forward to the future.
I achieve a new level of maturity and wisdom in grace.
I achieve a new wholeness of self in grace.
I maintain my individual rights and self-respect while working toward peace with my ex-spouse.
I am in control of my life, my responses, and my reactions.
I control my responses to my ex-spouse regardless of his or her actions.
I keep the best interests of the children at the forefront of my thoughts and actions.

I give my children the information they need based on their age and ability.
I speak the truth, tempered with love.
I make sure the children understand they are not at fault.
I am careful not to overwhelm the children with my own feelings.
I model healthy expression of feelings and resolving grief.
I understand children act out their feelings, and I see beneath the actions to the pain.
I understand when the children direct their anger toward me and lash out.
I recognize the connection between the divorce and the children's altered behavior patterns.
I encourage the children to express their feelings without demanding it.
I am always ready to listen, and I am comfortable hearing their feelings.
I accept and allow my children's feelings without denying or arguing with them.
I accept my children's feelings without guilt or shame.
I am thankful the children have the courage to accept and express their feelings.
I am thankful the children trust me enough to confide in me.
I accept my children feel differently toward my ex-spouse than I do.
I get the children help in all appropriate ways.
I encourage my children to spend time with my ex-spouse as appropriate.
I work to make the visitation time pleasant for all.
I make drop-offs and pickups as emotionally easy as possible.
I enjoy my free time without guilt, anxiety, or worry.
I create and maintain a new family structure that assures us peace and harmony.
I create and maintain new family patterns that assure us _____.

Exercising

Not all scripts work for all people, and this is an example of one that works for others and not for me. If I listen to the tape every night, I exercise regularly. When I stop listening to the tape, I stop exercising. I wish you better results!

The Emptying-the-Cup Script

Exercising and I are one.
I release and forgive myself for exercising.
I release and forgive myself for not exercising.
I release and forgive _____ for not teaching me how to exercise.

my family, school, society

I dissolve all false models and messages about exercise.
I dissolve all imbalances on the soul level around exercising.

I dissolve all imbalances on the soul level around fearing exercising.
I dissolve all imbalances on the soul level around judging exercising.
I dissolve all imbalances on the soul level around exercising too much.
I dissolve all imbalances on the soul level around exercising too little.
I dissolve all imbalances on the soul level around no pain–no gain messages.
I dissolve all imbalances on the soul level around wanting a perfect body.
I dissolve all imbalances on the soul level around associating exercise with _____ .

pain, shame, taking too much time, being too much trouble, approval

I dissolve my field of experience around exercising.
I transform my vibrational patterns around exercising.
I transcend exercising, and I am at peace with it.
I surrender to exercising, and I allow it in my life as appropriate.
I bring all past issues around exercising to an elegant completion in total grace.
I dissolve all future issues around exercising before they materialize.
I take total and complete responsibility for my exercise program.
I allow and assign others total and complete responsibility for their exercise program.
Exercising and _____ are separate for me now.

The Filling-the-Cup Script

Exercising has all positive outcomes for me now.
I am safe and protected when I exercise.
I am loved and accepted when I exercise.
I am nurtured and supported when I exercise.
I exercise for myself, not others.
I am motivated to exercise by my own goals and standards.
I am realistic and objective about my body.
I am realistic and objective about what my body can achieve.
I set realistic, achievable exercise goals, and I keep them.
I set a realistic, achievable exercise schedule, and I keep it.
I plan the exercise routine that is best for my body and lifestyle.
I make exercise a normal part of each day in some way.
I plan the best times and ways to exercise.
I modify exercise routines appropriately for me and my condition.
I am a steady, stable, reliable exerciser.
I make exercising a priority, and I set aside time and resources for it as appropriate.
I know the time I spend exercising is some of my most valuable time.
I work out regularly and systematically.
I methodically strengthen my body.
I exert the right amount of effort each time I exercise.

I am in touch with my body when I exercise, and I suspend all thoughts as appropriate.
I enjoy exercising and I feel good doing it.
I focus on exercising while I am doing it, and I flow with the time and the tempo.
I am adding years to my life exercising.
I feel good about my body becoming fit and conditioned.
I increase in fitness, stamina, vitality, and energy daily.
I feel good being physically fit and strong.
I am motivated to exercise regularly for the rest of my life, and I do so.
I feel productive when I exercise, knowing it renews and refreshes me.
I am proud to be a regular exerciser, and I am a role model for others.

Expectations

This script has helped me enormously, as I used to overthink things, which led to expecting outcomes. I'm different now—and much less frustrated! (Written for the recording "Loving Partnership 1"—the *Loving Partnership* series.)

The Emptying-the-Cup Script

Expectations and I are one.
I release and forgive myself for having expectations.
I release and forgive myself for not having expectations.
I release and forgive myself for expecting myself to be, have, or do _____.

What have you expected of yourself?

I release and forgive myself for not meeting my own expectations.
I release and forgive myself for not _____.

How have you disappointed yourself?

I release and forgive myself for not meeting others' expectations of me.
I release and forgive myself for not _____.

What have others expected you to do, be, or have?

I release and forgive everyone who had expectations of me.
I release and forgive _____ for expecting me to _____.

Whom have you disappointed, resisted or rebelled against?

I release and forgive everyone who did not meet my expectations.
I release and forgive _____ for _____.

How have others disappointed you?

I release, forgive and dissolve all expectations as appropriate.
I dissolve all imbalances on the soul level around expectations.
I dissolve all imbalances on the soul level around fearing expectations.
I dissolve all imbalances on the soul level around judging expectations.
I dissolve all imbalances on the soul level around conditioned and learned expectations.
I dissolve all imbalances on the soul level around family expectations.
I dissolve all imbalances on the soul level around societal and cultural expectations.
I dissolve all imbalances on the soul level around school and work expectations.
I dissolve all imbalances on the soul level around _____.

Who is expecting something of you now?

I dissolve all imbalances on the soul level around feeling shame or guilt when I don't meet my expectations of myself.
I dissolve all imbalances on the soul level around feeling anxiety when I don't meet my expectations of myself.
I dissolve all imbalances on the soul level around feeling shame or guilt when I don't meet others' expectations of me.
I dissolve all imbalances on the soul level around feeling anxiety when I don't meet others' expectations of me.
I dissolve all imbalances on the soul level around my expectations being too high.
I dissolve all imbalances on the soul level around my expectations being too low.
I dissolve my field of experience around expectations.
I transform my vibrational patterns around expectations.
I transcend expectations, and I am at peace with them.
I surrender to expectations, and I allow them in my life as appropriate.
I bring all past issues around expectations to an elegant completion in total grace.
I dissolve all future issues around expectations before they materialize.
I take total and complete responsibility for my expectations.
I allow and assign others total and complete responsibility for their expectations.
Having expectations and _____ are separate for me now.

being disappointed, disillusioned, let down

The Filling-the-Cup Script

I see my issues around expectations clearly.
Others' expectations and how I act, think, and feel are separate as appropriate.
Others' expectations and how I live are separate as appropriate.
Others' expectations and how I partner are separate as appropriate.
Others' expectations and how I parent are separate as appropriate.
Others' expectations and how I earn a living are separate as appropriate.

Others' expectations and how I _____ are separate as appropriate.

What areas of your life are driven by others' expectations?

I change, modify, and adjust my expectations at the right time for the right reasons.
I change, modify, and adjust my expectations in the right way for the right situations.
My expectations are healthy and natural.
My expectations are positive and healing.
I recognize my expectations and verbalize them clearly and simply.
I am at peace with the difference between what I expect and what I get as appropriate.
I bring my expectations into harmony with my daily living.
My expectations have all positive outcomes for me now.
My expectations serve my highest good.

Family Dysfunction

I don't know of a perfect family, so this script is for all of us! See Family—Loving for a script to create a loving family. (Written for the recording "Loving Family"—the *Loving Relationships* series.)

The Emptying-the-Cup Script

Family dysfunction and I are one.
I release and forgive my family for being dysfunctional.
I release and forgive myself for being part of a dysfunctional family.
I release and forgive myself for being dysfunctional.
I release and forgive myself for continuing dysfunctional family patterns.
I release and forgive all thoughts and beliefs that create, allow, and perpetuate family dysfunction.
I release and forgive all actions and reactions that create, allow, and perpetuate family dysfunction.
I release and forgive all customs, traditions, and rituals that create, allow, and perpetuate family dysfunction.
I release and forgive all organizations and institutions that create, allow, and perpetuate family dysfunction.
I release and forgive all fairy tales and fantasies that create, allow, and perpetuate family dysfunction.
I release and forgive all myths and archetypes that create, allow, and perpetuate family dysfunction.
I dissolve all imbalances on the soul level around denying my family's dysfunction.

I dissolve all imbalances on the soul level around accepting my family's dysfunction.

I dissolve all imbalances on the soul level around distorting my family's dysfunction and my role in it.

I dissolve all imbalances on the soul level around taking responsibility for my family's dysfunction.

I dissolve all imbalances on the soul level around taking responsibility for my dysfunction.

I dissolve all imbalances on the soul level around codependence with family.

I dissolve all imbalances on the soul level around counterdependence with family.

I dissolve all imbalances on the soul level around projections from and on to my family.

I dissolve all imbalances on the soul level around living my family's idealizing and distorting.

I dissolve all imbalances on the soul level around living my family's lies, pretenses, and exaggerations.

I dissolve all imbalances on the soul level around living my family's imbalances and unwholeness.

I dissolve my field of experience and transform my vibrational patterns around my family's dysfunction and my role in it.

I dissolve my field of experience and transform my vibrational patterns around having healthy, loving attachments with my family.

I dissolve my field of experience and transform my vibrational patterns around having basic trust in my family.

I dissolve my field of experience and transform my vibrational patterns around being trustworthy with my family.

I dissolve my field of experience and transform my vibrational patterns around my family's fears.

I dissolve my field of experience and transform my vibrational patterns around fearing my family.

I dissolve my field of experience and transform my vibrational patterns around being feared by my family.

I dissolve my field of experience and transform my vibrational patterns around my family's judgments.

I dissolve my field of experience and transform my vibrational patterns around judging my family.

I dissolve my field of experience and transform my vibrational patterns around being judged by my family.

I transcend family dysfunction, and I am at peace with it.

I surrender to family dysfunction, and I allow it in my life as appropriate.

I bring all past issues around family dysfunction to an elegant completion in total grace.

I dissolve all future issues around family dysfunction before they materialize.

I take total and complete responsibility for my part in family dysfunction.

I allow and assign others total and complete responsibility for their part in family dysfunction.

The Filling-the-Cup Script

I move beyond judgments of my family of origin to a state of acceptance and understanding.

I feel love and compassion for my family of origin as appropriate.

I feel honor and gratitude for my family of origin as appropriate.

I move beyond my family of origin role to a state of adult self-actualization.

I gracefully grow up into my authentic self, with or without my family of origin's acceptance and approval.

I gladly grow up into my authentic self, with or without my family of origin's support and nurturing.

I persistently grow up into my authentic self, with or without my family of origin's understanding and cooperation.

I open to and complete the process of healing my relationship with my family with love and compassion.

I open to and complete the process of healing my relationship with my family free and unafraid.

I work cooperatively with my family to heal our dysfunction as appropriate.

I move into and through the stages of healing with my family in harmony.

I move into and through the stages of completion and closure with my family in grace.

I heal my relationship with my family, whether or not they heal their relationship with me.

I heal my relationship with my family, with or without their participation and understanding.

I heal my relationship with my family, with or without their acceptance and approval.

I heal myself and my relationship with my family, with or without their understanding and support.

I heal my relationship with my family, whether or not they heal.

I move beyond family dysfunction to a state of healing, harmony, and self-actualization.

Family—Loving

I lived in Alaska for a decade—far from family of origin. I decided to create new family around me. I was nervous about telling my dad this plan, as he was a "staunch family man." I was surprised by his simple reply, "Family are the people around you who love you." Thanks, Dad! (Written for the recording "Loving Family"—the *Loving Relationships* series.)

The Clearing-the-Cup Script

Loving family and I are one.

I release and forgive myself for having a loving family.

I release and forgive myself for not having a loving family.

I release and forgive my family for not knowing how to be and become a loving family.

I release and forgive myself for not knowing how to be and become part of a loving family.

I release and forgive myself for creating and maintaining a loving family.

I release and forgive myself for not creating and maintaining a loving family.

I release and forgive myself for creating new and different family.

I release and forgive myself for not creating new and different family.

I dissolve all imbalances on the soul level around associating pain and loss with family.

I dissolve all imbalances on the soul level around associating pleasure and gain with family.

I dissolve my field of experience and transform my vibrational patterns around a loving family.

I dissolve my field of experience around creating and maintaining a loving family.

I dissolve my field of experience around creating an extended nonbiological family.

I dissolve my field of experience around continuing family patterns, traditions, and rituals.

I dissolve my field of experience around developing new family patterns, traditions, and rituals.

I transform my vibrational patterns around creating and maintaining a loving family.

I transform my vibrational patterns around creating an extended nonbiological family.

I transform my vibrational patterns around ancestors and future generations.

I transcend a loving family, and I am at peace with it.

I transcend creating and maintaining a loving family, and I am at peace with it.

I surrender to a loving family, and I allow it in my life as appropriate.

I surrender to creating and maintaining a loving family, and I allow it in my life as appropriate.

I bring all my past issues around a loving family to an elegant completion in total grace.

I dissolve all future issues around a loving family before they materialize.

I take total and complete responsibility for my part in a loving family.

I allow and assign others total and complete responsibility for their part in my loving family.

The Filling-the-Cup Script

I open to and allow the importance and meaning of a loving family in my life.

I honor my existing family for the part it has played in my life.

I am at peace with the paradox of leaving family and creating a loving family.

I move beyond existing family and family patterns to fulfill the promise of a loving family as appropriate.

I move beyond limiting definitions of family and redefine it in my own terms.

I reinvent family structure and function to increase family love, support, and mutuality in my life.

I create and maintain a loving family in harmony with my life and lifestyle.

I have the desire, intention, and ability to create and maintain a loving family for myself.

I have the heart, mind, and commitment to create and maintain a loving family for myself.

I allow the time and energy to create and maintain a loving family for myself.

I create and maintain a loving, honoring, and honorable family in peace and grace.

I consciously choose my loving family members based on my expanding awareness.

I open to, allow, and embrace creating new loving family roles that reflect my expanding awareness.

I create and maintain family models and roles based on love.

I create and maintain family foundations and structures free of dysfunction.

I create and maintain family values and traditions that fit me and my life as appropriate.

I create and maintain family rituals and ceremonies that fit me and my life as appropriate.

I create and maintain loving family relationships with people of like spirit, heart, and values.

I create and maintain loving family relationships with people of like mind, intentions, and actions.

I create and maintain a loving family with people who may or may not be biological relations as appropriate.

I create and maintain a loving family who may be very different than my biological family as appropriate.

I create and maintain a loving family who are capable of true intimacy.

I create and maintain a loving family who live up to their loving capacity.

I create and maintain a loving family who feel and express love in loving ways.

I create and maintain a loving family who are emotionally available.

I create and maintain a loving family who are open and caring.

I create and maintain a loving family who are generous and sharing.

I create and maintain a loving family who are honest and honorable.

I create and maintain a loving family who are trusting and trustworthy.

I create and maintain a loving family who are responsible and able to respond.

I create and maintain a loving family who have an attitude of gratitude.

I create and maintain a loving family who are fun, have fun, and share fun.

I create and maintain a loving family I enjoy being with.

I create and maintain a loving family who recognize and support my authentic self.

I create and maintain a loving family who recognize the sanctity of one another.

I create and maintain a loving family who mutually love, honor, and respect one another.

I create and maintain a loving family who joyfully explore and celebrate each other's lives.

I create and maintain a loving family who understand and respect each other's needs.

I create and maintain a loving family who share joys and sorrows.

I create and maintain a loving family who share thoughts and ideas.

I create and maintain a loving family who share feelings and values.

I create and maintain a loving family who share dreams and aspirations.

I create and maintain a loving family who are dedicated to the common good.

I create and maintain a loving family who see the commonality in all humanity.

I create and maintain a loving family who appreciate and allow diversity and difference.

I create and maintain a loving family who recognize and respond to spirit in children.

I create and maintain a loving family who recognize and respond to vitality in juniors.

I create and maintain a loving family who recognize and respond to wisdom in seniors.

I become the loving family member I wish to have in my life.

I go through life joyful, supported, and embraced by the loving family I create.

Fear

I was raised by a single mom who was fun, fearless, and feminine. So I gravitate to the philosophy of the Course in Miracles that states there are two emotions: love and fear. Therefore, all our emotions are based in one of the other. If we worry, it is fear-based. If we laugh, it is love-based. This approach has helped me play detective with my feelings (and those of my clients). When I am not in a positive place, I ask myself where my fear is coming from. I often get great insights. This script is to dissolve fear so we can operate from love-based emotions and motivations. (Written for the recording "Opening to Love"—the *Loving Relationships* series.)

The Emptying-the-Cup Script

Fear and I are one.

I release and forgive myself for being fearful and fear-based.

I release and forgive myself for not being fearful and fear-based.

I release and forgive my family, culture, and society for being fearful and fear-based.

I release and forgive every person that taught me fear or modeled fear to me.

I release and forgive myself for teaching or modeling fear to others.

I release and forgive every person, place, thing, or situation that created fear in me.

I release and forgive myself for creating fear in others.

I release and forgive my mother for creating fear in me in any way.

I release and forgive myself for fearing my mother in any way.

I release and forgive my mother for not opening to love.

I transcend my mother and I am at peace with her.

I release and forgive my father for creating fear in me in any way.

I release and forgive myself for fearing my father in any way.

I release and forgive my father for not opening to love.

I transcend my father and I am at peace with him.

I dissolve all imbalances on the soul level around fear.

I dissolve all imbalances on the soul level around being fearful or fear-based.

I dissolve all imbalances on the soul level around my basic survival instincts and fears.

I dissolve all imbalances on the soul level around my learned, automatic, or conditioned fears.

I dissolve all imbalances on the soul level around others creating fear in me.

I dissolve all imbalances on the soul level around others projecting their fear on to me.

I dissolve all imbalances on the soul level around creating fear in myself and others.

I dissolve all imbalances on the soul level around projecting my fear on to others.

I dissolve all imbalances on the soul level around adopting others' fears as my own.

I dissolve all imbalances on the soul level around cultural and societal fear.

I dissolve all imbalances on the soul level around traditional and historical fear.

I dissolve all imbalances on the soul level around religious and philosophical fear.

I dissolve all imbalances on the soul level around mythological and mythical fear.

I dissolve all imbalances on the soul level around superstitious and fanciful fear.

I dissolve all imbalances on the soul level around consensus reality and mass mind fear.

I dissolve all imbalances on the soul level around collective unconscious fear.

I dissolve all imbalances on the soul level around archetypal fear.

I dissolve all imbalances on the soul level around seeking or being addicted to fear.

I dissolve all imbalances on the soul level around associating fear with life, living, and feeling alive.

I dissolve all imbalances on the soul level around associating fear with love, loving, or being loved.

I dissolve all imbalances on the soul level around fear of not having my needs met.

I dissolve all imbalances on the soul level around fear of separation and loneliness.

I dissolve all imbalances on the soul level around fear of losing love, affection, and approval.

I dissolve all imbalances on the soul level around fear of losing security, stability, and the known.

I dissolve all imbalances on the soul level around fear of losing power and control.

I dissolve all imbalances on the soul level around having the courage to face my fear.

I dissolve all imbalances on the soul level around having the commitment to work through my fear.

I release and forgive myself for dissolving fear in this life and all others.

I release and forgive myself for not dissolving fear in this life and all others.

I dissolve my field of experience and transform my vibrational patterns around fear.

I dissolve my field of experience and transform my vibrational patterns around dissolving fear.

I dissolve the fear created by past experiences in total grace.

I dissolve the fear created by desire and attachment in complete harmony.

I dissolve cultural and organizational fear as appropriate in flowing peace.

I dissolve historical and consensus reality fear as appropriate in effortless joy.

I dissolve mythological and superstitious fear as appropriate in perfect equipoise.

I transcend fear and I am at peace with it.

I transcend dissolving fear and I am at peace with it.

I surrender to fear and I allow it in my life as appropriate.

I surrender to dissolving fear and I allow it in my life as appropriate.

I bring all past issues around fear to an elegant completion in total grace.

I bring all past issues around dissolving fear to an elegant completion in total grace.

I dissolve all future issues around fear before they materialize.

I dissolve all future issues around dissolving fear before they materialize.

I take total and complete responsibility for my fear as appropriate.

I take total and complete responsibility for dissolving my fear as appropriate.

I allow others total and complete responsibility for their fear as appropriate.

I allow others total and complete responsibility for dissolving their fear as appropriate.
I understand how others create and maintain fear in my life and I dissolve it.
I understand how I create and maintain fear in my life and I dissolve it.
I understand how I create and maintain fear in others' lives and I dissolve it.
I understand how others use fear to control and manipulate me and I dissolve it.
I understand how I use fear to control and manipulate myself and I dissolve it.
I understand how I use fear to control and manipulate others and I dissolve it.

The Filling-the-Cup Script

I choose love over fear and live my life accordingly.
I use my intuitive mind to understand the reason and significance of fear in my life.
I use my compassionate heart to dissolve fear at all times and places.
I use my soul understanding to replace fear with love moment to moment.
I have the courage and commitment to face my fear and I do so in grace.
I face my fear with awareness, clarity, and understanding.
I move beyond fear and a fearful state to a loving state.
I move beyond fear and a fearful state to a state of trust and grace.
I move beyond fear and fearful living to a state of peace, grace, and harmony.
I replace fearful thoughts with loving thoughts.
I replace fearful feelings with loving feelings.
I replace fearful actions and reactions with loving actions.
I replace fear with courage and bravery.
I replace fear with dignity and honor.
I replace fear with love and grace.
My thoughts and feelings are based in love.
My actions and reactions are based in love.
My life and the way I live it is based in love.

Feedback

In my various manager positions, I was recognized for my communication skills with my staff. This is the business approach to communication and feedback. (Written for the recording "Communicating Effectively"—the *Success* series.)

The Emptying-the-Cup Script

Feedback and I are one.
I release and forgive myself for giving positive feedback to myself.

I release and forgive myself for not giving positive feedback to myself.
I release and forgive myself for _____.

not recognizing or acknowledging the positive

I release and forgive myself for giving positive feedback to others.
I release and forgive myself for not giving positive feedback to others.
I release and forgive myself for _____.

not expressing gratitude, not giving praise, not saying nice things to others

I release and forgive myself for giving negative feedback to myself.
I release and forgive myself for _____.

being too hard on myself, being self-critical, focusing on the negative

I release and forgive myself for not giving negative feedback to myself.
I release and forgive myself for giving negative feedback to others.
I release and forgive myself for _____.

avoiding, lecturing, complaining, whining

I release and forgive myself for not giving negative feedback to others.
I release and forgive myself for _____.

What words would you take back if you could?

I release and forgive everyone who has been negative to me or about me.
I release and forgive _____ for _____.
I release, forgive, and dissolve my family model of giving feedback as appropriate.
I release, forgive, and dissolve the school model of giving feedback as appropriate.
I release, forgive, and dissolve the work model of giving feedback as appropriate.

How do you give feedback? How do others give you feedback?

I dissolve all imbalances on the soul level around feedback.
I dissolve all imbalances on the soul level around my ability to evaluate feedback objectively.
I dissolve all imbalances on the soul level around evaluating feedback through the filter of my feelings of self-worth.
I dissolve all imbalances on the soul level around _____.

taking it too personally, overreacting, not reacting

I dissolve all imbalances on the soul level around fearing being criticized.
I dissolve all imbalances on the soul level around fearing giving and receiving criticism.
I dissolve all imbalances on the soul level around judging being criticized.
I dissolve all imbalances on the soul level around judging giving and receiving criticism.

I dissolve all imbalances on the soul level around fear of rejection.
I dissolve all imbalances on the soul level around fear of _____.

not being good enough, not having friends

I dissolve all imbalances on the soul level around giving and receiving praise and compliments.
I dissolve all imbalances on the soul level around saying positive things to myself.
I dissolve all imbalances on the soul level around others saying positive things to me.
I dissolve all imbalances on the soul level around saying positive things to others.
I dissolve all imbalances on the soul level around inaccurate and insincere feedback.
I dissolve all imbalances on the soul level around honest, assertive feedback.
I dissolve all imbalances on the soul level around inappropriate responses to feedback.
I dissolve all imbalances on the soul level around feeling obligated to return compliments.
I dissolve all imbalances on the soul level around _____.

flattery, hollow compliments

I dissolve all imbalances on the soul level around wanting to defend myself against criticism.
I dissolve all imbalances on the soul level around _____.

vindictiveness, criticism, revenge

I dissolve my field of experience around giving and receiving negative feedback.
I dissolve my field of experience around giving and receiving positive feedback.
I transform my vibrational patterns around giving and receiving negative feedback.
I transform my vibrational patterns around giving and receiving positive feedback.
I transcend positive and negative feedback, and I am at peace with them.
I surrender to positive and negative feedback, and I allow them in my life as appropriate.
I bring all past issues around negative feedback to an elegant completion in total grace.
I bring all past issues around positive feedback to an elegant completion in total grace.
I dissolve all future issues around negative feedback before they materialize.
I dissolve all future issues around positive feedback before they materialize.
I take total and complete responsibility for how I give and receive negative feedback.
I take total and complete responsibility for how I give and receive positive feedback.

I allow and assign others total and complete responsibility for the way they give
and receive negative feedback.
I allow and assign others total and complete responsibility for the way they give
and receive positive feedback.
Positive feedback and _____ are separate for me now.
Negative feedback and _____ are separate for me now.

The Filling-the-Cup Script

Honest feedback has all positive outcomes for me now.
I am safe and protected when I give and receive honest feedback.
I am loved and accepted when I give and receive honest feedback.
I am nurtured and supported when I give and receive honest feedback.
I give positive feedback simply and honestly.
I give positive feedback directly and specifically.
I give positive feedback for the right things in the right ways.
I give positive feedback to the right people for the right reasons.
I respond to positive feedback with a simple thank-you as appropriate.
I respond to positive feedback with more positive feedback as appropriate.
I accept myself completely as an imperfect human being.
I recognize criticism for what it is, and I acknowledge it as appropriate.
I welcome valid criticism, and I learn from it.
I deflect or neutralize false criticism, and I respond appropriately.
I respond to criticism in perfect ways for me and the situation.
I receive all criticism in peace and calmness.
I am assertive and clear when I respond to criticism.
I remain calm, centered, and balanced while I handle criticism.
My voice stays steady and even while I handle criticism.
My words flow confidently while I handle criticism.
My breathing stays steady and rhythmic while I handle criticism.
My breathing stays deep and even while I handle criticism.
I earn my own respect when I give and receive feedback appropriately.
I earn the respect of others when I give and receive feedback appropriately.

Feelings

When I am writing a script for myself or a client, it is often challenging to verbalize the right feeling for each issue. I wrote this script for (1) overall emotional clearing and balance, and (2) as a reference tool for other scripts. Scan it to find the appropriate word when you are creating your personalized scripts.

The Emptying-the-Cup Script

Feelings and I are one.
I release and forgive myself for having feelings.
I release and forgive myself for ignoring or denying my feelings.
I release and forgive myself for suppressing my feelings.
I release and forgive myself for _____.
I release and forgive myself for ignoring and denying others' feelings.
I release and forgive myself for teaching others to suppress their feelings.
I release and forgive everyone who denied my feelings.
I release and forgive everyone who taught me to suppress my feelings.
I release and forgive everyone who _____ my feelings.

ridiculed, belittled, criticized

I release and forgive _____ for _____.

telling me I was too emotional, misunderstanding my feelings, using my feelings against me, using my feelings to manipulate me

I dissolve all imbalances on the soul level around my feelings.
I dissolve all imbalances on the soul level around fearing my feelings.
I dissolve all imbalances on the soul level around judging my feelings.
I dissolve all imbalances on the soul level around feeling _____.

abandoned	beaten	cheated
accused	belittled	choked
aching	belligerent	cold
aggravated	bereaved	competitive
aggressive	betrayed	conflicted
agonized	bitter	confused
alienated	bored	consumed
alone	bothered	crabby
aloof	bound up	cranky
angry	boxed in	crappy
anguished	bristling	critical
annoyed	broken up	criticized
anxious	bruised	crushed
apologetic	bugged	deceived
apprehensive	burdened	deceptive
argumentative	burned out	degraded
attached	callous	demeaned
attacked	careless	demoralized
badgered	carried away	dependent
baited	cautious	depressed
battered	chased	derived

[Continued on next page]

[feelings, *continued*]

deserted
despairing
desperate
destroyed
dirty
disappointed
disconnected
disgraced
disgruntled
disgusted
distant
distraught
distressed
distrusted
distrustful
dominated
domineering
doomed
double-crossed
down
dreadful
edgy
embarrassed
empty
enraged
exasperated
exposed
foolish
forced
forceful
frightened
frustrated
furious
greedy
grim
grouchy
guarded
hard
hassled
hateful
helpless
hesitant
hollow

hopeless
horrified
hostile
humiliated
hurt
ignorant
impatient
impotent
incompetent
incomplete
insecure
insignificant
insincere
insulted
intolerant
irate
irked
irresponsible
irritated
jealous
jittery
left out
lonely
lost
low
lustful
mad
malicious
mean
miserable
misunderstood
moody
nasty
nervous
numb
obsessed
offended
ornery
out of control
overwhelmed
panicky
paralyzed
peeved

perturbed
petrified
phony
powerless
pressured
pulled apart
put down
puzzled
quarrelsome
raped
ravished
regretful
rejected
rejecting
removed
repulsed
repulsive
resentful
resistant
revengeful
rotten
ruined
scared
scolded
scorned
screwed
seduced
self-centered
self-conscious
selfish
separated
shattered
shocked
shot down
shy
sickened
silly
sinking
smothered
smug
sneaky
sorry
spiteful

squelched	timid	unstable
starved	tired	upset
stiff	tormented	uptight
stifled	torn	violated
strangled	tortured	violent
stubborn	trapped	vulnerable
stupid	tricked	weak
subdued	ugly	whipped
submissive	unapproachable	wild
suffocated	unaware	wiped out
tainted	uncertain	withdrawn
tense	uncomfortable	worried
terrified	unfriendly	wounded
ticked	unhappy	zapped
tight	unimportant	

I dissolve my field of experience around my feelings.
I transform my vibrational patterns around my feelings.
I transcend my feelings, and I am at peace with them.
I surrender to my feelings, and I allow them in my life as appropriate.
I bring all past issues around my feelings to an elegant completion in total grace.
I dissolve all future issues around my feelings before they materialize.
I take total and complete responsibility for my feelings.
I allow and assign others total and complete responsibility for their feelings.

The Filling-the-Cup Script

Feeling my feelings has all positive outcomes for me now.
I am safe and protected when I acknowledge and experience my feelings.
I am loved and accepted when I acknowledge and experience my feelings.
I am nurtured and supported when I acknowledge and experience my feelings.
I experience and express my feelings at the right times in the right ways.
I experience and express my feelings with the right people for the right reasons.
I give myself permission to experience all of my feelings completely.
I give myself permission to feel my positive, life-affirming feelings completely.
I allow myself to feel _____.

accepted	amused	beautiful
affectionate	appreciative	brave
agreeable	assertive	bubbly
alive	attentive	calm
alluring	attractive	capable
altruistic	aware	carefree

[Continued on next page]

[feelings, *continued*]

caring	genuine	safe
certain	giving	satisfied
cheerful	grateful	secure
comfortable	handsome	silly
comforted	healthy	sincere
comforting	helpful	smart
compassionate	high	soft
complete	independent	soothed
confident	innocent	soothing
considerate	inspired	spontaneous
content	humorous	strong
cuddly	loved	successful
curious	loving	sure
daring	lucky	sympathetic
delighted	open	tender
desirable	overjoyed	terrific
desirous	pampered	tolerant
different	patient	tremendous
eager	peaceful	trusted
ecstatic	perceptive	trusting
elated	pleased	understanding
enraptured	powerful	understood
enthusiastic	quiet	useful
esteemed	real	valuable
fascinated	refreshed	valued
fortunate	refreshing	warm
friendly	relaxed	whole
full	relieved	willing
funny	responsible	wonderful
generous	responsive	worthy

I live a rich, full, healthy emotional life.
I experience positive, life affirming feelings moment to moment.

Forgiving

All religious and philosophical systems refer to the power of forgiveness, and research on the mind/body connection suggests this is a key to health. As you know, releasing and forgiving is a cornerstone of every *Change Your Mind* script. Consider doing a forgiveness script to get as clear as possible.

The Emptying-the-Cup Script

Forgiving and I are one.
I release and forgive myself for being forgiving.
I release and forgive myself for not being forgiving.
I release and forgive myself for not forgiving myself.
I release and forgive myself for not forgiving myself for _____.

What do you think the worst things you have done are?

I release and forgive myself for not forgiving myself for _____.

holding a grudge, being vengeful, wanting revenge, being arrogant

I release and forgive myself for not forgiving _____ for _____.

Who did what to you that you are still holding on to? Who are you holding a grudge against?

I release and forgive everyone who did not forgive me.
I release and forgive _____ for _____.

Who is still holding a grudge against you?

I release and forgive everyone who taught me not to be forgiving.
I release and forgive others to go to their highest good so that I may go to mine.
I dissolve all imbalances on the soul level around forgiving.
I dissolve all imbalances on the soul level around fearing forgiving.
I dissolve all imbalances on the soul level around judging forgiving.
I dissolve all imbalances on the soul level around confusing forgiving with forgetting.
I dissolve all imbalances on the soul level around confusing forgiving with approving.
I dissolve all imbalances on the soul level around confusing forgiving with agreeing.
I dissolve all imbalances on the soul level around confusing forgiving with weakness.
I dissolve all imbalances on the soul level around confusing forgiving with _____.

allowing more of the same, being vulnerable, not being safe

I dissolve my field of experience around forgiving.
I transform my vibrational patterns around forgiving.
I transcend forgiving, and I am at peace with it.
I surrender to forgiving, and I allow it in my life as appropriate.
I bring all past issues around forgiving to an elegant completion in total grace.
I dissolve all future issues around forgiving before they materialize.

I take total and complete responsibility for my own feelings of forgiveness.
I allow and assign others total and complete responsibility for their feelings of forgiveness.
Forgiving and _____ are separate for me now.

betraying my values, being immoral, feeling prideful, feeling superior

The Filling-the-Cup Script

Forgiving myself has all positive outcomes for me now.
Forgiving others has all positive outcomes for me now.
I am safe and protected when I forgive myself and others.
I am loved and accepted when I forgive myself and others.
I am nurtured and supported when I forgive myself and others.
I understand the true nature of forgiveness and its benefits for me.
I understand the true nature of forgiveness and its benefits for my loved ones.
I understand the true nature of forgiveness and its benefits for the world.
I am protected by my knowledge and understanding of the past.
I am protected by my loving, forgiving nature.
My past is now complete and resolved in grace.
The more I release and forgive, the lighter I feel.
The lighter I feel, the more love I experience.
I live a positive, loving, forgiving life.

Global Citizenship

I look forward to the day we each serve as a global citizen in a truly global community, united in mutual cooperation, support, and empowerment.

The Emptying-the-Cup Script

The global community and I are one.
I release and forgive myself for being a global citizen.
I release and forgive myself for not being a global citizen.
I release and forgive my family for not teaching me about global citizenship.
I release, forgive, and dissolve all false models of being a global citizen.
I dissolve all imbalances on the soul level around being a global citizen.
I dissolve all imbalances on the soul level around fearing being part of the global community.
I dissolve all imbalances on the soul level around fearing other cultures.
I dissolve all imbalances on the soul level around judging my culture.
I dissolve all imbalances on the soul level around judging other cultures.
I dissolve all imbalances on the soul level around judging being part of the global community.

I dissolve all imbalances on the soul level around cultural diversity.

I dissolve all imbalances on the soul level around cultural barriers.

*I dissolve all imbalances on the soul level around cultural prejudices and stereo-
types.*

I dissolve all imbalances on the soul level around global competition.

I dissolve all imbalances on the soul level around global hatred and prejudice.

I dissolve all imbalances on the soul level around global hostility and conflict.

What is most upsetting to you about the global situation?

*I dissolve all imbalances on the soul level around confusion about the global com-
munity.*

*I dissolve all imbalances on the soul level around confusion about my rightful
place in the global community.*

I dissolve my field of experience around my part in the global community.

I transform my vibrational patterns around my part in the global community.

I transcend the global community, and I am at peace with it.

I transcend my part in the global community, and I am at peace with it.

I surrender to the global community, and I allow it in my life as appropriate.

*I surrender to my part in the global community, and I allow it in my life as ap-
propriate.*

*I bring all past issues around the global community to an elegant completion in
total grace.*

*I bring all past issues around my part in the global community to an elegant com-
pletion in total grace.*

I dissolve all future issues around the global community before they materialize.

*I dissolve all future issues around my part in the global community before they
materialize.*

I take total and complete responsibility for my part in the global community.

*I allow and assign others total and complete responsibility for their part in the
global community as appropriate.*

Being part of the global community and _____ are separate for me now.

The Filling-the-Cup Script

Being a part of the global community has all positive outcomes for me now.

I am safe and protected when I am part of the global community.

I am safe and protected when I work on the global level.

I am loved and accepted when I am part of the global community.

I am loved and accepted when I work on the global level.

I am nurtured and supported when I am part of the global community.

I am nurtured and supported when I work on the global level.

I work on the global level for the right reasons.

I work on the global level in the right way at the right time.

I work on the global level for the right causes with the right people.

I participate effectively in global experiences.
I provide value to others through my global experiences.
I live the principles of global community—equality, liberty, and justice.
I live the principles of global community—compassion, harmony, and peace.
I live the principles of global community—_____.
I am sensitive to my culture and the culture of others.
I recognize what is involved in my own cultural self-image, and I allow it.
I recognize what is involved in others' cultural self-image, and I allow it.
I understand what is involved in self- and group identity.
I am aware of the impact of culture shock on my sense of identity.
I am aware of the impact of culture shock on others' sense of identity.
I extend compassion to myself and others during culture shock.
I enjoy learning about other cultures, and I do so.
I immerse myself in other cultures as appropriate.
I immerse myself in other cultures to feel their feelings.
I immerse myself in other cultures to think their thoughts.
I adjust and adapt to other cultures with ease.
I translate what I learn into appropriate actions automatically.
I flow with people and situations different from my culture and background.
I respect myself and others equally, and I express that respect in all appropriate ways.
I build on our differences for mutual understanding, cooperation, and growth.
I recognize similarities and common concerns.
I am tolerant, flexible, and patient with myself in other cultures.
I am tolerant, flexible, and patient with others in my culture.
I transform my personal attitudes and perceptions to be an effective global citizen.
I communicate effectively across all barriers.
I am at peace with differences, complexity, and paradox.
I realize love brings people together across cultures.
I work to become the change I wish to see in the world.

Goals

In my teaching/training/consulting, I have found that people who aren't comfortable writing goals are (1) people who are highly creative and fear goals will be restricting, (2) people with no model for goal setting, and (3) people who don't know the difference between a purpose, wish, fantasy, goal, dream, and so on. This script is to support you in creating goals that suit you and your lifestyle. Do it your way! (Written for the recording "Being Proactive"—the *Success* series.)

The Emptying-the-Cup Script

Goals and I are one.
I release and forgive myself for having goals and achieving them.
I release and forgive myself for having goals and not achieving them.
I release and forgive myself for not having goals.
I release and forgive myself for not knowing how to write goals.
I release and forgive myself for not knowing how to achieve my goals.
I release and forgive myself for not achieving _____.

What goals have you not achieved?

I release and forgive everyone who didn't teach me how to set and achieve goals.
I release and forgive everyone who told me I couldn't have my goals.
I release and forgive everyone who didn't support my goals.
I release and forgive _____ for _____.

Who told you you couldn't have your goals, called you a dreamer, impractical?

I release, forgive, and dissolve my family model of goal setting.
I release, forgive, and dissolve my family's goals as appropriate.
I dissolve all imbalances on the soul level around goals.
I dissolve all imbalances on the soul level around fearing goals.
I dissolve all imbalances on the soul level around fearing achieving my goals.
I dissolve all imbalances on the soul level around fearing not achieving my goals.
I dissolve all imbalances on the soul level around resisting goals.
I dissolve all imbalances on the soul level around judging goals.
I dissolve all imbalances on the soul level around everyone who judged my goals.
I dissolve all imbalances on the soul level around fear of success.
I dissolve all imbalances on the soul level around fear of failure.
I dissolve all imbalances on the soul level around not achieving my goals.
I dissolve all imbalances on the soul level around not knowing my true goals.
I dissolve all imbalances on the soul level around confusing others' goals for mine.
I dissolve all imbalances on the soul level around writing the wrong goals for me.
I dissolve all imbalances on the soul level around not being committed to my goals.
I dissolve all imbalances on the soul level around not having the energy to achieve my goals.
I dissolve all imbalances on the soul level around not having the resources to achieve my goals.
I dissolve all imbalances on the soul level around not having the _____ to achieve my goals.

Why haven't you achieved your goals?

I dissolve all imbalances on the soul level around being proactive and positive.
I dissolve my field of experience around having goals and achieving them.
I transform my vibrational patterns around having goals and achieving them.
I transcend having goals, and I am at peace with it.
I transcend achieving my goals, and I am at peace with it.
I surrender to having goals, and I allow them in my life as appropriate.
I surrender to achieving my goals, and I allow it in my life as appropriate.
I bring all past issues around having goals to an elegant completion in total grace.
I bring all past issues around achieving my goals to an elegant completion in total grace.
I take total and complete responsibility for having goals and achieving them.
I allow and assign others total and complete responsibility for their goals as appropriate.
Setting goals and _____ are separate for me now.

being locked in, restricted, rigid, limited

The Filling-the-Cup Script

Setting goals and achieving them has all positive outcomes for me now.
I am safe and protected when I set goals and achieve them.
I am loved and accepted when I set goals and achieve them.
I am nurtured and supported when I set goals and achieve them.
I allow myself to feel positive and powerful when I achieve my goals.
I am the artist of my own creation.
I take responsibility for who I am and where I am going.
I am now creating my life exactly as I want it.
My creation is appropriate to my personality and desired lifestyle.
My goals are appropriate to my personality and desired lifestyle.
I have a great attitude toward myself and my goals.
I enjoy planning my life and setting goals.
I take pleasure in setting balanced life goals.
My goals are reasonable and reachable.
My goals are challenging and motivating.
My goals are well thought out.
My goals support my personal and professional growth.
My goals support my personal and professional freedom.
My goals support my emotional and spiritual growth.
My goals support my emotional and spiritual freedom.
My goals promote my financial growth and freedom.
My goals promote _____.
My personal values are reflected in my goals.

I feel empowered when I set goals.
I keep my goals in a style effective for me.
I review and update my goals regularly.
I change and modify my goals as appropriate.
I match my behavior to my goals.
I am determined and persistent in the pursuit of my goals.
I focus on my goals at the right times in the right way.
The process of achieving my goals is fun for me.
I make detailed plans to achieve my goals as appropriate.
I make daily "to do lists" that include goal-reaching activities.
It is easy to take the steps to achieve my goals.
I do something every day to put me one step closer to my goals as appropriate.
I enjoy taking the steps to achieve my goals.
I visualize my goals already achieved.

Gratitude

I was extolling my many blessings to my daughter one day, and I asked her why she thought I was so lucky. Her immediate reply was "because you're so grateful." If she is right, this script can make you lucky.

The Emptying-the-Cup Script

Being grateful and I are one.
I release and forgive myself for being grateful and expressing it.
I release and forgive myself for being grateful and not expressing it.
I release and forgive myself for not being grateful.
I release and forgive myself for not being grateful for _____.

my health, mind, income, home, family, circumstances, faith, talent

I release everyone who is not grateful.
I release, forgive, and dissolve the way my family expressed gratitude.
I release, forgive, and dissolve all false models of gratitude.
I release and forgive _____ for _____ my gratitude.

Who ridiculed you, embarrassed you, called you an optimist?

I dissolve all imbalances on the soul level around gratitude.
I dissolve all imbalances on the soul level around being grateful.
I dissolve all imbalances on the soul level around expressing gratitude.
I dissolve all imbalances on the soul level around fearing gratitude.
I dissolve all imbalances on the soul level around fearing _____.

being grateful is weakness or dependence; gratitude toward me obligates me

I dissolve all imbalances on the soul level around denying my blessings.
I dissolve all imbalances on the soul level around judging gratitude.
I dissolve all imbalances on the soul level around being too grateful.
I dissolve all imbalances on the soul level around not being grateful enough.
I dissolve all imbalances on the soul level around wanting others to be grateful to me.
I dissolve all imbalances on the soul level around any and all discomfort with gratitude.
I dissolve all imbalances on the soul level around any and all discomfort with feeling grateful.
I dissolve all imbalances on the soul level around expressing gratitude in inappropriate ways.
I dissolve all imbalances on the soul level around substituting _____ for gratitude.

money, gifts, tithing, sarcasm, hardness

I dissolve my field of experience around gratitude and being grateful.
I transform my vibrational patterns around gratitude and being grateful.
I transcend gratitude and being grateful, and I am at peace with them.
I surrender to gratitude and being grateful, and I allow them in my life as appropriate.
I bring all past issues around gratitude and being grateful to an elegant completion in total grace.
I dissolve all future issues around gratitude and being grateful before they materialize.
I take total and complete responsibility for my gratitude and how I express it.
I allow and assign others total and complete responsibility for their gratitude and how they express it.

The Filling-the-Cup Script

Being grateful has all positive outcomes for me now.
I am safe and protected when I am grateful.
I am loved and accepted when I am grateful.
I am nurtured and supported when I am grateful.
I am grateful for _____.
I express my gratitude at the right time in the right way.
I express my gratitude to the right people for the right reasons.
I am filled with an attitude of gratitude, and it enriches my life.

Grieving

Because my life involves continual change, I get the chance to do continual grieving, releasing, and letting go. I have accelerated the process to an advanced state—I now grieve in advance and am often clear when the change occurs. (Written for the recording "Releasing Past Relationships"—the *Loving Relationships* series).

The Emptying-the-Cup Script

Grieving and I are one.
I release and forgive myself for grieving.
I release and forgive myself for not grieving.
I release and forgive myself for denying my grief.
I release and forgive everyone who denied their grief.
I release and forgive myself for prolonging my grief.
I release and forgive everyone who prolonged their grief.
I release, forgive, and dissolve all false models of grieving.
I release and forgive _____ for _____.

How does your family grieve? your gender, culture, religion?

I dissolve all imbalances on the soul level around grieving.
I dissolve all imbalances on the soul level around fearing grieving.
I dissolve all imbalances on the soul level around judging grieving.

How do you feel about grief and grieving?

I dissolve all imbalances on the soul level around moving through the stages of
*   grieving.*
I dissolve all imbalances on the soul level around denial.
I dissolve all imbalances on the soul level around fearing denial.
I dissolve all imbalances on the soul level around judging denial.
I dissolve all imbalances on the soul level around moving beyond denial.
I dissolve all imbalances on the soul level around anger.
I dissolve all imbalances on the soul level around fearing anger.
I dissolve all imbalances on the soul level around judging anger.
I dissolve all imbalances on the soul level around moving beyond anger.
I dissolve all imbalances on the soul level around bargaining.
I dissolve all imbalances on the soul level around fearing bargaining.
I dissolve all imbalances on the soul level around judging bargaining.
I dissolve all imbalances on the soul level around moving beyond bargaining.
I dissolve all imbalances on the soul level around depression.
I dissolve all imbalances on the soul level around fearing depression.
I dissolve all imbalances on the soul level around judging depression.
I dissolve all imbalances on the soul level around moving beyond depression.

I dissolve all imbalances on the soul level around acceptance.
I dissolve all imbalances on the soul level around fearing acceptance.
I dissolve all imbalances on the soul level around judging acceptance.
*I dissolve all imbalances on the soul level around moving to acceptance natu-
    rally.*
I dissolve my field of experience around grieving.
I transform my vibrational patterns around grieving.
I transcend grieving, and I am at peace with it.
I surrender to grieving, and I allow it in my life as appropriate.
I bring all past issues around grieving to an elegant completion in total grace.
I dissolve all future issues around grieving before they materialize.
I take total and complete responsibility for my grief and grieving process.
*I allow and assign others total and complete responsibility for their grief and
    grieving process as appropriate.*
Grieving and _____ are separate for me now.

The Filling-the-Cup Script

Grieving has all positive outcomes for me now.
I am safe and protected when I grieve and complete the grieving process.
I am loved and accepted when I grieve and complete the grieving process.
I am nurtured and supported when I grieve and complete the grieving process.
I am in touch with my loss, and I grieve it in all appropriate ways.
I understand my need to grieve, and I accept it.
I am open to my grief, and I embrace it.
I am in touch with my grief, and I welcome it.
I take sufficient time to grieve and do so in all healthy, healing ways.
*I move through each phase and stage of the grieving process to completion in
    grace.*
I move to acceptance in peace, love, and grace.
I move to acceptance in dignity, love, and understanding.
I move to acceptance in compassion and clarity.
I give myself over to the spirit of change and transition as appropriate.
I claim the power of change and transition as my own.

Guilt

I've always enjoyed the saying "Don't should on yourself." The shoulds,
have to's, need to's, ought to's, and musts are a basis for guilt. I have eliminated 95 percent of those comments from my vocabulary. (Written for the
recording "Releasing Your Past"—the *Empowerment* series.)

The Emptying-the-Cup Script

Guilt and I are one.
I release and forgive myself for feeling guilty.
I release and forgive myself for not feeling guilty.
I release and forgive myself for not feeling guilty about _____.
I release and forgive every person and situation that made me feel guilty.
I release and forgive _____ for making me feel guilty.

myself, my parents, partner, friends, society, religion

I release and forgive myself for allowing others to make me feel guilty.
I release and forgive myself for making others feel guilty.
I release and forgive myself for making _____ feel guilty.

children, partner, coworkers

I dissolve all imbalances on the soul level around guilt.
I dissolve all imbalances on the soul level around fearing guilt.
I dissolve all imbalances on the soul level around judging guilt.
I dissolve all imbalances on the soul level around feeling guilty about _____.

standing up for myself, challenging authority, telling the truth, express-ing my feelings, confronting, being confused, not understanding, making mistakes, having fun, feeling good

I dissolve all imbalances on the soul level around others using guilt to motivate
or manipulate me.
I dissolve all imbalances on the soul level around using guilt to motivate myself.
I dissolve all imbalances on the soul level around using guilt to manipulate or
motivate others.
I dissolve all imbalances on the soul level around using guilt to _____.

punish myself, punish others, get the upper hand

I dissolve my field of experience around guilt.
I transform my vibrational patterns around guilt.
I transcend guilt, and I am at peace with it.
I surrender to guilt, and I allow it in my life as appropriate.
I bring all past issues around guilt to an elegant completion in total grace.
I dissolve all future issues around guilt before they materialize.
I take total and complete responsibility for my guilt.
I allow and assign others total and complete responsibility for their guilt.
Guilt and _____ are separate for me now.

feeling righteous, feeling moral

The Filling-the-Cup Script

I recognize guilt for what it is in my life.
I recognize the sources of guilt in my life.
I replace guilt with peace and harmony.
I replace guilt with understanding and acceptance.
I replace guilt with compassion and love.
I replace guilt with positive motivation.
I replace guilt with _____.

Healing: Christian

This script was adapted from the book *Jesus Christ Heals* by Charles Fillmore.

The Filling-the-Cup Script

I recognize God as the all-encompassing Mind.
I recognize Christ as the all loving.
I recognize Spirit as the all-active manifestation.
I am soul; I am body; I am spirit; and the three are one.
The Kingdom of God is within me.
I am the vessel of God, and I express God.
In God, I love and move and express my feelings.
I am a tower of strength and stability in the realization that God is my health.
God, heaven, earth, and all the healing powers are united in healing me.
I press forward with courage and boldness in the power of God, and I am healed.
The peace of God wells up within me.
I trust in God in all things, and I am obedient to God.
God lives in me now.
By the grace of God, through Christ Jesus, I am made whole.
I welcome Christ into my body.
I recognize Christ as the embodiment of the God-Mind.
My mind is cleansed by Christ.
I have new life in Christ, and I am healed.
My new life in Christ fills me with zeal to live, and I am healed.
The Christ quickens and heals me.
Eternal life and strength are here, and I am made whole through Jesus Christ.
I am in unity with the spirit of truth.
My life source is spiritual energy.
I recognize truth as it is in principle.
The spirit of wholeness quickens me and heals me.
I am strengthened and healed by the power of the spirit of the inner me.

I daily praise and thank the spirit of life and health for constantly restoring me to perfection of body.

I praise and give thanks that the strength and power of Spirit now restore me to harmony and health.

I have the power to release the divine life imprisoned in my cells and project it as spiritual energy.

The vitalizing energy floods my whole being, and I am healed.

I rejoice because thy harmonizing love makes me whole.

My life flows swift and strong.

My soul bursts forth in song.

I will sing unto the Lord a new song of harmony and health.

I am one with divine mind—serene, orderly, and placid.

I sow seeds of love and the enjoyment of life.

I acknowledge fulfillment.

I am upright and honest in all that I think and do.

I do unto others as I would have them do unto me.

I have order in my physical life.

I have order in my mental life.

I have order in my emotional life.

I have order in my spiritual life.

I establish myself in the spiritual law.

I am the offspring of God.

I am one with His perfect wisdom, which is now ordering my life in divine harmony and health.

I affirm divine order daily.

My faith is constant and unchanging.

My word is the measure of my power.

I use my mind for right thinking.

My thoughts radiate with the speed of spiritual light.

I diligently seek God in all I do.

I mentally concentrate on a perfect body.

I focus all of my mental powers on a perfect body.

I pray daily.

I lift my mortal mind to the plane of spirit daily.

All things are possible to me when I exercise spiritual power under divine law.

I leverage my mind's energies through daily prayer.

I create a spiritual aura through daily prayer.

Though my prayers, I adjust my mind and body in harmony with God's creative laws.

I pray from a still place within my self.

I am persistent in prayer.

I am one with pure Being.

I am immersed in the Holy Spirit of life, love and wisdom.

The law of perfect harmony and I are one.

I am open to learn truth.
I am unlimited in my power.
I increase daily in health and strength, life and love.
I increase daily in wisdom and boldness, freedom and charity.
I am now in harmony with the Father, and stronger than any mortal law.
I know my birthright in pure Being, and I boldly assert my perfect freedom.
I am dignified and definite, yet meek in all that I think and do.
I am one with and I now manifest love, charity, justice, kindness, and generosity.
I am one with and I now fully manifest infinite goodness and mercy.
Peace flows through me like a river through my mind, and I thank thee, O God.
I rejoice daily in my healing.
Healing and I are one.
I am healed.

Health: General

This script is general, as theories on diet and exercise are contradictory and changing rapidly (i.e., high protein versus low protein; salt creates high blood pressure versus salt lowers high blood pressure). One way to complete the script is to locate a book you believe in on health and integrate its principles. Please add lots of "as appropriates" to avoid false beliefs of the moment. Best of luck with your new healthy lifestyle. (Written for the recording "Opening to Healing"—the *Healing* series.)

The Emptying-the-Cup Script

Being healthy and I are one.
I release and forgive myself for being healthy.
I release and forgive myself for not being healthy.
I release and forgive _____ for not teaching me how to be healthy.

my family, school, medical profession, doctors

I release, forgive, and dissolve all false models of health.
I release, forgive, and dissolve all false models of _____.

longevity, nutrition, exercise, supplements, herbs, medicine, alternative medicine

I dissolve all imbalances on the soul level around being healthy.
I dissolve all imbalances on the soul level around abusing my body.
I dissolve all imbalances on the soul level around _____ my body.

neglecting, pushing, ignoring, abusing

I dissolve all imbalances on the soul level around fearing being healthy.
I dissolve all imbalances on the soul level around _____.

What is your health issue?

I dissolve all imbalances on the soul level around fearing being sick.
I dissolve all imbalances on the soul level around judging being healthy.
I dissolve all imbalances on the soul level around judging being sick.
I dissolve all imbalances on the soul level around everyone who judged me for being sick.
I dissolve all imbalances on the soul level around believing I have to be sick.
I dissolve all imbalances on the soul level around believing in miracle cures.
I dissolve all imbalances on the soul level around believing _____.

medicine cures me, being old means being sick, fasting will make me well

I dissolve all imbalances on the soul level around focusing on illness in place of wellness.
I dissolve all imbalances on the soul level around focusing on symptoms in place of cause.
I dissolve all imbalances on the soul level around feeling betrayed by _____.

my body, doctors, modern medicine, the educational system

I dissolve all imbalances on the soul level around bonding with others through illness.
I dissolve all imbalances on the soul level around associating being sick with _____.

What were your childhood experiences around getting sick? Did you get out of chores, not have to go to school, get special attention, get criticized?

I dissolve all imbalances on the soul level around feeling _____ about being sick.

How did your family feel about sickness—guilty, ashamed, weak, normal, angry, special?

I dissolve all imbalances on the soul level around not understanding the nature of health.
I dissolve all imbalances on the soul level around not understanding the intelligence within.
I dissolve all imbalances on the soul level around not understanding my own body and how it works.
I dissolve all imbalances on the soul level around not understanding that disease is caused by low resistance.
I dissolve all imbalances on the soul level around not understanding how food and lifestyle affect my health.

I dissolve all imbalances on the soul level around not understanding _____.

acid/base balances, heart rates, glandular functions, calories, grams

I dissolve all imbalances on the soul level around not understanding how to correct my imbalances.
I dissolve all imbalances on the soul level around waiting for a health crisis to change.
I dissolve all imbalances on the soul level around substituting medicine for health.
I dissolve all imbalances on the soul level around substituting _____ for health.
I dissolve all imbalances on the soul level around following health fads.
I dissolve my field of experience around being well.
I dissolve my field of experience around cellular toxicity.
I dissolve my field of experience around inappropriate responses to stimuli.
I dissolve my field of experience around stress-producing thoughts.
I transform my vibrational patterns around being well.
I transform my vibrational patterns around cellular toxicity.
I transform my vibrational patterns around stress-producing thoughts.
I transcend being well, and I am at peace with it.
I surrender to being well, and I allow it in my life as appropriate.
I bring all past issues around being well to an elegant completion in total grace.
I dissolve all future issues around being well before they materialize.
I take total and complete responsibility for my wellness.
I allow and assign others total and complete responsibility for their wellness.
Being well and being _____ are separate for me now.

alone, isolated, ignored, assigned more work

The Filling-the-Cup Script

Being healthy and feeling good has all positive outcomes for me now.
I am safe and protected when I am healthy and feel good.
I am loved and accepted when I am healthy and feel good.
I am nurtured and supported when I am healthy and feel good.
I believe in the wellness principle that good health is natural.
I understand good health is my natural birthright, and I claim it in grace.
I am committed to living a long, happy, satisfying, and productive life.
I have the courage and determination to live a long, happy, satisfying, and productive life.
I have the knowledge and discipline to live a long, happy, satisfying, and productive life.
I choose to make the journey to wellness, and I enjoy the trip.
I take the steps to achieve a long, happy, satisfying, and productive life in grace.

I accept health does not mean the absence of disease; rather it means normal phys-
iological function.
I understand my health depends on me first.
My first responsibility is to promote my health, and I do it.
I recognize the causes of imbalance in my body: toxicity, timing, and thoughts.
I recognize only my body can heal itself, and I provide it with the tools to do that.
I change the circumstances that create malfunctions.
I give my body every opportunity to repair injured and impaired areas.
I give myself time to heal and flow with the process.
I maintain a healthy immune system and vitally healthy cells.
I respond to external stimuli in all positive and healthy ways.
I think thoughts that are positive and health-inducing.
I provide myself with the proper exercise, serenity, diet, and environment.
I flow with the process of returning my body to its healthy functioning.
I respect my body, my life energy, and my health.
I heal myself naturally every day.
I choose health and healthy environments.
I choose health and healthy habits.
I choose health and healthy thoughts.
I choose health and _____.
Everything I do adds to my health.
I make the decisions daily that add to my good health.
I take the actions daily that add to my good health.
I take good care of myself every day.
I give my body the rest it needs.
I sleep deeply, peacefully, and restfully.
I awaken invigorated and refreshed, ready to experience another day.
I eat what is best for my continuing health.
I eat fresh, live, healthy food daily.
I eat whole grains daily.
My food is naturally salty.
Water is my favorite fitness drink.
I only eat when I am hungry.
I eat slowly and chew each bit thoroughly.
I maintain a healthy balance of diet and exercise.
I schedule my exercise, and I stick to my schedule.
I exercise in some form every day.
I increase in health and vitality daily.
Energy flows through my body easily.
Oxygen flows through my body easily.
I breathe deeply and evenly, fully and freely.
I love to breathe down into my abdomen.
The more I breathe, the healthier I get.
My immune system is functioning properly.

My thalmus is balanced and active.
My white blood cells are activated and efficient.
My heart is open and clear.
My heart is charged with blood flow continually.
My liver is operating effectively.
My kidneys operate efficiently.
My stomach and intestinal tract are balanced and healthy.
My reproductive organs are clear and open.
My acid-base balance remains healthy for me.
I am in touch and in tune with my body.
I recognize the signals my body sends me.
I honor the signals my body sends me, and I act on them as appropriate.
I balance my physical, emotional, and mental bodies.
I understand the interconnectedness of these bodies for me.
I recognize signals from each of these bodies as valid.
I listen to these body signals, and I make changes accordingly.
My mind is sending health signals to my entire body.
My brain is directing my cellular structures to increasing health.
My mind transforms ideas of health into my healthy physical condition.
My mind transforms images of health into my healthy physical condition.
My mind transforms feelings of health into my healthy physical condition.
I focus on health, and I see myself healthy.
I am in harmony with the universe.
I am vibrantly healthy, and I love life.
I am full of radiant health and energy.
I give thanks for my increasing health and vitality.

Holographic Universe

I believe in a holographic universe, and I have weird and wonderful experiences around these beliefs.

The Emptying-the-Cup Script

The holographic universe and I are one.
I release and forgive myself for seeing myself as part of the holographic universe.
I release and forgive myself for not seeing myself as part of the holographic universe.
I release and forgive myself for not understanding the holographic universe with my mind.
I release and forgive myself for not understanding the holographic universe with my body.

I release and forgive myself for not understanding the holographic universe with my emotions.

I dissolve all imbalances on the soul level around being part of the holographic universe.

I dissolve all imbalances on the soul level around fearing being part of the holographic universe.

I dissolve all imbalances on the soul level around judging being part of the holographic universe.

I dissolve my field of experience around being part of the holographic universe.

I transform my vibrational patterns around being part of the holographic universe.

I transcend being part of the holographic universe, and I am at peace with it.

I surrender to being part of the holographic universe, and I allow it in my life as appropriate.

I bring all past issues around being part of the holographic universe to an elegant completion in total grace.

I dissolve all future issues around being part of the holographic universe before they materialize.

I take total and complete responsibility for being part of the holographic universe.

I allow and assign others total and complete responsibility for their part in being part of the holographic universe.

Being part of the holographic universe and _____ are separate for me now.

The Filling-the-Cup Script

Being part of the holographic universe has all positive outcomes for me now.
I am safe and protected when I am part of the holographic universe.
I am loved and accepted when I am part of the holographic universe.
I am nurtured and supported when I am part of the holographic universe.
I am a hologram of love and harmony.
I am a hologram of gratitude and compassion.
I am a hologram of abundance and prosperity.
I am a hologram of freedom and joy.
I am a hologram of light and illumination.
I am a hologram of conscious evolution.
I am a hologram of world peace.
I am a hologram of _____.

Humor

I believe a great goal is to laugh every day—in positive and healthy ways. Many of my fondest memories are around laughter with my family and friends. May this script support that in your life.

The Emptying-the-Cup Script

Humor and I are one.

I release and forgive myself for having a sense of humor.

I release and forgive myself for not having a sense of humor.

I release and forgive myself for taking myself and my life too seriously.

I release and forgive everyone who does not have a sense of humor.

I release and forgive everyone who denies my humor.

Laughing and I are one.

I release and forgive myself for not laughing enough.

I release and forgive myself for laughing too much.

I release and forgive myself for not having fun and laughing every day.

I release and forgive everyone who does not laugh enough.

I release and forgive everyone who punished me for being humorous and laughing.

I dissolve all imbalances on the soul level around humor.

I dissolve all imbalances on the soul level around fearing humor.

I dissolve all imbalances on the soul level around stifling humor.

I dissolve all imbalances on the soul level around being punished for my humor and laughter.

I dissolve all imbalances on the soul level around being shamed for my humor and laughter.

I dissolve all imbalances on the soul level around being _____ for my humor.

I dissolve all imbalances on the soul level around fearing a positive emotional state.

I dissolve all imbalances on the soul level around the misuse of humor and laughter.

I dissolve all imbalances on the soul level around fearing being laughed at.

I dissolve all imbalances on the soul level around laughing at myself.

I dissolve all imbalances on the soul level around self-ridicule.

I dissolve all imbalances on the soul level around laughing at others.

I dissolve all imbalances on the soul level around laughter as a social sanction.

I dissolve all imbalances on the soul level around being tickled and tickling others.

I dissolve all imbalances on the soul level around teasing and being teased.

I dissolve all imbalances on the soul level around teasing as an expression of aggression.

I dissolve all imbalances on the soul level around judging humor.

I dissolve all imbalances on the soul level around misunderstanding humor.

I dissolve all imbalances on the soul level around the misuse of humor.

I dissolve all imbalances on the soul level around inappropriate, excessive humor.

I dissolve all imbalances on the soul level around negative, dysfunctional humor.

I dissolve all imbalances on the soul level around abusive humor.

I dissolve all imbalances on the soul level around cruel, aggressive humor.

I dissolve all imbalances on the soul level around harmful, hurting humor.
I dissolve all imbalances on the soul level around insulting humor.
I dissolve all imbalances on the soul level around sadistic humor.
I dissolve all imbalances on the soul level around sexist humor.
I dissolve all imbalances on the soul level around ridicule and satire.
I dissolve all imbalances on the soul level around using humor to deliver insults and hostility.
I dissolve all imbalances on the soul level around substituting humor for honesty.
I dissolve all imbalances on the soul level around substituting humor for anger.
I dissolve all imbalances on the soul level around substituting humor for _____.
I dissolve all imbalances on the soul level around being funny to hide sadness, depression.
I dissolve all imbalances on the soul level around being a comedian.
I dissolve all imbalances on the soul level around clowning.
I dissolve all imbalances on the soul level around telling jokes.
I dissolve all imbalances on the soul level around being a practical joker.
I dissolve all imbalances on the soul level around being a punster.
I dissolve all imbalances on the soul level around laughing to hide nervousness.
I dissolve all imbalances on the soul level around laughing to hide _____.

insecurity, confusion, fear, discomfort, embarrassment

I dissolve all imbalances on the soul level around silly, vacant laughter.
I dissolve all imbalances on the soul level around forced laughter.
I dissolve all imbalances on the soul level around manic, hysterical laughter.
I dissolve all imbalances on the soul level around sardonic, cynical, derisive laughter.
I dissolve all imbalances on the soul level around aberrant laughter.
I dissolve all imbalances on the soul level around contrary laughter.
I dissolve my field of experience around humor and laughter.
I transform my vibrational patterns around humor and laughter.
I transcend humor and laughter, and I am at peace with them.
I surrender to humor and laughter, and I allow them in my life as appropriate.
I bring all past issues around humor and laughter to an elegant completion in total grace.
I dissolve all future issues around humor and laughter before they materialize.
I take total and complete responsibility for my sense of humor and laughter.
I allow and assign others total and complete responsibility for their sense of humor and laughter.
Humor and _____ are separate for me now.

The Filling-the-Cup Script

I understand the role humor and laugher play in my life, and I welcome it.
I recognize and accept my unique sense of humor as appropriate.

I easily distinguish between healthy and unhealthy humor and laughter.
I am safe and protected when I am happy and laughing.
I am loved and accepted when I am happy and laughing.
I am nurtured and supported when I am happy and laughing.
I use humor in fine and elevating ways, and it liberates me.
I use humor to express love, affection, and caring in all appropriate ways.
I use humor within the context of mutually understanding, loving, and support-
  ing relationships.
I laugh with people, enfolding them in the humor.
I have a laughing attitude toward life in all healthy and positive ways.
I find humor in commonplace and ordinary everyday events as appropriate.
I can laugh at events while remaining positively emotionally connected with them.
I perceive life comically without losing love or respect for myself and others.
My humor is automatic and spontaneous.
I have an unlimited ability to laugh.
I understand my ability to laugh is a sign of my emotional health.
I use laughter as a release of tension and surplus energy as appropriate.
I laugh at the right things for the right reasons.
I laugh at the right times in the right way.
I use my sense of humor in a positive, healing way.
I use humor and laughter to cope with stress in all appropriate ways.
I use humor to promote social harmony.
I use humor in socially beneficial ways.
I use humor in therapeutic ways.
I use humor and laughter in joyous, free ways.

Inner Peace

I have dedicated my life to harmony, freedom, and creativity, for those bring me inner peace. May this script—aptly placed between humor and intelligence—support you in attaining inner peace your way. (Written for the recording "Attaining Inner Peace"—the *Spirituality* series.)

The Emptying-the-Cup Script

Attaining inner peace and I are one.
I release and forgive myself for having inner peace.
I release and forgive myself for not having inner peace.
I release and forgive myself for holding on to unpeaceful states of mind, body,
  and emotions.
I release and forgive myself for holding on to _____.
I dissolve all past agreement that disturb my inner peace on any level.
I dissolve all imbalances on the soul level around inner peace.

I dissolve all imbalances on the soul level around trying to attain inner peace in dysfunctional ways.

I dissolve all imbalances on the soul level around desiring and striving for inner peace.

I dissolve all imbalances on the soul level around fearing and avoiding inner peace.

I dissolve all imbalances on the soul level around creating or allowing obstacles, blocks, and disturbances to my inner peace.

I dissolve all imbalances on the soul level around becoming frustrated, discouraged, or disheartened by my lack of inner peace.

I dissolve all imbalances on the soul level around thoughts and feelings of separation, rejection, and disapproval.

I dissolve all imbalances on the soul level around thoughts and feelings of disruption, discontent, and dissatisfaction.

I dissolve all imbalances on the soul level around thoughts and feelings of deception, distrust, doubt, and worry.

I dissolve all imbalances on the soul level around thoughts and feelings of frustration, confusion, and illusion.

I dissolve all imbalances on the soul level around thoughts and feelings of agitation, anxiety, and restlessness.

I dissolve all imbalances on the soul level around thoughts and feelings of anger, ignorance, and jealousy.

I dissolve all imbalances on the soul level around thoughts and feelings of pride, envy, greed, and avarice.

I dissolve all imbalances on the soul level around thoughts and feelings of hopelessness, helplessness, and powerlessness.

I dissolve all imbalances on the soul level around valuing my thoughts, feelings, and actions over inner peace.

I dissolve all imbalances on the soul level around valuing my personality, image, and identity over inner peace.

I dissolve all imbalances on the soul level around valuing physical possessions, stimulation, and excitement over inner peace.

I dissolve all imbalances on the soul level around needing or creating strain, struggle, and effort.

I dissolve all imbalances on the soul level around needing or creating perfectionism and criticism.

I dissolve all imbalances on the soul level around needing or creating drama and intensity.

I dissolve all imbalances on the soul level around identifying with loss and gain.

I dissolve all imbalances on the soul level around identifying with pleasure and pain.

I dissolve all imbalances on the soul level around identifying with my inner struggles, conflicts, confusions, and fears.

I dissolve all imbalances on the soul level around identifying with chronic tensions and habitual reactions.

I dissolve all imbalances on the soul level around identifying with cravings and desires.

I dissolve all imbalances on the soul level around identifying with dysfunctions, addictions, and compulsions.

I dissolve all imbalances on the soul level around faulty actions feeling right and correct actions feeling wrong.

I transcend inner peace, and I surrender to it in grace.

I surrender to inner silence and quiet presence and embrace them in my life.

I bring all past issues around attaining inner peace to an elegant completion in total grace.

I dissolve all future issues around attaining inner peace before they materialize.

I take total and complete responsibility for my own inner peace.

I allow others total and complete responsibility for their own inner peace.

The Filling-the-Cup Script

I understand there is no possession finer than inner peace.

I open to, invite, and embrace inner peace into my life moment to moment.

I recognize inner peace is at the center of my being, and I claim it as mine.

I allow peace to flow throughout my mind and body with each breath I take.

I am objective about my lifestyle and its cause and effect relationship.

I use my free will to make conscious choices to live in a state of inner peace.

I choose the right path and right actions that deepen my serenity and inner peace.

I increase in direct and profound experience of serenity and inner peace daily.

I am Divinely Guided as to how to create a lifestyle of inner peace and I follow that guidance.

I open to, invite, allow, and embrace a lifestyle of serenity and inner peace.

I live my lifestyle with inner serenity and calm awareness.

I am serene in the face of all obstacles and difficulties.

I am peaceful in the face of all persons, places, and things.

When I experience disharmony, I become love.

When I experience injury, I become forgiveness.

When I experience doubt or despair, I become faith.

When I experience sadness or grief, I become joy.

When I experience darkness, I become light.

I carefully attend all virtuous beings with worship and reverence.

I carefully attend all unvirtuous beings with unconditional love.

I carefully attend helpful beings with helpfulness and show gratitude.

I carefully attend all harmful beings with supreme compassion and appropriate action.

I maintain my inner peace and harmony at all times and places.

I live a life that is outwardly simple and inwardly rich with inner peace.

Intelligence

As a parent and former university professor and college dean, this script is dear to my heart. I urge all parents, educators, counselors, career consultants, supervisors, and others related to assessing individuals' performance to record this script. I thank my family for recognizing and honoring all forms of intelligence, and for requiring me to be more than a "high IQ" in life. May we live to see this kind of balance established for each of us, and for every child.

The Emptying-the-Cup Script

Intelligence and I are one.
I release and forgive myself for believing I am intelligent.
I release and forgive myself for believing I am not intelligent.
I release and forgive myself for believing I am _____.

slow, stupid, dumb

I release and forgive myself for _____.

having learning difficulties, being a late bloomer, not doing math well, being confused, not understanding

I release and forgive everyone who taught me I was not intelligent.
I release and forgive myself for telling others they are not intelligent.
I release and forgive everyone who treated me like I wasn't intelligent.
I release and forgive myself for treating others like they are not intelligent.
I release and forgive _____.

What were your family's beliefs about intelligence and learning? Your school experiences around intelligence and learning? Your current situation?

I dissolve all imbalances on the soul level around intelligence.
I dissolve all imbalances on the soul level around my intelligence.
I dissolve all imbalances on the soul level around fearing intelligence.
I dissolve all imbalances on the soul level around fearing my intelligence.
I dissolve all imbalances on the soul level around fearing _____.

tests, intelligence tests, IQ tests, standardized tests, being labeled, being misunderstood: teachers, professors, classes, school, textbooks, situations that require reading

I dissolve all imbalances on the soul level around judging my intelligence.
I dissolve all imbalances on the soul level around associating intelligence by _____.

book learning, academics, grades, test scores, verbal skills

I dissolve all imbalances on the soul level around society valuing and honoring one intelligence more highly than others.
I dissolve all imbalances on the soul level around linguistic intelligence.
I dissolve all imbalances on the soul level around my intelligence of words.
I dissolve all imbalances on the soul level around logical mathematical intelligence.
I dissolve all imbalances on the soul level around my intelligence of numbers and logic.
I dissolve all imbalances on the soul level around spatial intelligence.
I dissolve all imbalances on the soul level around my intelligence with pictures and images.
I dissolve all imbalances on the soul level around musical intelligence.
I dissolve all imbalances on the soul level around my intelligence with rhythm and melody.
I dissolve all imbalances on the soul level around body-kinesthetic intelligence.
I dissolve all imbalances on the soul level around my intelligence of my physical body.
I dissolve all imbalances on the soul level around interpersonal intelligence.
I dissolve all imbalances on the soul level around my intelligence of understanding and working with people.
I dissolve all imbalances on the soul level around intrapersonal intelligence.
I dissolve all imbalances on the soul level around my intelligence of my inner self.
I dissolve all imbalances on the soul level around any and all blocks to developing my intelligences.
I dissolve all imbalances on the soul level around letting my learning difficulties block my development as a successful person.
I dissolve all imbalances on the soul level around shutting down or neglecting one of my intelligences.
I dissolve all imbalances on the soul level around neglecting one of my intelligences because _____.

of a negative experience, being shamed, threatened, ridiculed about it, Dad said it was stupid, Mom said I'd never make a living doing it, I didn't have time/money to develop it, of financial/career/family pressure

I dissolve all imbalances on the soul level around focusing on developing one intelligence.
I dissolve all imbalances on the soul level around focusing on developing one intelligence to _____.

please my parents, fit in, perform at school, for my career, do what was expected

I dissolve my field of experience around my intelligences.

I transform my vibrational patterns around my intelligences.

I transcend my intelligences, and I am at peace with them.

I surrender to my intelligences, and I allow them in my life as appropriate.

I bring all past issues around my intelligences to an elegant completion in total grace.

I dissolve all future issues around my intelligences before they materialize.

I take total and complete responsibility for my intelligences.

I allow and assign others total and complete responsibility for their intelligences as appropriate.

The Filling-the-Cup Script

My intelligences have all positive outcomes for me now.

I am safe and protected when I develop and express my intelligences.

I am loved and accepted when I develop and express my intelligences.

I am nurtured and supported when I develop and express my intelligences.

I understand IQ tests measure verbal and logical thinking without assessing other ways of knowing.

I understand IQ tests measure school giftedness, not life success skills.

I understand intelligence is the ability to respond successfully to new situations.

I understand intelligence is the capacity to learn from experience.

I understand intelligence depends on the context, task, and demands that life presents.

I understand the expression of intelligences is culturally determined.

I realize there are multiple intelligences that can be found in every walk of life.

I understand there are at numerous kinds of intelligences, and I have my own unique blend of them.

I recognize verbal intelligence and word smartness *in myself and others.*

I recognize visual intelligence and picture smartness in myself and others.

I recognize melody intelligence and music smartness in myself and others.

I recognize kinesthetic intelligence and body smartness in myself and others.

I recognize mathematical and scientific intelligence and logic smartness in myself and others.

I recognize interpersonal intelligence and social smartness in myself and others.

I recognize intrapersonal intelligence and self-smartness in myself and others.

I am in touch with my own unique type of intelligences, and I celebrate them.

I honor the many sides of my intelligences, and I develop them further.

I understand each of my intelligences has its own unique developmental pattern, and I flow with it.

I allow each intelligence to come forward in its own way and time as appropriate.

I recognize my intelligences by honestly appraising how I function in day-to-day living and everyday activities.

I realize the paradox of my greatest strength may be found within my learning difficulties.

I understand how I naturally think and learn, and I claim it as my own.
I match my intelligences to my work and leisure life, and I live a fulfilled life.
I choose work that allows the expression of my intelligences, and I prosper.
I work with my most powerful intelligences, and I have a sense of purpose and vision.
I understand how my intelligences affect the way I relate to others.
I understand how others' intelligences affect the way they relate to me.
I use my understanding of multiple intelligences to support self-esteem in myself and others.
I use my understanding of multiple intelligences to support teaching and learning.
I use my understanding of multiple intelligences to support harmony and goodwill.
I use my understanding of multiple intelligences to support _____.

Intimacy

I was "middle-aged" before I realized how unusual my definition of intimacy was. My paternal family was a loving extended farm family. For them, love was normal, inclusive, and nonsexual. Person-to-person relationships were about intimacy and love, and partnering was about intimacy, love, and sex. This script is about intimacy. (Written for the recording "Loving Intimacy"—the *Loving Partnership* series.)

The Emptying-the-Cup Script

Intimacy and I are one.
I release and forgive myself for having intimacy in my life.
I release and forgive myself for not having intimacy in my life.
I release and forgive myself for being intimate with myself first.
I release and forgive myself for not being intimate with myself first.
I release and forgive myself for being intimate with others.
I release and forgive myself for not being intimate with others.
I release and forgive myself for not knowing how to create and maintain intimacy.
I release and forgive everyone who has not been intimate with me.
I release and forgive Mom and Dad for their intimacy patterns with each other.
I release and forgive Mom and Dad for their intimacy patterns with me and others.
I release and forgive Mom and Dad for not teaching me how to create and maintain intimacy.
I dissolve all imbalances on the soul level around intimacy.

I dissolve all imbalances on the soul level around all false models and false standards of intimacy.

I dissolve all imbalances on the soul level around intimacy myths, fantasies, and fairy tales.

I dissolve all imbalances on the soul level around cultural and religious models of intimacy.

I dissolve all imbalances on the soul level around societal and media models of intimacy.

I dissolve all imbalances on the soul level around family and transgenerational models of intimacy.

I dissolve all imbalances on the soul level around childhood patterns of intimacy.

I dissolve all imbalances on the soul level around fearing and judging intimacy.

I dissolve all imbalances on the soul level around fear of giving and receiving intimacy.

I dissolve all imbalances on the soul level around avoiding and blocking intimacy.

I dissolve all imbalances on the soul level around fear of engulfment and loss of identity.

I dissolve all imbalances on the soul level around fear of self-discovery and knowledge.

I dissolve all imbalances on the soul level around desiring and craving intimacy.

I dissolve all imbalances on the soul level around fear of isolation and being alone.

I dissolve all imbalances on the soul level around fear of inadequacy, vulnerability, and weakness.

I dissolve all imbalances on the soul level around fear of abandonment and rejection.

I dissolve all imbalances on the soul level around confusing anything else with intimacy.

I dissolve all imbalances on the soul level around substituting anything else for intimacy.

I dissolve all imbalances on the soul level around emotionally detached and disconnected interactions.

I dissolve all imbalances on the soul level around automatic and mechanical interactions.

I dissolve all imbalances on the soul level around superficial and shallow interactions.

I dissolve all imbalances on the soul level around bored and lifeless interactions.

I dissolve all imbalances on the soul level around dishonest and deceptive interactions.

I dissolve all imbalances on the soul level around creating or maintaining intimacy in dysfunctional ways.

I dissolve all imbalances on the soul level around allowing others to create or maintain intimacy with me in dysfunctional ways.

I dissolve my field of experience and transform my vibrational patterns around intimacy.

I dissolve my field of experience and transform my vibrational patterns around re-creating my childhood intimacy experiences.

I dissolve my field of experience and transform my vibrational patterns around engaging in nonintimate relationships.

I dissolve my field of experience and transform my vibrational patterns around any and all betrayals of intimacy in my life.

I transcend intimacy, and I am at peace with it.

I surrender to intimacy, and I allow it in my life as appropriate.

I take total and complete responsibility for my willingness and ability to be intimate.

I allow and assign others total and complete responsibility for their willingness and ability to be intimate as appropriate.

I bring all my past issues around intimacy to an elegant completion in total grace.

I dissolve all future issues around intimacy before they materialize.

The Filling-the-Cup Script

I open to, allow, and embrace loving intimacy in my life.

I open to, allow, and embrace the openness, honesty, and vulnerability needed to experience true intimacy.

I am safe, protected, and supported when I am intimate.

I am loved, accepted, and nurtured when I am intimate.

I am intimate at the right time in the right ways.

I am intimate for the right reasons with the right people.

I live an intimate life full of love, joy, peace, and harmony.

I live an intimate life full of compassion, reverence, and gratitude.

I live an intimate life full of purpose and meaning.

I claim my divine birthright to have an intimate relationship with myself first.

I realize true intimacy is the deepest level of connecting with and sharing my authentic self.

I transform the abstraction of intimacy into common everyday loving interactions.

I develop and nurture the talents, skills, and emotions of true intimacy in grace.

I engage in self-revelation and discovery of others and develop fully mindful intimate relationships.

I share loving intimacy mutually and wholeheartedly as appropriate.

I accept the paradox of unity and separateness inherent in intimacy.

I accept the paradox of increased intimacy creating increased individuality.

I accept the paradox of irregular intimacy strengthening the continuity of relationship.

I strive for mutual transparency and extend our boundaries of honesty and truth.

I move with the tides of intimacy and allow their ebb and flow as appropriate.

I accept the stages of intimacy and their unique demands, frustrations, joys, and satisfactions in grace.

I use the stages of intimacy to add new depth and fullness to my ways of relating.

I develop and maintain balance among the various types and dimensions of intimacy.

I develop and maintain a multifaceted intimacy by sharing myself and my life.

I develop and maintain emotional intimacy and share my depth of awareness.

I develop and maintain recreational intimacy and share stress relieving play.

I develop and maintain intellectual intimacy and share a world of ideas.

I develop and maintain creative and aesthetic intimacy and share experiences of beauty.

We develop and maintain work intimacy and support each other in bearing responsibilities and tasks.

I develop and maintain spiritual intimacy and share a reverence for the power of spirit and soul.

My intimate relationships are based on mutual companionship, trust, and enjoyment.

My intimate relationships are powerful, purposeful, and peaceful.

My intimate relationships are a path to deeper awareness, depth, and spirit.

My intimate relationships are an unfolding process of personal and spiritual discovery.

My intimate relationships are mutually satisfying, pleasurable, and joyful.

My intimate relationships are mutually supportive, nurturing, and validating.

My intimate relationships thrive on uniqueness and individuality.

My intimate relationships are a mutual communion with others' spirits and souls.

I give the gift of intimacy freely and unconditionally to those who earn my trust as appropriate.

I receive the gift of intimacy from those who give it freely and unconditionally as appropriate.

Intuition

I believe we are all intuitive, and our intuitive insights often met criticism, disapproval, fear, etc. My intuition has been a guiding principle in my life, and I share this script to support your developing and using yours. (Written for the recording "Trusting Your Guidance"—the *Spirituality* series.)

The Emptying-the-Cup Script

Being intuitive and I are one.

I release and forgive myself for being intuitive.

I release and forgive myself for not being intuitive.

I release and forgive everyone who denied my intuition.

I release and forgive myself for using my intuition.

I release and forgive myself for not using my intuition.

I release and forgive myself for ignoring, denying, or burying my own intuition.

I release and forgive myself for arguing, resisting, and rebelling against my intuition.

I release and forgive myself for overriding my intuition with worry and doubt.

I release and forgive myself for overriding my intuition with logic and rationale.

I release and forgive myself for overriding my intuition with _____.

I release and forgive myself for being afraid to acknowledge and follow my intuition in all times and places.

I release and forgive myself for betraying my intuitive knowing in this life and all others.

I release, forgive, and dissolve my fear of misusing my intuitive power in this life and all others.

I release, forgive, and dissolve all false models and messages about intuition.

I dissolve all imbalances on the soul level around being intuitive.

I dissolve all imbalances on the soul level around fearing intuition.

I dissolve all imbalances on the soul level around judging intuition.

I dissolve all imbalances on the soul level around _____.

I dissolve my field of experience and transform my vibrational patterns around being intuitive.

I transcend intuition, and I am at peace with it.

I surrender to intuition, and I allow it in my life as appropriate.

I bring all my past issues around intuition to an elegant completion in total grace.

I dissolve all future issues around intuition before they materialize.

I gently dissolve all blocks and barriers to accessing my intuition.

I dissolve the barrier of self-doubt from my connection to own intuition.

I take total responsibility for my intuition and how I use it.

I allow and assign others total responsibility for their intuition and how they use it.

The Filling-the-Cup Script

Being intuitive has all positive outcomes for me now.

Being true to myself and being true to my intuition are the same for me now.

I am loved and accepted when I am intuitive.

I am safe and protected when I am intuitive.

I am nurtured and supported when I am intuitive.

I create a trusting relationship with my intuitive self.

I determine my higher purpose for accessing my intuition.

I am clear in my desire and readiness for connection with my intuitive self.
I take the necessary steps to increase my intuition daily.
I recognize the intuitive sense is the sense of the nonphysical world.
I recognize intuition is developed through divine knowledge and devotional love.
I recognize intuition is developed through meditation and selfless service.
I experience my intuition through stillness, nonjudgment, and meditation.
I give myself permission to receive and act on intuitive messages.
I open myself to the information and experience of my intuitive self and translate it perfectly.
I become aware of what I am feeling and knowing intuitively, and I trust it.
I become aware of what I am hearing and seeing intuitively, and I trust it.
I structure and organize my intuitive experiences in perfect ways.
I interpret and evaluate my intuitive experiences in perfect ways.
I trust my intuitive impressions and process them without editing or explaining.
I realize dreams are work being done at other levels of awareness, and I honor them.
I acknowledge symbols, pictures, songs, and other signals of intuition as appropriate.
I easily discern between true intuition and false guidance.
I hear true intuition accurately and dissolve all else as appropriate.

Letting Go

I think the American phenomenon of thrift shops and garage sales is a great example of our cultural pattern of overacquiring. I feel we do the same with thoughts, feelings, people, etc. Personalize this script to address whatever you resist letting go of. (Written for the recording "Releasing Past Relationships"—the *Loving Partnership* series.)

The Emptying-the-Cup Script

Letting go and I are one.
I release and forgive myself for letting go.
I release and forgive myself for not letting go.
I release and forgive myself for holding on to _____.

people, things, habits, ideas

I release and forgive myself for modeling or teaching others not to let go.
I release and forgive all who modeled or taught me not to let go.
I release and forgive everyone who didn't let go.
I release and forgive everyone who held on to me.

Is someone holding on to you?

I release and forgive myself for wanting others to hold on to me.
I release and forgive myself for giving _____ power over me by holding on to them.

people, animals, possessions/belongings, roles, status, habits

I dissolve all false models of holding on and letting go.
I dissolve all imbalances on the soul level around letting go.
I dissolve all imbalances on the soul level around fearing letting go.
I dissolve all imbalances on the soul level around associating holding on with pleasure.
I dissolve all imbalances on the soul level around associating holding on with power.
I dissolve all imbalances on the soul level around associating holding on with control.
I dissolve all imbalances on the soul level around associating holding on with _____.
I dissolve all imbalances on the soul level around justifying holding on.
I dissolve all imbalances on the soul level around holding on too long.
I dissolve all imbalances on the soul level around holding on to the wrong things.
I dissolve all imbalances on the soul level around holding on for the wrong reasons.
I dissolve all imbalances on the soul level around holding on to _____.

a person, a job, security, obligation, duty, a title, recognition, furniture, clothes

I dissolve all imbalances on the soul level around letting go of my emotional wounds.
I dissolve all imbalances on the soul level around letting go of _____.

fear, pride, my past, memories, fantasies, children, family, rituals, habits

I dissolve all imbalances on the soul level around letting go of frightening and painful experiences.
I dissolve all imbalances on the soul level around letting go of _____.

What past experience replays in your mind and emotions?

I dissolve all imbalances on the soul level around letting go of separation and suffering.
I dissolve all imbalances on the soul level around letting go of attachment and desire.
I dissolve all imbalances on the soul level around letting go of pride and ego.
I dissolve all imbalances on the soul level around letting go of disappointment and disillusionment.
I dissolve all imbalances on the soul level around letting go of insecurity and dependence.

I dissolve all imbalances on the soul level around letting go of inadequacy and failure.

I dissolve all imbalances on the soul level around letting go of judgment and blame.

I dissolve all imbalances on the soul level around letting go of guilt and self-punishment.

I dissolve all imbalances on the soul level around letting go of disowning, projecting, and scapegoating.

I dissolve all imbalances on the soul level around letting go of anger and drama.

I dissolve all imbalances on the soul level around letting go of bitterness and hatred.

I dissolve all imbalances on the soul level around letting go of vindictiveness, vengeance, and revenge.

I dissolve all imbalances on the soul level around letting go of recrimination and retribution.

I dissolve all imbalances on the soul level around letting go of jealousy, rivalry, and possessiveness.

I dissolve all imbalances on the soul level around letting go of nostalgia, regret, and resentment.

I dissolve all imbalances on the soul level around letting go of expectations.

I dissolve all imbalances on the soul level around letting go of illusion and fantasy.

I dissolve all imbalances on the soul level around letting go of distorted perceptions and interpretations.

I dissolve all imbalances on the soul level around letting go of false hopes, dreams, and promises.

I dissolve all imbalances on the soul level around letting go of false memories.

I dissolve all imbalances on the soul level around letting go of false ideas and ideals.

I dissolve all imbalances on the soul level around letting go of false duty and obligation.

I dissolve all imbalances on the soul level around letting go of unfulfilled wishes, dreams, and desires.

I dissolve all imbalances on the soul level around letting go of wanting the past to be different.

I dissolve all imbalances on the soul level around letting go of wanting my life to be different.

I dissolve all imbalances on the soul level around letting go of wanting _____ to be different.

I dissolve all imbalances on the soul level around associating letting go with pain and loss.

I dissolve all imbalances on the soul level around associating letting go with fear and uncertainty.

I dissolve all imbalances on the soul level around associating letting go with quitting and weakness.

I dissolve all imbalances on the soul level around associating letting go with loss of control.

I dissolve all imbalances on the soul level around associating letting go with loss of security.

I dissolve all imbalances on the soul level around associating letting go with loss of love.

I dissolve my field of experience and transform my vibrational patterns around letting go.

I dissolve my field of experience and transform my vibrational patterns around holding on.

I transcend letting go, and I am at peace with it.

I surrender to letting go, and I allow it in my life.

I bring all past issues around letting go to an elegant completion in total grace.

I dissolve all future issues around letting go before they materialize.

I take total and complete responsibility for letting go in my life.

I allow others total and complete responsibility for letting go in their lives.

The Filling-the-Cup Script

I am at peace letting go of the past before I know the future.

I have the emotional courage to let go.

I am loved and accepted when I let go.

I am safe and protected when I let go.

I am nurtured and supported when I let go.

I know when to let go and when to hold on, and I do so appropriately.

I let go of the right things at the right times for the right reasons.

I recognize the special characteristics of my own letting go experience and flow with them.

I recognize the effects and results of letting go, and I accept them in peace.

I send unconditional love to the parts of myself struggling with letting go.

I am at peace with the paradox of letting go and taking hold of myself.

I let go and create space for new and better thoughts, feelings, actions, and situations in my life.

Listening

Listening has been identified as the weakest skill for most of us. This addresses that weakness. (Written for the recording "Loving Communication"—the *Loving Relationships* series.)

The Emptying-the-Cup Script

Listening and I are one.

I release and forgive myself for listening to myself.

I release and forgive myself for not listening to myself.

I release and forgive myself for listening to others.

I release and forgive myself for not listening to others.

I release and forgive everyone who did not listen to me.

I release, forgive, and dissolve all false models of listening from all times and places.

I dissolve all imbalances on the soul level around fearing and judging listening to my inner dialogue.

I dissolve all imbalances on the soul level around unloving, critical, negative inner dialogue.

I dissolve all imbalances on the soul level around fearing and judging listening to my outer dialogue.

I dissolve all imbalances on the soul level around unloving, critical, negative outer dialogue.

I dissolve all imbalances on the soul level around fearing and judging listening to others.

I dissolve all imbalances on the soul level around unloving, critical, negative messages from others.

I dissolve all imbalances on the soul level around my blocks to actively listening.

I dissolve all imbalances on the soul level around being unwilling to hear what another is saying.

I dissolve all imbalances on the soul level around distorting or misunderstanding what I hear.

I dissolve all imbalances on the soul level around my conditioned responses while I'm listening.

I dissolve all imbalances on the soul level around my expectations while I'm listening.

I dissolve all imbalances on the soul level around selecting what I will hear.

I dissolve all imbalances on the soul level around hearing messages consistent with my own agendas and beliefs.

I dissolve all imbalances on the soul level around filtering messages inconsistent with my beliefs and thoughts.

I dissolve all imbalances on the soul level around filtering messages inconsistent with my values, feelings, and attitudes.

I dissolve all imbalances on the soul level around filtering messages inconsistent with my hopes, dreams, and desires.

I dissolve all imbalances on the soul level around being a lazy listener.

I dissolve all imbalances on the soul level around daydreaming and drifting mentally.

I dissolve all imbalances on the soul level around being a compliant, passive listener.

I dissolve all imbalances on the soul level around ignoring or forgetting what I hear.

I dissolve all imbalances on the soul level around being a critical, evaluative listener.

I dissolve all imbalances on the soul level around thinking about my reply while listening.

I dissolve all imbalances on the soul level around being a domineering listener.

I dissolve all imbalances on the soul level around being a bored, distracted listener.

I dissolve all imbalances on the soul level around being a hurried, tired, preoccupied listener.

I dissolve all imbalances on the soul level around being an overloaded, overwhelmed listener.

I dissolve all imbalances on the soul level around being a stonewalling nonlistener.

I dissolve all imbalances on the soul level around being a reactive listener.

I dissolve all imbalances on the soul level around arguing, discounting, and denying what I hear.

I dissolve all imbalances on the soul level around jumping to conclusions about what I hear.

I dissolve all imbalances on the soul level around being a take-it-personally defensive listener.

I dissolve all imbalances on the soul level around feeling attacked, wronged, or misunderstood while I listen.

I dissolve all imbalances on the soul level around feeling righteously indignant while I listen.

I dissolve all imbalances on the soul level around feeling smug, prideful, or superior while I listen.

I dissolve all imbalances on the soul level around being an active, involved listener.

I dissolve all imbalances on the soul level around being a neutral observer listener.

I dissolve all imbalances on the soul level around opening to receive others' feelings and perceptions.

I dissolve all imbalances on the soul level around opening to receive others' facts and viewpoints.

I dissolve all imbalances on the soul level around opening to receive negative feedback.

I dissolve all imbalances on the soul level around opening to receive positive feedback.

I dissolve all imbalances on the soul level around being empathetically connected with the speaker.

I dissolve all imbalances on the soul level around responding nonverbally.

I dissolve all imbalances on the soul level around mirroring the speaker.

I dissolve all imbalances on the soul level around acknowledging the speaker.

I dissolve all imbalances on the soul level around confusing acknowledgment and validation with agreement.

I dissolve my field of experience and transform my vibrational patterns around actively listening to myself and others.

I transcend listening, and I am at peace with it.

I surrender to listening, and I allow it in my life.

I take total and complete responsibility for actively listening to myself and others.

I allow and assign others total and complete responsibility for actively listening to themselves and to me.

The Filling-the-Cup Script

I increase my active, responsible, purposeful listening daily.

I maintain consistent attention and listen openly and compassionately.

I convey a positive, supportive, encouraging energy and attitude while I listen.

I easily discern the purpose for others' communications and their underlying emotions.

I receive the literal message.

I listen for the emotions behind the message.

I open to, allow, and accept others' emotions and points of view with ease.

I acknowledge the speaker in appropriate, appreciative ways.

I listen from an open, unassuming, clear place within myself.

I listen from a still, silent, peaceful place within myself.

I listen from a compassionate, nonjudgmental place within myself.

I listen for what has heart and meaning.

I listen with my ears, eyes, heart, and mind.

I am a good listener, and it shows.

I am a good listener, and I enjoy the process of listening.

Manifesting

Manifestation is the spiritual approach to "making things happen." I believe we are manifesting continually—mostly unconsciously. I have experienced many "miracles" in my life—consciously created. This script supports your opening to and creating your own miracles consciously. (Written for the recording "Manifesting with Ease"—the *Spirituality* series.)

The Emptying-the-Cup Script

Manifesting and I are one.

I release and forgive myself for manifesting consciously.

I release and forgive myself for not manifesting consciously.

I release and forgive myself for believing in my powers of manifestation.

I release and forgive myself for not believing in my powers of manifestation.

I release and forgive everyone who taught me I couldn't manifest.

I release and forgive everyone who did not believe in my power of manifestation.

I release and forgive _____.

I release, forgive, and dissolve all teachings and models of limitation and lack.

I release, forgive, and dissolve all teachings and models of straining and struggling.

I release and forgive myself for imposing artificial or meaningless constraints on me or my life in any way.

I dissolve all imbalances on the soul level around manifestation.

I dissolve all imbalances on the soul level around manifesting unconsciously.

I dissolve all imbalances on the soul level around manifesting consciously.

I dissolve all imbalances on the soul level around developing the power of manifesting.

I dissolve all imbalances on the soul level around fearing manifestation.

I dissolve all imbalances on the soul level around judging manifestation.

I dissolve all imbalances on the soul level around limitation and lack.

I dissolve all imbalances on the soul level around strain and struggle.

I dissolve all imbalances on the soul level around substituting strain and struggle for the power of manifestation.

I dissolve all imbalances on the soul level around substituting strain and struggle for achievement and self-worth.

I dissolve all imbalances on the soul level around manifesting from anything but ease, grace, and pure intention.

I dissolve all imbalances on the soul level around misunderstanding and misusing the power of manifestation.

I dissolve all imbalances on the soul level around substituting power over externals for power within myself.

I dissolve all imbalances on the soul level around misusing my powers of manifestation.

I dissolve all inner conflicts around my intentions in ease and grace.

I dissolve all imbalances on the soul level around having unclear or impure intentions.

I dissolve all imbalances on the soul level around having self-defeating or unhealthy intentions.

I dissolve all imbalances on the soul level around adopting others' intentions.

I dissolve all imbalances on the soul level around distrusting the power of my intention.

I transcend manifesting, and I am at peace with it.
I surrender to manifesting, and I allow it in my life.
I bring all my issues around manifesting to an elegant completion in total grace.
Manifesting and _____ are separate for me now.

selfishness, pride, ego, disharmony, imbalance

The Filling-the-Cup Script

I open to experiencing ease and grace in my life moment to moment.
I open to have magic and miracles fill my life moment to moment.
My mind is filled with miracle consciousness and my heart is filled with love.
I am a vehicle for miracles to work through, and I am a miracle in action.
I am at peace with the paradox of making things happen and allowing things to happen.
I am at peace with the paradox of having intense desire and having no attachment to outcome.
I am at peace with the paradox of unshakable serenity and intense commitment to my intentions.
I am at peace with the paradox of having desires for the future while living fully in the present.
Time is my ally and my friend and we are in gracious partnership for manifestation.
I recognize the present as my point of power where matter meets with spirit.
I create intention and choices in keeping with universal law.
My intentions are in alignment with natural law, universal truth, and justice.
My thoughts, emotions, and actions are in alignment with my intentions at all times in all places.
I am clear and pure in my intentions and feel them in my heart.
I organize my space/time events around my intention and desire.
My intentions, grounded in spiritual nonattachment, work in natural ways to create my heart's desires.
I hold my intentions in fixity of purpose to the total exclusion of obstacles from any source.
I recognize my present circumstances are an opportunity to manifest something new and beautiful.
I realize I create my own opportunities by becoming prepared for them.
I know my own heart and mind, and I am true to that knowing in all times and places.
My hearts desires and intention come into pure alignment for my perfect healing and automatic manifestation.
Imaginary obstacles to my manifesting my heart's desires disintegrate and disappear.

Realistic obstacles to my manifesting my heart's desires are transmuted into opportunities and shifted accordingly.

My power of manifestation becomes more potent and more accessible to me moment to moment.

I step forward into my own driving force and power of manifestation in true humility and total grace.

All of my personality and soul forces work together to achieve my heart's desires.

I step into my true magical self that is my essential state.

I recognize my true abilities are the result of practice, discipline, and patience.

I experience my personal magic as an expression of who I am, not what I do.

I recognize the fullness of my true magical self and I am divinely guided to its perfect use.

I recognize the fullness of my true miracle self and I am divinely guided to its perfect use.

I step into the mastery of manifestation easily and effortlessly and in pure grace.

I channel abundance and prosperity through me in perfect ways for myself and others.

I have a new evolutionary template and I take quantum leaps into states of grace.

I simplify everything until it vibrates in accord with the true me.

I reach new octaves of harmony, peace, and oneness daily.

I maintain a new spiral of conscious manifestation, joy, and prosperity.

I am in divine partnership with higher power to make conscious responsible choices.

I am in divine partnership with higher power to manifest my heart's desires.

I trust higher power to support my manifestations at all times and all places.

I have already received in spirit the fulfillment of my heart's desires, and it is manifesting through me in ease and grace.

I joyously swim in the universal ocean of opportunity and manifest great things for myself and others.

I use my true magical powers to create peace, love, and prosperity for myself and my planet.

I manifest magic and miracles that serve universal good.

Meditation

I began meditating in the 1970s, and it has been on ongoing source of remarkable experiences. This script took me to a new level. (Written for the recording "Attaining Inner Peace"—the *Spirituality* series.)

The Emptying-the-Cup Script

Meditation and I are one.

I release and forgive myself for meditating.

I release and forgive myself for not meditating.

I dissolve all false models and methods of meditating.

I dissolve all imbalances on the soul level around meditating.

I dissolve all imbalances on the soul level around substituting symbols, rituals, or ceremonies for true meditation.

I dissolve all imbalances on the soul level around restless, superficial, unwholesome states of mind.

I dissolve all imbalances on the soul level around fear of or attachment to my internal dialogues and distractions.

I dissolve all imbalances on the soul level around meditating in dry, habitual, and mechanical ways.

I dissolve all imbalances on the soul level around the blueprint of my thought forms.

I dissolve all imbalances on the soul level around mass consciousness and collective unconscious.

I dissolve all imbalances on the soul level around the paradox of mind as both a block and path to inner peace.

I dissolve my field of experience and transform my vibrational patterns around meditation.

I transcend meditation, and I am at peace with it.

I transcend having and doing for being.

I surrender to meditation, and I embrace it into my life.

I take total and complete responsibility for my meditations.

I allow others total and complete responsibility for their meditations.

The Filling-the-Cup Script

I tailor my meditation to my individual needs and circumstances.

I joyfully engage in the self-examination, study, and analysis that support my ongoing meditations.

I improve the quality of my meditation daily.

I partner with my subconscious to deepen my meditations.

I engage in meditation at the right times in the right ways for the right reasons.

I engage in meditation with regularity and consistency.

I engage in meditation with persistence and patience.

I engage in meditation with focus and clear intent.

I engage in meditation with awareness and alertness.

I engage in meditation fully conscious and fully present.

I direct my meditations to calm and neutralize my ego and personality.

I direct my meditations to make connection with the Divine.

I open to, invite, and allow meditations that open me to grace.

I open to, invite, and allow meditations that support my direct personal experience with the Divine.

I open to, invite, and allow meditations that open me to Divine awareness.
I flow effortlessly from my meditations to my worldly living.

Moving On

I am often asked, "When the releasing and forgiving and letting go are done, how do I move on with my life?" This is in answer to that question. (Written for the recording "Releasing Past Relationships"—the *Loving Partnership* series.)

The Emptying-the-Cup Script

Moving on and I are one.
I release and forgive myself for moving on.
I release and forgive myself for not moving on.
I release and forgive everyone who didn't move on.
I release and forgive myself for not wanting others to move on.
I release and forgive everyone who didn't want me to move on.
I release and forgive everyone who taught or modeled not moving on to me.
I release and forgive myself for teaching and modeling not moving on to others.
I dissolve all false models and messages of moving on from all times and places.
I dissolve all imbalances on the soul level around moving on.
I dissolve all imbalances on the soul level around fearing moving on.
I dissolve all imbalances on the soul level around judging moving on.
I dissolve all imbalances on the soul level around associating moving on with pain and loss.
I dissolve all imbalances on the soul level around associating moving on with loss of control.
I dissolve all imbalances on the soul level around associating moving on with loss of security.
I dissolve all imbalances on the soul level around associating moving on with loss of love.
I dissolve my field of experience and transform my vibrational patterns around moving on.
I transcend moving on, and I am at peace with it.
I surrender to moving on, and I allow it in my life as appropriate.
I bring all past issues around moving on to an elegant completion in total grace.
I dissolve all future issues around moving on before they materialize.
I take total and complete responsibility for moving on with my life.
I allow others total and complete responsibility for moving on with their lives.

The Filling-the-Cup Script

I recognize when holding on holds me back, and I take timely right action.
I have the courage to move on, and I do so as appropriate.
I have the commitment to move on, and I do so as appropriate.
I have the discipline to move on, and I do so as appropriate.
I have the _____ to move on, and I do so as appropriate.

What is keeping you from moving on? What would you have to have, do, or be to move on?

I am loved and accepted when I move on.
I am safe and protected when I move on.
I am nurtured and supported when I move on.
I move on in the right way at the right time for the right reasons.
I move on and attain mental clarity and harmony.
I move on and attain emotional clarity and harmony.
I move on and attain physical clarity and harmony.
I move on and attain spiritual clarity and harmony.
I move on to attain _____.

What would you like to gain by moving on?

I move on to a positive satisfying present and a fulfilling future.
I move on wise, free, and unafraid—in clarity, peace, grace, and harmony.

Neatness

I created this script for a client who reported back that it worked. I hope it works for you too.

The Emptying-the-Cup Script

Being neat and I are one.
I release and forgive myself for being neat.
I release and forgive myself for not being neat.
I release and forgive everyone in my life who isn't neat.
Clutter and I are one.
I release and forgive myself for creating clutter and allowing it in my life.
I release and forgive everyone who taught me to accumulate material things.
I release, forgive, and dissolve all models of clutter.
I dissolve all imbalances on the soul level around being neat.
I dissolve all imbalances on the soul level around fearing being neat.
I dissolve all imbalances on the soul level around judging being neat.
I dissolve all imbalances on the soul level around everyone who judged me for not being neat.

I dissolve all imbalances on the soul level around clutter.

I dissolve all imbalances on the soul level around fearing clutter.

I dissolve all imbalances on the soul level around judging clutter.

I dissolve all imbalances on the soul level around having a cluttered mind.

I dissolve all imbalances on the soul level around creating a cluttered environment.

I dissolve all imbalances on the soul level around substituting shuffling clutter for meaningful action.

I dissolve all imbalances on the soul level around crowding myself, my life, and my environment.

I dissolve all imbalances on the soul level around my accumulations.

I dissolve all imbalances on the soul level around externalizing my feelings onto things.

I dissolve all imbalances on the soul level around substituting things for love in my life.

I dissolve all imbalances on the soul level around trying to fill feelings of emptiness with things.

I dissolve all imbalances on the soul level around trying to fill feelings of loneliness with things.

I dissolve all imbalances on the soul level around everyone who substituted things for love in my life.

I dissolve all imbalances on the soul level around substituting possessions for unmet childhood needs.

I dissolve all imbalances on the soul level around substituting possessions for

_____.

feeling my emotions, living my life fully, having a relationship, personal confidence, self-worth

I dissolve all imbalances on the soul level around everyone who denied me the things I wanted or needed.

I dissolve all imbalances on the soul level around measuring who I am by what I own or possess.

I dissolve all imbalances on the soul level around controlling the clutter and junk in my life.

I dissolve all imbalances on the soul level around eliminating the clutter from my life.

I dissolve all imbalances on the soul level around growing up and letting go.

I dissolve all imbalances on the soul level around cleaning things up and clearing things out.

I dissolve all imbalances on the soul level around keeping what I have outgrown.

I dissolve all imbalances on the soul level around keeping things I don't need or use.

I dissolve all imbalances on the soul level around keeping what is obsolete or broken.

I dissolve all imbalances on the soul level around keeping _____.

collections, keepsakes, gifts, certificates, awards, trophies, curios, collectibles, gadgets, trinkets, tools, fabric, books, hobby supplies

I dissolve all imbalances on the soul level around spending on things in place of enriching experiences.

I dissolve all imbalances on the soul level around overdecorating _____.

myself, my home, my office, my vacation home, my boat, my car

I dissolve all imbalances on the soul level around not being able to let go.

I dissolve all imbalances on the soul level around confusing letting go with loss.

I dissolve my field of experience around _____.

I transform my vibrational patterns around _____.

I transcend being neat, and I am at peace with it.

I transcend holding on to things, and I release them.

I surrender to being neat, and I allow it in my life as appropriate.

I bring all past issues around being neat to an elegant completion in total grace.

I dissolve all future issues around being neat before they materialize.

I take total and complete responsibility for my own neatness.

I allow and assign others total and complete responsibility for their own neatness as appropriate.

Being neat and _____ are separate for me now.

The Filling-the-Cup Script

Being neat has all positive outcomes for me now.

I am safe and protected when I am neat.

I am loved and accepted when I am neat.

I am nurtured and supported when I am neat.

I establish internal satisfaction, no longer substituting external satisfaction as appropriate.

I understand there is no possession finer than good feelings, happy times, and memories.

I accept the task of simplifying and decluttering as a lifelong process.

I understand simplicity doesn't mean hard times.

I understand luxury doesn't mean good times.

I understand more is not better, and I establish simplicity, cleanliness, and clarity in my home, business, and office.

I avoid locations and events that tempt me to add clutter and junk to my life.

I easily recognize and admit when I have bought the wrong things, and I dispose of them.

I decide what to keep in my life based on my lifestyle and what makes my life easier.

I decide what to keep in my life based on what adds to my feelings of aliveness.

I decide what to keep in my life based on functionality.

I decide what to keep in my life based on what saves time and does the job well.

I decide what to keep in my life based on when and how often I use it.

I decide what to keep in my life based on how much time and effort it takes to care for it.

I decide what to keep in my life based on how it enhances my life.

I decide what to keep in my life based on how it contributes to a happy, free, resourceful life.

I decide what to keep in my life based on _____.

I allow my possessions to change as my needs and lifestyle change.

I keep, use, and store what is genuinely useful to me as appropriate.

I keep what I need for my journey of life.

I keep what generates love and good feelings in my life.

I keep what helps me in my business and work.

I keep what provides true value for me, my work, and my loved ones.

I maintain a clear, organized, and efficient closet.

I acquire and keep clothes that I consistently wear and feel and look good wearing.

I easily distinguish between appropriate accessories and over decoration.

I dispose of clothes that no longer suit me or my lifestyle.

I keep my vehicles clean and uncluttered.

I maintain a trash container in my vehicle and use it.

I keep cleaning supplies in my vehicle and use them as appropriate.

It is fun for me to identify the necessary steps to declutter my life, and I take them in grace.

It is fun for me to identify the necessary steps to declutter my environment, and I take them in grace.

I maintain my environment and possessions in a neat, uncluttered manner easily and effortlessly.

Negativity

My most recent self-improvement effort is to motivate myself with only positive. For instance, instead of telling myself, "Don't forget your plane ticket." I tell myself, "Remember your plane ticket." Being positive is a subtle reworking on all levels. I keep working on it!

The Emptying-the-Cup Script

Being negative and I are one.

I release and forgive myself for being negative.

I release and forgive myself for not being negative.

I release and forgive everyone who has been negative in my life.

I release and forgive everyone who modeled negativity to me.

I release, forgive, and dissolve all models of negativity in grace.
I dissolve all imbalances on the soul level around negativity.
I dissolve all imbalances on the soul level around fearing negativity.
I dissolve all imbalances on the soul level around fearing positiveness.
I dissolve all imbalances on the soul level around judging negativity.
I dissolve all imbalances on the soul level around judging positiveness.
I dissolve all imbalances on the soul level around my family model of negativity.
I dissolve all imbalances on the soul level around societal models of negativity.
I dissolve all imbalances on the soul level around cultural models of negativity.
I dissolve all imbalances on the soul level around educational models of negativity.
I dissolve all imbalances on the soul level around religious models of negativity.
I dissolve all imbalances on the soul level around _____ models of negativity.
I dissolve all imbalances on the soul level around _____.

What form does your negativity take—complaining, criticism, overreacting, lecturing? What form of negativity do others use with you?

I dissolve my field of experience around negativity.
I transform my vibrational patterns around negativity.
I transcend negativity, and I am at peace with it.
I surrender to negativity, and I allow it in my life as appropriate.
I bring all past issues around negativity to an elegant completion in total grace.
I dissolve all future issues around negativity before they materialize.
I take total and complete responsibility for my negativity.
I allow and assign others total and complete responsibility for their negativity.
Being positive and being _____ are separate for me now.

innocent, naive, dumb, air-headed, impractical, taken advantage of

The Filling-the-Cup Script

Being positive has all positive outcomes for me now.
I am safe and protected when I am positive.
I am loved and accepted when I am positive.
I am nurtured and supported when I am positive.
I see the good in each situation.
I am positive at the right time in the right way.
I am positive in the right way with the right people.

Passive-Aggression

Anger is covered separately. Use this script to address your specific events and issues. (Written for the recording "Speaking Up for Yourself"—the *Empowerment* series.)

The Emptying-the-Cup Script

Passive-aggression and I are one.
I release and forgive myself for being passive-aggressive.
I release and forgive myself for not being passive-aggressive.
I release and forgive everyone who was passive-aggressive with me.
I release and forgive _____ who modeled passive-aggression to me.
I dissolve all imbalances on the soul level around passive-aggression.
I dissolve all imbalances on the soul level around fearing passive-aggression.
I dissolve all imbalances on the soul level around fearing _____.

feeling anger, expressing anger, being overpowering, losing control

I dissolve all imbalances on the soul level around judging passive-aggression.
I dissolve all imbalances on the soul level around judging _____.

anger, assertiveness, not being a nice person

I dissolve all imbalances on the soul level around _____.
I dissolve my field of experience around passive-aggression.
I transform my vibrational patterns around passive-aggression.
I transcend passive-aggression, and I am at peace with it.
I surrender to passive-aggression, and I allow it in my life as appropriate.
I bring all past issues around passive-aggression to an elegant completion in total grace.
I dissolve all future issues around passive-aggression before they materialize.
I take total and complete responsibility for my anger.
I take total and complete responsibility for my passiveness.
I allow and assign others total and complete responsibility for their anger.
I allow and assign others total and complete responsibility for their passiveness.
I replace passivity with assertiveness in all positive ways.
I replace anger with understanding of myself and others.
I move beyond passive-aggression to a healthy way of expressing my emotions.

Perfectionism

I have a tendency toward perfectionism. In the past, I strove to be fault-less in all things. After clearing perfectionism, I am selectively "perfect." I work diligently to create the "perfect" script before I produce and release a tape for you, which I feel is appropriate. Look at the scripts *Expectations, Self-love,* and *Shame* for related issues. (Written for the recording "Loving Your-self"—the *Loving Relationships* series.)

The Emptying-the-Cup Script

Perfectionism and I are one.
I release and forgive myself for being perfect.

I release and forgive myself for not being perfect.
I release and forgive myself for believing I should be perfect.
I release and forgive everyone who told me I had to be perfect.
I release and forgive everyone who tried to make me perfect.
I release and forgive everyone who withheld love for perfection.
I release and forgive everyone who withheld _____ for perfection.

dinner, playtime, good grades, raises

I dissolve all imbalances on the soul level around perfectionism.
I dissolve all imbalances on the soul level around fearing perfectionism.
I dissolve all imbalances on the soul level around fearing not being perfect.
I dissolve all imbalances on the soul level around fearing not _____ perfectly.

behaving, performing, dressing, speaking, playing basketball

I dissolve all imbalances on the soul level around judging myself as imperfect.
I dissolve all imbalances on the soul level around judging others as imperfect.
I dissolve all imbalances on the soul level around competing to be perfect.
I dissolve all imbalances on the soul level around comparing myself to someone perfect.
I dissolve all imbalances on the soul level around being compared with _____.
I dissolve all imbalances on the soul level around confusing being perfect with being loved and lovable.
I dissolve all imbalances on the soul level around confusing being perfect with _____.
I dissolve my field of experience and transform my vibrational patterns around perfectionism.
I transcend perfectionism, and I am at peace with it.
I surrender to perfectionism, and I allow it in my life as appropriate.
I take total responsibility for my perfectionism.
I allow and assign others total responsibility for their perfectionism.

The Filling-the-Cup Script

I am loved and accepted whether or not I am perfect.
I am loved and accepted whether or not I _____ perfectly.
I am safe and protected whether or not I am perfect.
I am safe and protected whether or not I _____ perfectly.
I am nurtured and supported whether or not I am perfect.
I am nurtured and supported whether or not I _____ perfectly.
I am _____ whether or not I am perfect.
I motivate myself with compassion and self-love in place of striving for perfection.
I motivate myself with _____ in place of striving for perfection.
I reconcile and balance the conflicting desire for perfection with the reality of the human condition.

I love and accept myself completely regardless of my talents, abilities, and achieve-
ments.
I love and accept myself completely regardless of _____.

Performing Well

Include perfectionism with this script to create balance—not extremes.

The Emptying-the-Cup Script

Performing well and I are one.
I release and forgive myself for performing well.
I release and forgive myself for not performing well.
I release and forgive everyone who withheld _____ for performance.

love, approval, food, play, raises, promotions

I release everyone who told me I did not perform well.
I release everyone who _____ my performance.

criticized, ridiculed, rejected

I dissolve all imbalances on the soul level around performing well.
I dissolve all imbalances on the soul level around fearing performing well.
I dissolve all imbalances on the soul level around judging performing well.
I dissolve all imbalances on the soul level around being judged for what I do in
place of who I am.
I dissolve all imbalances on the soul level around judging myself by my perfor-
mance.
I dissolve all imbalances on the soul level around _____ judging people by
their performance.

my family, school, society, work, religion, church, team sports, clubs, organizations

I dissolve all imbalances on the soul level around being motivated to perform
well.
I dissolve all imbalances on the soul level around being capable of performing
well.
I dissolve all imbalances on the soul level around _____.
I dissolve my field of experience around performing well.
I transform my vibrational patterns around performing well.
I transcend performing well, and I am at peace with it.
I surrender to performing well, and I allow it in my life as appropriate.
I bring all past issues around performing well to an elegant completion in total
grace.

I dissolve all future issues around performing well before they materialize.
I take total and complete responsibility for my performance issues.
I allow and assign others total and complete responsibility for their performance issues as appropriate.
Performing well and being a perfectionist are separate for me now.
Performing well and _____ are separate for me now.

pushing myself, not having time for myself, not having time for my family, not enjoying life, sacrificing relationships, sacrificing my health

The Filling-the-Cup Script

Performing well has all positive outcomes for me now.
I am safe and protected when I perform well.
I am loved and accepted when I perform well.
I am nurtured and supported when I perform well.
I accept myself as imperfect and unique at the same time.
I enjoy knowing I am responsible for my actions.
I take pleasure in motivating myself.
I am reasonable and realistic in the performance standards I set for myself.
I know I can perform well and succeed, and I do it.
I have a great attitude about my performance.
I enjoy doing high-quality work.
I enjoy doing high-quality _____.

parenting, quilting, gardening, cooking, sailing, consulting, writing

I consistently do high-quality work.
I have many talents, and I use them well as appropriate.
I enjoy programming my mind positively for performance daily.
I improve daily in attitude and ability.
Each day, I nourish and improve my mind.
Each day, I nourish and improve my body.
Each day, I nourish and improve my emotions.
Each day, I nourish and improve my spirit.
My horizons are constantly expanding.
Life holds endless opportunities for me.
I give and receive value equally.
I believe in myself and my future.
What others have done, I can do.
I rise to new heights consistently.
I grow stronger with each challenge.
I am willing to be successful and happy.
I am willing for my life to work.
I am an achiever.

I apply myself to tasks with eagerness and confidence.
I apply myself to tasks with _____.
I take great pleasure in achieving excellence.
I make excellence a part of my daily life.
I focus on excellence and what it means to me.
I am comfortable with excellence and all it brings.
I am safe with excellence and peak performance.
I choose excellence and peak performance for myself.

Personal Power

When I was taking flying lessons, my instructor explained the developmental process of flying—from scared to cocky to mature—if you lived through the cocky stage. From this, I developed a "power curve" model I used in workshops. As we increase in power, we can become overconfident and egotistical. Often, we have a "significant emotional event" (SEE) in which we crash and burn and have the opportunity to SEE things differently. I've experienced several of those curves, from my days as a white-water guide (beginning to think I was invincible) to days teaching (beginning to think I had all the answers). I hope this script helps you claim your personal power without experiencing a SEE! (Written for the recording "Claiming Your Personal Power"—the *Empowerment* series.)

The Emptying-the-Cup Script

Personal power and I are one.
I release and forgive myself for having personal power.
I release and forgive myself for not having personal power.
I release and forgive myself for using my personal power.
I release and forgive myself for not using my personal power.
I release and forgive everyone who took my personal power.
I release and forgive _____ for _____.

Who told you to be powerless? Who dominated you? Who made you wrong when you were in your power?

I release and forgive myself for giving my power away.
I release and forgive myself for _____.

What did you do when others tried to take your power—give up, manipulate, get passive aggressive? How do you act when you feel powerless?

I release and forgive myself for taking others' power.
I release and forgive myself for _____.

What have you done to others when they showed power?

I release and forgive my mother and father for their power issues.

I release and forgive myself for confusing control with personal power.

I release and forgive myself for confusing money and possessions with personal power.

I release and forgive myself for confusing position and prestige with personal power.

I release and forgive myself for confusing education and credentials with personal power.

I release and forgive myself for confusing appearance and looks with personal power.

I release and forgive myself for confusing excitement and drama for personal power.

I release and forgive myself for confusing _____ with personal power.

What are your symbols of power? Your responses to being powerless?

I dissolve all imbalances on the soul level around personal power.

I dissolve all imbalances on the soul level around fearing and judging personal power.

I dissolve all imbalances on the soul level around my family's issues with personal power.

I dissolve all imbalances on the soul level around cultural and societal patterns of personal power.

I dissolve all imbalances on the soul level around gender and age models of personal power.

I dissolve all imbalances on the soul level around religious and racial models of personal power.

I dissolve all imbalances on the soul level around associating claiming my power with pain.

I dissolve all imbalances on the soul level around associating claiming my power with losing love.

I dissolve all imbalances on the soul level around associating claiming my power with losing security.

I dissolve all imbalances on the soul level around associating claiming my power with losing _____.

What did you lose when you acted powerfully?

I dissolve my field of experience and transform my vibrational patterns around having personal power.

I transcend personal power, and I at peace with it.

I surrender to personal power, and I allow it in my life.

The Filling-the-Cup Script

Claiming, having, and using my personal power have all positive outcomes for me now.

It is now safe for me to grow up and express my personal power fully.

It is natural for me to empower myself to the fullest.

It is natural for me to have and use personal power.

I am safe and protected when I have and use personal power.

I am loved and accepted when I have and use personal power.

I am nurtured and supported when I have and use personal power.

I use my personal power for the highest good for myself and others.

I move beyond my family model of power as appropriate.

As I increase in power, my self-love and acceptance increases.

As I increase in power, my health increases.

As I increase in power, my relationships increase in power.

As I increasingly claim my personal power, my life fills with more love, prosperity, and grace.

My self-love and acceptance are bases of my personal power.

My openness and vulnerability are bases of my personal power.

My harmony and balance are bases of my personal power.

My giving and receiving are bases of my personal power.

My acceptance and flow are bases of my personal power.

My total healing and wellness are bases of my personal power.

My ability to feel, love, and express is a base of my personal power.

My ability to understand and trust is a base of my personal power.

My ability to love and heal is a base of my personal power.

My ability to recognize and acknowledge truth is a base of my personal power.

My faith, spirituality, and inner peace are bases of my personal power.

I use my power in the right way at the right time in the right situations.

I use my power with the right people for the right reasons.

I go boldly forward claiming my personal power in all appropriate ways.

Prayer

The power of prayer is undeniable. Many of the ideas in this script came from Larry Dossey's work on prayer and healing. (Written for the recording "Opening to Healing"—the *Healing* series.)

The Emptying-the-Cup Script

Prayer and I are one.

I release and forgive myself for praying.

I release and forgive myself for not praying.

I release and forgive everyone who forced me to pray.

I release and forgive everyone who taught me inappropriate ways to pray.

I release, forgive, and dissolve all false models of prayer.

I release and forgive myself for not having prayer as a natural part of my life.

I release, forgive, and dissolve every time I thought my prayers went unanswered.

I release and forgive myself and others for losing faith in the power of prayer.

I dissolve all imbalances on the soul level around prayer.

I dissolve all imbalances on the soul level around fearing and judging prayer.

I dissolve my field of experience and transform my vibrational patterns around prayer.

I transcend prayer and I am at peace with it.

I surrender to prayer and I allow it in my life.

I bring all my past issues around prayer to an elegant completion in total grace.

The Filling-the-Cup Script

My life is a prayer and I live my prayer life moment to moment.

I accept and flow with my unique and personal prayer style.

I pray at the right times in the right ways for the right reasons.

I engage in prayer fully conscious and fully present.

I use prayers of gratitude, worship, and devotion at appropriate times in appropriate ways.

I use open-ended prayers of Thy Will Be Done at appropriate times in appropriate ways.

I use directed prayers for a specific outcome at appropriate times in appropriate ways.

My prayer time is my intimate time with the Divine.

My prayer time is a state of being and an attitude of devotion.

My prayer time is a state of relaxation and quietude.

My prayer time is a state of focused and sustained attention.

My prayer time is a self-loving state calling out for a perfect match of love.

My prayers are my invitation and respectful request for the world to manifest in benevolent ways.

I realize prayer does not change the science of being but brings me into harmony with it.

I have absolute faith that all things are possible in the Divine.

I recognize faith is self-generating energy I can summon in all times and places.

My faith is constant and unchanging, and I know when my prayers have been answered.

I praise and give thanks that the strength and power of Spirit are with me in prayer.

Prejudice

We're all prejudiced about something. I'm prejudiced about people who knowingly do the "wrong things," especially in positions of power (injustice). I've done several clearings on that topic, and I no longer feel angry, frustrated, or powerless in the face of injustice. Now I selectively choose which of the injustices I will work to change, and I do so with a sense of peace. Work with your prejudices honestly, and enjoy your new peace and harmony.

The Emptying-the-Cup Script

Prejudice and I are one.
I release and forgive myself for being prejudiced.
I release and forgive myself for not being prejudiced.
I release and forgive everyone who taught me prejudice.
I release and forgive everyone who is prejudiced against me.
I release and forgive _____ for _____.

Who was prejudiced in your past? What experiences of prejudice do you have?

I dissolve all imbalances on the soul level around prejudice.
I dissolve all imbalances on the soul level around fearing prejudice.
I dissolve all imbalances on the soul level around judging prejudice.
I dissolve all imbalances on the soul level around judgment.
I dissolve all imbalances on the soul level around false information and ideas.
I dissolve all imbalances on the soul level around stereotypes.
I dissolve all imbalances on the soul level around discrimination.
I dissolve all imbalances on the soul level around discrimination based on _____.

gender, race, age, intelligence, religion, appearance, weight, clothing, money

I dissolve all imbalances on the soul level around superiority.
I dissolve all imbalances on the soul level around inferiority.
I dissolve all imbalances on the soul level around _____.

What actions do you associate with prejudice—snobbery, hatred, violence, hostility, condescension?

I dissolve my field of experience around prejudice.
I transform my vibrational patterns around prejudice.
I transcend prejudice, and I am at peace with it.
I surrender to prejudice, and I allow it in my life as appropriate.
I bring all past issues around prejudice to an elegant completion in total grace.

I dissolve all future issues around prejudice before they materialize.
I take total and complete responsibility for my prejudices.
I allow and assign others total and complete responsibility for their prejudices.

The Filling-the-Cup Script

I am calm and peaceful in the face of prejudice.
I am centered and balanced in the face of prejudice.
I am safe and protected when I face prejudice.
I am loved and accepted when I face prejudice.
I am nurtured and supported when I face prejudice.
I flow with prejudice while I work to eliminate it.
I flow with prejudiced people while I work to change their viewpoint.
I maintain clear objectivity while I hear others' points of view.
I accept the person without accepting the point of view.
I see myself and others clearly and objectively.
I see myself and others free of the distortion of stereotypes and prejudices.
I treat others as I would like to be treated.

Prosperity

Prosperity is an issue for all of us in some form—mental, physical, emotional, spiritual, or financial. I love working with prosperity scripts, and I created the *Money* series to support all of us in being wealthy on all levels (see the *Wealth* script.)

The Emptying-the-Cup Script

Prosperity and I are one.
I release and forgive myself for being prosperous.
I release and forgive myself for not being prosperous.
I release and forgive myself for _____.

struggling, living in lack or poverty, overspending

I release and forgive everyone who told me I would never be prosperous.
I release and forgive everyone who expected me to be prosperous.
I release and forgive _____.

being judged for my income, assets, earning potential

I release, forgive, and dissolve all false models of prosperity.
I dissolve all imbalances on the soul level around prosperity.
I dissolve all imbalances on the soul level around fearing prosperity.

I dissolve all imbalances on the soul level around judging prosperity.
I dissolve all imbalances on the soul level around misunderstanding the nature of prosperity.
I dissolve all imbalances on the soul level around misunderstanding the source of prosperity.
I dissolve all imbalances on the soul level around _____.
I dissolve all imbalances on the soul level around confusing prosperity with _____.

money, possessions, income, love, acceptance

I dissolve my field of experience around prosperity.
I transform my vibrational patterns around prosperity.
I transcend prosperity, and I am at peace with it.
I surrender to prosperity, and I allow it in my life as appropriate.
I bring all past issues around prosperity to an elegant completion in total grace.
I dissolve all future issues around prosperity before they materialize.
I take total and complete responsibility for my prosperity as appropriate.
I allow and assign others total and complete responsibility for their prosperity as appropriate.
Prosperity and _____ are separate for me now.

sacrifice, struggle

The Filling-the-Cup Script

Being prosperous has all positive outcomes for me now.
I am safe and protected when I am prosperous.
I am loved and accepted when I am prosperous.
I am nurtured and supported when I am prosperous.
I choose prosperity mentally, physically, emotionally, and spiritually.
There is no limit to my supply and the sources of my supply.
My supply comes from all points in the universe.
My supply comes from all avenues of life.
I open to, allow, invite and embrace my highest good now.
I am ready to receive prosperity now.
I am ready to receive unlimited good in all areas of my life now.
I picture only good, and I receive only good.
New channels of prosperity open to me daily.
My infinite intelligence makes contact with the source daily.
I thank the source for unlimited increase in mind, money and substance.
I always have something to give.
I give richly and I receive richly.
I give consistently and open the way to receive consistently.
I tithe in appropriate amounts to appropriate sources.

I expect the best in every experience.
The law of mental attraction opens every channel of supply to me.
I invite power and love into my life, and every need is met.
I take only the good from each experience and release all else.
I see beyond appearances and recognize another set of circumstances.
My progress toward total prosperity is swift and joyous.
My prosperity is omnipresent.
I am grateful for all I have, and I give thanks for it.

Public Speaking

The first time I spoke in public, I stuttered, lost my breath, and nervously perspired enough to ruin what I was wearing. Now public speaking is as natural as talking on the phone. Give this script a try, and practice, practice, practice.

The Emptying-the-Cup Script

Public speaking and I are one.
I release and forgive myself for being a good public speaker.
I release and forgive myself for not being a good public speaker.
I release and forgive everyone who told me I wasn't a good public speaker.
I release and forgive _____.

What negative experiences have you had around public speaking?

I dissolve all imbalances on the soul level around public speaking.
I dissolve all imbalances on the soul level around fearing public speaking.
I dissolve all imbalances on the soul level around judging public speaking.
I dissolve all imbalances on the soul level around sharing my ideas in public.
I dissolve all imbalances on the soul level around my audience.
I dissolve all imbalances on the soul level around _____ when I speak in public.

stuttering, forgetting what I wanted to say, reading, faltering, being monotone

I dissolve all imbalances on the soul level around _____ when I speak in public.

being embarrassed, humiliated, questioned, disagreed with, attacked, ignored

I dissolve my field of experience around pubic speaking.
I transform my vibrational patterns around public speaking.
I transcend public speaking, and I am at peace with it.

I surrender to public speaking, and I allow it in my life as appropriate.
I bring all past issues around public speaking to an elegant completion in total grace.
I dissolve all future issues around public speaking before they materialize.
I take total and complete responsibility for my public speaking.
I allow and assign others total and complete responsibility for their public speaking.
Public speaking and _____ are separate for me now.

The Filling-the-Cup Script

Public speaking has all positive outcomes for me now.
I am safe and protected when I speak in public.
I am loved and accepted when I speak in public.
I am nurtured and supported when I speak in public.
I am an easy, confident, competent, effective public speaker.
I am a powerful speaker in my own way, and I appear that way to others.
I look forward to making public presentations.
It is fun for me to speak in public.
I enjoy sharing my ideas and information.
I am always deeply relaxed and calm.
My breathing is deep and even throughout my speech.
My voice is clear, forceful, and dynamic as appropriate.
My voice is _____ as appropriate.

even, soft, persuasive

I put emotion in my voice, and the audience responds well.
My hands are loose and easy throughout my speech.
I smile a lot as I speak as appropriate.
I gesture effectively when I speak.
I blend spontaneity with planning perfectly.
I use an outline and notes, and I speak naturally and effortlessly.
I have prepared visuals as appropriate.
I use my visuals at the right time in the right way for the right reasons.
My words and ideas flow when I speak in public.
My sense of timing is perfect.
I say the right things at the right time in the right way.
I speak from my heart as well as my head.
I maintain my head and heart connection while I speak.
I stay fully conscious while I speak.
I know my purpose for speaking, and it shows.
I understand my material, and it shows.
I know what I want from my audience, and I get it.
I know who my audience is, and I speak appropriately.

I match my presentation to my audience as appropriate.
I get in tune with my audience right away, and they feel it.
I create a bond of goodwill with my audience.
I flow with who they are, and they flow with who I am.
I start with an attention-getting opening.
I tell my audience what I am going to tell them; then I tell them; then I tell them what I told them.
I limit my number of main points as appropriate.
I cover the perfect amount of material for the time frame.
I present the material in an interesting, relevant way.
I relate the material to the audience in appropriate ways.
I help my audience understand the material.
My descriptions are visual and clear.
I tell stories as appropriate.
I am a natural storyteller, and I enjoy it.
My audience enjoys the way I tell a story.
I use humor as appropriate.
I sum up my talk when I am finished.
My summary is clear and concise.
I do a good job speaking, and I know it.
I get a good response to my presentation, and I am pleased.
I accept compliments about my speaking simply and graciously.

Quit Smoking

I get about 50 percent success with clients who try to quit smoking. Stick with it, and I am sure you will be one of the 50 percent that succeeds!

The Emptying-the-Cup Script

Smoking and I are one.
Quitting smoking and I are one.
I release and forgive myself for smoking.
I release and forgive myself for not smoking.
I release and forgive myself for not being able to quit smoking before.
I release, forgive, and dissolve all my old responses to quitting smoking.
I release and forgive everyone who smokes.
I release and forgive everyone who taught me to smoke.
I release and forgive everyone who modeled smoking to me.
I dissolve all imbalances on the soul level around smoking.
I dissolve all imbalances on the soul level around fearing smoking.
I dissolve all imbalances on the soul level around judging smoking.
I dissolve all imbalances on the soul level around bonding through smoking.

I dissolve all imbalances on the soul level around relating to the world though my dependencies.

I dissolve all imbalances on the soul level around smoking fantasies, illusions, and archetypes.

I dissolve all imbalances on the soul level around living out unconscious fantasies with smoking.

I dissolve all imbalances on the soul level around my need and desire for the forbidden.

I dissolve all imbalances on the soul level around desiring a cigarette.

I dissolve all imbalances on the soul level around all smoking represents and symbolizes.

I dissolve all imbalances on the soul level around being seduced by advertising.

I dissolve all imbalances on the soul level around oral gratification.

I dissolve all imbalances on the soul level around associating being daring and adventurous with smoking.

I dissolve all imbalances on the soul level around being risk-taking and sensation-seeking.

I dissolve all imbalances on the soul level around being impulsive and making snap decisions.

I dissolve all imbalances on the soul level around being nervous, overwrought, and hyperactive.

I dissolve all imbalances on the soul level around being anxious, restless, and pessimistic.

I dissolve all imbalances on the soul level around having chronic depression.

I dissolve all imbalances on the soul level around believing I am not in control of myself, my habits, and my life.

I dissolve all imbalances on the soul level around the immediate satisfaction I get from smoking.

I dissolve all imbalances on the soul level around associating _____ with smoking.

being independent, free, rebellious, beyond authority, one of the gang, accepted

I dissolve all imbalances on the soul level around trying to change or escape who I am with smoking.

I dissolve all imbalances on the soul level around smoking to change or escape my feelings.

I dissolve all imbalances on the soul level around using smoking to suppress divergent activities.

I dissolve all imbalances on the soul level around being addicted to smoking.

I dissolve all imbalances on the soul level around denying my addiction to smoking.

I dissolve all imbalances on the soul level around my emotional addictions that support smoking.

I dissolve all imbalances on the soul level around my mental addictions that support smoking.

I dissolve all imbalances on the soul level around physical addictions that support smoking.

I dissolve all imbalances on the soul level around my psychological addictions that support smoking.

I dissolve all imbalances on the soul level around my physical dependence on smoking.

I dissolve all imbalances on the soul level around my emotional dependence on smoking.

I dissolve all imbalances on the soul level around my mental dependence on smoking.

I dissolve all imbalances on the soul level around my cravings, urges, and compulsions to smoke.

I dissolve all imbalances on the soul level around the ritual, routine, and habit of smoking.

I dissolve all imbalances on the soul level around the ritual of inhaling and exhaling smoke.

I dissolve all imbalances on the soul level around all that motivates me to smoke.

I dissolve all imbalances on the soul level around eliminating my motivators to smoke.

I dissolve all imbalances on the soul level around thinking about smoking.

I dissolve all imbalances on the soul level around unconsciously smoking.

I dissolve all imbalances on the soul level around comforting myself with smoking.

I dissolve all imbalances on the soul level around smoking _____.

to end boredom, be alert, relax, fit in, alter my mood, be in altered state, as a stimulant, as a sedative

I dissolve all imbalances on the soul level around quitting smoking.

I dissolve all imbalances on the soul level around _____.

Why did you start smoking? When do you reach for a cigarette now? What makes it hard to quit?

I dissolve all imbalances on the soul level around my obstacles to quitting smoking easily.

I dissolve all imbalances on the soul level around my internal state that obstructs my quitting smoking.

I dissolve all imbalances on the soul level around my external surroundings that obstruct my quitting smoking.

I dissolve all imbalances on the soul level around feeling discouraged or guilty for not quitting.

I dissolve all imbalances on the soul level around quitting smoking and relapsing.

I dissolve all imbalances on the soul level around withdrawal symptoms.
I dissolve all imbalances on the soul level around using _____ as an excuse to not quit smoking.

withdrawal symptoms, gaining weight, lack of self-control

I dissolve my field of experience around smoking and quitting smoking.
I transform my vibrational patterns around smoking and quitting smoking.
I transcend smoking and its effects on my health.
I surrender to smoking, and I allow it in my life as appropriate.
I bring all past issues around quitting smoking to an elegant completion in total grace.
I dissolve all future issues around quitting smoking before they materialize.
I take total and complete responsibility for my smoking habit.
I allow and assign others total and complete responsibility for their smoking habit.
I recognize my barriers to quitting smoking, and I dissolve them.
Smoking and _____ are separate for me now.

gaining weight, being irritable

The Filling-the-Cup Script

Quitting smoking has all positive outcomes for me now.
I realize smoking is a human behavior that can be controlled.
I know I have the power to quit smoking now and forever.
I have the desire and commitment to quit smoking.
I have the courage and discipline to quit smoking.
I have the knowledge and ability to quit smoking.
Everything I need to quit smoking is inside me, and I embrace and use it in grace.
I quit smoking the best way for me to become smoke-free for my lifetime.
I am totally and completely dedicated to quitting smoking, and I allow myself the full spectrum of that learning experience.
I make a take-charge quit-smoking contract with myself, and I keep it easily.
I choose the best method, tools, and techniques for quitting smoking for me.
I do sufficient planning to assure success.
I set a quit date and get support for myself and my decision.
I am nurtured and supported while I quit smoking.
I am safe and protected while I quit smoking.
I am loved and accepted while I quit smoking.
I am peaceful and calm while I quit smoking.
I identify my emotional smoking triggers, and I stay ahead of them.
I identify my physical smoking triggers, and I stay ahead of them.
I get rid of smoking-related cues in my environment.
I avoid smoking environments as appropriate.
I wait out my cravings and neutralize them in all healthy ways.

I recognize my relapse situations and neutralize them in all healthy ways.
I see any relapses as opportunities to learn better coping methods.
I overcome my addiction to nicotine in healthy ways.
I minimize the discomfort of nicotine withdrawal in healing ways.
I recognize my withdrawal symptoms as positive signs of progress.
I am free of cravings for cigarettes.
I reward myself at each step of my successful quit-smoking program.
I know the benefits of quitting smoking, and I review them regularly as appropriate.
Each day is easier for me to stay smoke-free.
I stay smoke-free for the rest of my life.
I take control of my life and my habits, and I feel good about myself.

Sales Calls/Cold-calling

This script is very general. If you have a favorite sales book or manual, integrate its principles, for example, developing relationship with customers, etc.

The Emptying-the-Cup Script

Sales and I are one, and cold-calling and I are one.
Ethical self-promotion and I are one.
I release and forgive myself for promoting myself through sales.
I release and forgive myself for not promoting myself through sales.
I release and forgive everyone who taught me not to promote myself.
I release and forgive everyone who told me _____.

not to stand out, not to be pushy, I couldn't do it

I dissolve all imbalances on the soul level around sales calls and cold-calling.
I dissolve all imbalances on the soul level around ethical self-promotion.
I dissolve all imbalances on the soul level around fearing sales calls and cold-calling.
I dissolve all imbalances on the soul level around fearing ethical self-promotion.
I dissolve all imbalances on the soul level around fearing rejection and failure.
I dissolve all imbalances on the soul level around fearing acceptance and success.
I dissolve all imbalances on the soul level around fearing _____.

prospecting, making presentations, closing

I dissolve all imbalances on the soul level around judging sales calls and cold-calling.
I dissolve all imbalances on the soul level around judging ethical self-promotion.
I dissolve all imbalances on the soul level around the sales process.

I dissolve all imbalances on the soul level around achieving and success.
I dissolve all imbalances on the soul level around outperforming my _____ level of performance.

expected, planned, projected, last quarter, last year, father's, manager's, mentor's, trainer's, consultants'

I dissolve all imbalances on the soul level around _____.
I dissolve my field of experience around sales calls, cold-calling, and ethical self-promotion.
I transform my vibrational patterns around sales calls, cold-calling, and ethical self-promotion.
I transcend sales calls and cold-calling, and I am at peace with them.
I transcend ethical self-promotion, and I am at peace with it.
I surrender to sales calls and cold-calling, and I allow them in my life as appropriate.
I surrender to ethical self-promotion, and I allow it in my life as appropriate.
I bring all past issues around sales calls and cold-calling to an elegant completion in total grace.
I bring all past issues around ethical self-promotion to an elegant completion in total grace.
I dissolve all future issues around sales calls and cold-calling before they materialize.
I dissolve all future issues around ethical self-promotion before they materialize.
I take total and complete responsibility for my performance making sales calls.
I allow and assign others total and complete responsibility for their responses to my sales calls.
Making sales calls and _____ are separate for me now.

being uncomfortable, being defensive, being aggressive

The Filling-the-Cup Script

Making sales calls has all positive outcomes for me now.
Cold-calling has all positive outcomes for me now.
Ethical self-promotion has all positive outcomes for me now.
I am safe and protected when I make sales calls.
I am safe and protected when I make cold calls.
I am safe and protected when I promote myself ethically.
I am safe and protected when I am visible and stand out.
I am loved and accepted when I make sales calls.
I am loved and accepted when I make cold calls.
I am loved and accepted when I promote myself ethically.
I am loved and accepted when I am visible and stand out.
I am nurtured and supported when I make sales calls.

I am nurtured and supported when I make cold calls.

I am nurtured and supported when I promote myself ethically.

I am nurtured and supported when I am visible and stand out.

I am now willing to feel good about myself all the time.

I accept myself completely as I am, knowing I am improving daily.

I provide value with who I am.

I provide value with what I do.

I give and receive value equally.

I feel wonderful receiving the monetary rewards of my business.

I feel wonderful receiving the emotional rewards of my business.

I feel wonderful receiving the _____ rewards of my business.

I recognize the balance of monetary and emotional rewards in selling my product.

I find emotional satisfaction in selling with sensitivity and empathy.

I find intellectual satisfaction in selling with knowledge and skill.

I find spiritual satisfaction in selling with honesty and integrity.

All of my sales and prospecting actions are appropriate, and I am rewarded for them.

I balance my self-promotional activities with respect for the rights and needs of others.

I am competent in my field, and I appear that way to others.

It is fun for me to learn about my product and field, and I learn more every day.

I feel good with my level of product knowledge.

I provide the right information in the right way at the right time to the right people.

I provide the right services to the right people at the right time in the right ways.

I feel good about providing information to others about my product.

It is natural for me to mix business and pleasure as appropriate.

It is natural for me to approach family and friends with my product.

I meet new friends often when I prospect and make sales calls.

I enjoy having social involvement with individuals and groups.

I am comfortable with all types of people.

I am equally comfortable with all levels of society.

I am at home with the top economic and social levels of society.

I am consistent in my approach and performance, regardless of the types of people.

I am at home making presentations to all types of people.

I feel good presenting to one person or to a group of people.

I am adequately prepared for each presentation.

I balance my presentation skills and techniques with my human skills.

I balance information with genuine emotion.

I balance realism and objectivity with emotion.

It is fun for me to prospect, present, and close.

I see prospecting as the primary base of my sales.

I understand the prospecting cycle, and I follow it.

I have specific prospecting goals.

I have a prospecting formula that works for me, and I stick to it as appropriate.

I know how many calls to make a day, and I make them easily and effortlessly.

I feel good when I achieve my prospecting goals.

I make new friends and gather new information prospecting.

I find new ways to motivate myself to make my calls.

I make my prospecting calls at my best time of day.

I am on top of it when I do my prospecting.

I keep accurate records of my prospecting which I enjoy reviewing.

I see prospecting as the pipeline to my success.

I feel good about being in sales.

I feel good being responsible for my performance.

I get personal satisfaction doing my job well.

I am always deeply centered and relaxed about myself and my profession.

I am at peace with who I am and what I do.

I am full of dignity and respect for who I am and what I do.

I take pride and pleasure in my role as a professional salesperson.

I have a mature understanding of my profession, and I feel good about that.

My mind is filled with positive thoughts and positive thinking.

I see the possibilities of my profession daily.

I see new opportunities for myself and my business daily.

I see how my product can benefit all types of people.

I balance organization and planning with action and results.

I am consistently assertive and use persuasion as appropriate.

It is natural for me to put myself forward and stand out.

I am comfortable being public and self-disclosing to others.

It is okay for me to be perceived as forward.

I feel good when I am spontaneous as appropriate.

I feel good showing my emotions as appropriate.

I feel good asking for what I want.

I am comfortable taking social and emotional risks.

I have complete trust that everything is working for my highest good now.

I am at peace with the intensity of my own emotions.

I experience enthusiasm daily and show it.

I take pleasure in setting my career goals and achieving them.

I set goals that are achievable with who I am and where I am now.

My goals are well thought out and specific as appropriate.

I have a specific plan to achieve my goals.

I balance my goal planning with my action to achieve them.

I see sales as the road to my wealth and status as appropriate.

I am clear on my values, both personally and professionally.

I deserve to have all the education, wealth, and status I want.

I deserve to have all the love, peace, and security I want.

I let go and let it flow when appropriate.

Self-love

This may be the most important script of all. I spent thirteen years researching and writing the "Loving Yourself" recording, and this is an excerpt from it (from the *Loving Relationships* series.)

The Emptying-the-Cup Script

Loving myself and I are one.

I release and forgive everyone who did not love me unconditionally.

I release and forgive myself for not loving myself unconditionally.

I release and forgive everyone who did not have mercy, understanding, and compassion for me.

I release and forgive myself for not having mercy, understanding, and compassion for myself.

I release and forgive everyone who taught or modeled anything but self-love to me.

I release and forgive myself for teaching and modeling anything but self-love to others.

I release and forgive myself for confusing self-love with conceit, arrogance, or pride.

I dissolve all imbalances on the soul level around loving myself.

I dissolve all imbalances on the soul level around being conceived in anything but love.

I dissolve all imbalances on the soul level around feeling unwelcome or like a mistake or accident.

I dissolve all imbalances on the soul level around Mom and Dad loving me conditionally.

I dissolve all imbalances on the soul level around Mom and Dad and how they demonstrated love.

I dissolve all imbalances on the soul level around judgmental and contradictory messages about the nature of love and self-love.

I dissolve all imbalances on the soul level around the connection between love, responsibility, resentment, and rage.

I transcend Mom and Dad and I am at peace with them.

I bring all past issues with Mom and Dad to an elegant completion in total grace.

I dissolve all future issues with Mom and Dad before they materialize.

I take total and complete responsibility for my part in relationship with Mom and Dad.

I allow Mom and Dad total and complete responsibility for their part in relationship with me.

I dissolve all imbalances on the soul level around not loving myself unconditionally.

I dissolve all imbalances on the soul level around substituting ego, conceit, vanity, or pride for self-love.

I dissolve all imbalances on the soul level around substituting possessions and accomplishments for self-love.

I dissolve all imbalances on the soul level around confusing or substituting nonloving thoughts, emotions, and actions for self-love.

I dissolve all imbalances on the soul level around linking self-love with anything but the innate worth of my authentic self.

I dissolve all imbalances on the soul level around linking self-love with anything unlike itself.

I dissolve all imbalances on the soul level around feeling unworthy or undeserving of loving myself.

I dissolve all imbalances on the soul level around feeling alienated, alone, isolated, lonely, and incomplete.

I dissolve all imbalances on the soul level around having a dysfunctional relationship with myself.

I dissolve all imbalances on the soul level around treating myself in nonloving ways.

I dissolve all imbalances on the soul level around allowing others to treat me in nonloving ways.

I dissolve all imbalances on the soul level around betraying, neglecting, rejecting, or abandoning myself.

I dissolve all imbalances on the soul level around renouncing, avoiding, or rejecting self-love.

I dissolve all imbalances on the soul level around denying, displacing, or externalizing self-love.

I dissolve all imbalances on the soul level around seeking validation, love, and completeness outside of myself.

I dissolve all imbalances on the soul level around being controlled by the need to love and be loved.

I dissolve all imbalances on the soul level around linking my self-love with the love from others.

I dissolve all imbalances on the soul level around needing to love others to experience the feelings of love.

I dissolve all imbalances on the soul level around being codependent or counterdependent.

I dissolve all imbalances on the soul level around striving to be what others want me to be to get love.

I dissolve all imbalances on the soul level around having a social mask or role that conflicts with my authentic self.

I dissolve all imbalances on the soul level around family, societal, and cultural models that limit, obstruct, or distort my self-love.

I dissolve all imbalances on the soul level around myths and archetypes that limit, obstruct, or distort my self-love.

I dissolve all imbalances on the soul level around the collective unconscious that limits, obstructs, or distorts my self-love.

I dissolve my field of experience and transform my vibrational patterns around self-love.

I transcend loving myself unconditionally and I am at peace with it.

I surrender to loving myself unconditionally and I allow it in my life.

I bring all past issues around loving myself unconditionally to an elegant completion in total grace.

I dissolve all future issues around loving myself unconditionally before they materialize.

I take total and complete responsibility for loving myself and my own self-loving state.

I allow others total and complete responsibility for loving themselves and their own self-loving state as appropriate.

The Filling-the-Cup Script

I claim my Divine birthright to have a loving relationship with myself.

I open to, invite, allow and embrace my self-honoring, self-loving state.

I open to, allow, and embrace my sacred right to be fully human.

I accept and trust in the human condition and myself as a representative of that condition.

I open to, allow, and embrace my sacred right to be honored and honorable as fully human.

I open to, allow, and embrace acceptance of myself and others as fully human.

I recognize I am a person in process and I am at peace with my process.

I open to, allow, and embrace times of reevaluation and clarification.

I open to, allow, and embrace the full knowledge of my virtues, assets, and strengths without pride or arrogance.

I open to, allow, and embrace the full knowledge of my problems, limitations, and failures without denial, distortion, or self-hate.

My self-loving state is independent of achievements, accomplishments, and possessions as appropriate.

My self-loving state is independent of others opinions and judgments as appropriate.

I neutralize all that makes me feel less than human through superhuman demands.

I neutralize all that makes me feel less than human through any form of abuse.

I neutralize all that makes me love myself less in any form.

I neutralize people whose effect is to dilute my ability to love myself.

I neutralize people whose effect is to dilute my honoring of my authentic self.

I align with those who support my humanness and self-loving state.

I align with those who recognize and support my authentic self.

I recognize and honor my authentic self as a I recognize and honor others' authentic selves.

I care for, nourish, nurture, and cherish my authentic self.

I open to, allow, and embrace self-love, self-acceptance, and validation in its healthiest forms.

I transform my field of experience to be self-loving in all times and places.

I am safe and protected when I feel and demonstrate my self-love and self-loving state.

I am loved and accepted when I feel and demonstrate my self-love and self-loving state.

I am nurtured and supported when I feel and demonstrate my self-love and self-loving state.

I participate in life in place of performing for it and experience being in place of doing.

I am self-loving and loyal to myself and I put myself first as appropriate.

I nurture the habit and process of loyalty to myself and my self-loving state.

I treat myself with kindness, generosity, respect, and dignity at all times and places.

My self-loving state supports my life of peace, joy, harmony, and abundance.

I open to a state of self-loving grace within myself.

I open to, allow, and embrace all feelings that support my self-loving grace.

I open to, allow, and embrace all actions that demonstrate my self-loving grace.

I open to, allow, and embrace all knowledge and insights that increase my state of self-loving grace.

I am filled with life-sustaining self-loving grace.

I step into the full radiant power of my authentic self and my self-loving state of grace.

I redefine self-loving grace as spirit flowing through me.

I experience self-loving grace as a powerful way to express spirit in the world.

Benevolence, compassion, and self-loving grace reign supreme within me moment to moment.

Shame

I consider fear, judgment, forgiveness, guilt, and shame the "Big Five" to clear. Try it and watch your life change. (Written for the recording "Healing Your Childhood"—the *Empowerment* series.)

The Emptying-the-Cup Script

Shame and I are one.
I release and forgive myself for feeling shame.
I release and forgive myself for feeling shame about _____ .

procrastination, divorce, failure, overeating, overspending, sex

I release and forgive myself for not feeling shame.

I release and forgive myself for denying shame.
I release and forgive myself for displacing shame.
I release and forgive myself for projecting shame.
I release and forgive myself for acting out shame.
I release and forgive _____ for having shame.
I release and forgive _____ for giving me shame.
I release and forgive _____ for making me feel ashamed.
I release and forgive _____ for being shame-based.
_____'s shame and my shame are separate for me now.

father, mother, partner, school, society, religion

I dissolve all imbalances on the soul level around shame.
I dissolve all imbalances on the soul level around fearing shame.
I dissolve all imbalances on the soul level around judging shame.
I dissolve all imbalances on the soul level around taking on others' shame.
I dissolve all imbalances on the soul level around being controlled with shame.
I dissolve all imbalances on the soul level around controlling others with shame.
I dissolve all imbalances on the soul level around being manipulated with shame.
I dissolve all imbalances on the soul level around manipulating others with shame.
I dissolve my field of experience around shame.
I transform my vibrational patterns around shame.
I transcend shame, and I am at peace with it.
I surrender to shame, and I allow in my life as appropriate.
I bring all past issues around shame to an elegant completion in total grace.
I dissolve all future issues around shame before they materialize.
I take total and complete responsibility for my shame.
I allow and assign others total and complete responsibility for their shame.
Shame and _____ are separate for me now.

The Filling-the-Cup Script

I accept my shame for what it is, and I acknowledge it.
I am safe and protected when I move beyond shame.
I am loved and accepted when I move beyond shame.
I am nurtured and supported when I move beyond shame.
I am _____ when I move beyond shame.
I replace shame with understanding and compassion.
I replace denial with acceptance and harmony.
I replace repression with honest expression and peace.
I replace displacement with clarity and ownership.
I release and heal all mental memories of shame in peace and harmony.
I release and heal all emotional memories of shame in peace and harmony.
I release and heal all physical memories of shame in peace and harmony.

I release and heal all spiritual memories of shame in peace and harmony.
I move forward free of shame and full of compassion.

Spirituality

I define spirituality as connection to spirit, and I feel it is the most important aspect of our lives. In the spirituality scripts, I strive to use words and concepts that are equally comfortable, relevant, and applicable for all religions and spirit based belief systems. Modify the wording to fit yours. (Written for the recording "Grounding Your Spirituality"—the *Spirituality* series.)

The Emptying-the-Cup Script

Spirituality and I are one.
I release and forgive myself for being spiritual.
I release and forgive myself for not being spiritual.
I release and forgive myself for denying my spirituality.
I release and forgive everyone who denied their spirituality.
I release and forgive everyone who denied my spirituality.
I release and forgive myself for denying others' spirituality.
I release and forgive _____.
I release, forgive, and dissolve all false models and messages around spirituality.
I dissolve all imbalances on the soul level around spirituality.
I dissolve all imbalances on the soul level around fearing spirituality.
I dissolve all imbalances on the soul level around judging spirituality.
I dissolve all imbalances on the soul level around being confused about spirituality.
I dissolve all imbalances on the soul level around _____.
I dissolve all imbalances on the soul level around others trying to take my spirit.
I dissolve all imbalances on the soul level around giving up my spirit to anyone or anything.
I dissolve all imbalances on the soul level around not believing fully in my spirituality.
I dissolve all imbalances on the soul level around not standing fully in my spirituality.
I dissolve all imbalances on the soul level around not feeling my spirituality.
I dissolve all imbalances on the soul level around cultures, religions, and philosophies that misunderstand spirituality.
I dissolve all imbalances on the soul level around cultures, religions, and philosophies that misrepresent spirituality.
I dissolve all imbalances on the soul level around cultures, religions, and philosophies that suppress spirituality.

I dissolve all imbalances on the soul level around substituting religion for spirituality.

I dissolve all imbalances on the soul level around substituting _____ for spirituality.

I dissolve all imbalances on the soul level around contradictions between religion, morality, and spirituality in my life.

I dissolve my field of experience and transform my vibrational patterns around spirituality.

I transcend spirituality, and I am at peace with it.

I transcend simple morality for the subtle complexity of spirituality.

I surrender to spirituality, and I allow it in my life.

I surrender to my spiritual quest, and I am at peace with it.

I surrender to the true nature and source of my spiritual power.

I bring all my past issues around spirituality to an elegant completion in total grace.

I bring all my issues around being spiritual to an elegant completion in total grace.

I bring all my issues around standing in my spirituality to an elegant completion in total grace.

I bring all my issues around believing in my spirituality to an elegant completion in total grace.

I bring all my issues around feeling my spirituality to an elegant completion in total grace.

I dissolve all future issues around spirituality before they materialize.

I take total and complete responsibility for my spirituality.

I take responsibility for my spiritual power, and I express it in right action.

I allow others total and complete responsibility for their spirituality as appropriate.

Being spiritual and being self-absorbed are separate for me now.

Being spiritual and _____ are separate for me now.

being cloistered, solitude, poverty, abstinence, sacrifice

The Filling-the-Cup Script

I welcome and embrace spirituality in all its forms wherever I find it.

I open to spirituality in my life and it flows throughout all parts of my being.

I deserve a rich spiritual life and I give myself permission to live it.

I give myself permission to experience and live the fullness of my spiritual power.

I move into the development and expression of my spiritual power in joy and freedom.

I am at peace with my infinite and unfathomable spiritual power.

I accept the multidimensional nature of my own spirituality in joy and harmony.

I embrace the mysteries of spirituality in peace.

My spirituality is grounded in my connection to my Higher Self and Universal Source.

My spirituality is grounded in universal moral principles and eternal truth.

My spirituality is grounded in the reverence and honoring of all life.

My spirituality is grounded in a sense of sacredness for all that is.

My spirituality is grounded in my ability to experience unconditional love.

My spirituality is grounded in my ability to be fully present.

My spirituality is grounded in my own moral courage and ability to confront my personality.

My spirituality is grounded in self-knowledge and self-acceptance of all aspects of my being.

My spirituality is grounded in my understanding of cause and effect.

My spirituality is grounded in my own life experiences and the good that comes from them.

I am at peace with the paradox of grounding my spirituality while freeing my Spirit.

Living and expressing my spiritual power have all positive outcomes for me now.

I flow with the the paradox of being humble about my spiritual power.

My spirituality shines forth in my radiance and energetic vibrancy.

I stand firmly in my spirituality and genuineness.

I ignite the spiritual fire within peace, love, joy, and harmony.

I easily distinguish between the ritual and story of religion and the depth and glory of spirituality.

I invite _____ into my life and accept the natural consequences.

God, Goddess, Universal Source, Buddha, Divine Spirit

I open to, allow and embrace _____ as my constant companion.

God, Goddess, Universal Source, Buddha, Divine Spirit

_____ surrounds me, enfolds me, and protects me in perfect ways for me.

God, Goddess, Universal Source, Buddha, Divine Spirit

_____ watches over me, guides me, and enriches me in perfect ways for me.

God, Goddess, Universal Source, Buddha, Divine Spirit

Strategic Thinking

This is a good business script; consider balancing it with the *Intuition* script. (Written for the recording "Solving Problems Wisely"—the *Success* series.)

The Emptying-the-Cup Script

Strategic thinking and I are one.
I release and forgive myself for thinking strategically.
I release and forgive myself for not thinking strategically.
I release and forgive myself for believing I can't think strategically.
I release and forgive everyone who told me I didn't know how to think.
I release, forgive, and dissolve all false models of strategic thinking.
I dissolve all imbalances on the soul level around strategic thinking.
I dissolve all imbalances on the soul level around fearing thinking strategically.
I dissolve all imbalances on the soul level around judging thinking strategically.
I dissolve all imbalances on the soul level around any and all blocks to my thinking strategically.
I dissolve all imbalances on the soul level around substituting strategic thinking for feeling.
I dissolve my field of experience around strategic thinking.
I transform my vibrational patterns around strategic thinking.
I transcend strategic thinking, and I am at peace with it.
I surrender to strategic thinking, and I allow it in my life as appropriate.
I bring all past issues around strategic thinking to an elegant completion in total grace.
I dissolve all future issues around strategic thinking before they materialize.
I take total and complete responsibility for my strategic thinking.
I allow and assign others total and complete responsibility for their strategic thinking.
Strategic planning and _____ are separate for me now.

The Filling-the-Cup Script

Strategic thinking has all positive outcomes for me now.
I am safe and protected when I think strategically.
I am loved and accepted when I think strategically.
I am nurtured and supported when I think strategically.
I conduct a situational review at the right time in the right way for the right reasons.
I identify and list my concerns in terms of desired outcomes.
I use action verbs to list my concerns.
I separate my concerns into small, manageable pieces.
I determine if one cause, action, or decision is enough to explain the concern.
I determine if one cause, action, or decision is enough to resolve the concern.
If necessary, I reduce each concern to an even smaller unit.
I establish priorities by relative impact, urgency, and trend.
I determine the seriousness of each concern in comparison to other concerns.

I identify the deadline for resolving each concern.

I decide if each concern is stable, improving, or getting worse.

I recognize what will most likely happen if I do nothing.

I conduct a cause analysis at the right time in the right way for the right reasons.

I select the appropriate thinking skill by determining what I want when I'm through analyzing.

I am clear on the difference between symptoms, cause, and effect.

I realize the visible parts of the problem are not necessarily the problem.

I recognize the cause is what creates the effect I recognize as the problem.

I realize the effect is the impact of the problem.

I determine what has gone right and what has gone wrong.

I determine what sets this problem apart from others.

I determine what has changed, if anything.

I determine what are the likely causes, and how I will verify them.

I determine what's working and making a difference.

I determine what's not working that would make a difference if it were.

I determine what's missing that would make a difference if it were provided.

I determine what's working that doesn't make a difference.

I generate a likely cause.

I move to decision making at the right time in the right way for the right reasons.

I know what I have to decide.

I identify and assess risks.

I determine the purpose of the decision.

I determine the need for a decision now.

I do something temporary to gain more time as appropriate.

I learn to adapt and live with the problem as appropriate.

I fix or eliminate the problem at the true root cause as appropriate.

I prepare a plan analysis at the right time in the right way for the right reasons.

I determine the plan and how it will work.

I establish guidelines so I know if it is working or not.

I establish alarms or alerts along the way to let me know when the plan is off.

I state the objective of the plan clearly and simply.

I identify problems with the plan.

I identity opportunities with the plan.

I develop preventive and facilitative actions for the plan.

I create a contingency plan so I know what I will do if the plan doesn't work.

I implement the plan and track its progress.

I evaluate the plan and modify as appropriate.

I learn from each process and improve myself and my skills and abilities.

I use my strategic thinking skills at the right times in the right situations.

I use my strategic thinking skills in the right ways for the right reasons.

Struggle

When I first addressed this issue for myself, it was a major SHIFT. I experienced deep loneliness for several days as if a friend had died. I believe that was because such a significant part of me had dissolved—the struggler-against-all-odds-achiever part of me—which had been my dominating operating mode. Now, over a decade later, I feel the release from struggle on nearly all levels. This reverses my transgenerational patterns, and it is a delight to recognize, experience, and celebrate the transformation.

The Emptying-the-Cup Script

Struggle and I are one.
I release and forgive myself for struggling and straining.
I release and forgive myself for struggling with _____.

What were your experiences with family members, in school, at work, in business, with money, with relationships?

I release and forgive myself for not struggling and straining.
I release and forgive everyone who told me life was a struggle.
I release and forgive everyone who told me I had to struggle.
I release and forgive _____ for modeling struggle to me.
I release, forgive, and dissolve all false messages around struggle.
I dissolve all imbalances on the soul level around struggle and strain.
I dissolve all imbalances on the soul level around fearing struggle and strain.
I dissolve all imbalances on the soul level around judging struggle and strain.
I dissolve all imbalances on the soul level around judging myself by my struggles.
I dissolve all imbalances on the soul level around creating struggle and strain.
I dissolve all imbalances on the soul level around my family pattern of struggle and strain.
I dissolve all imbalances on the soul level around my transgenerational patterns of struggle and strain.
I dissolve all imbalances on the soul level around societal and cultural patterns of struggle and strain.
I dissolve all imbalances on the soul level around religious and philosophical patterns of struggle and strain.
I dissolve all imbalances on the soul level around _____.
I dissolve all imbalances on the soul level around all no pain–no gain messages.
I dissolve all imbalances on the soul level around believing struggle develops character.
I dissolve all imbalances on the soul level around believing I have to struggle to make it.
I dissolve all imbalances on the soul level around believing _____.
I dissolve all imbalances on the soul level around trying too hard.

I dissolve all imbalances on the soul level around not trying hard enough.
I dissolve all imbalances on the soul level around believing I have to struggle to _____ .

be a good person, get ahead, make money, control my habits, have a good relationship

I dissolve my field of experience around struggling and straining.
I transform my vibrational patterns around struggling and straining.
I transcend struggle and strain, and I am at peace with them.
I surrender to struggle and strain, and I allow them in my life as appropriate.
I bring all past issues around struggling to an elegant completion in total grace.
I dissolve all future issues around struggling before they materialize.
I take total and complete responsibility for the struggles in my life as appropriate.
I allow and assign others total and complete responsibility for the struggles in their lives as appropriate.
I recognize my issues around struggle, and I dissolve them in grace.
I know the difference between work and struggle, and I work in all appropriate ways.
Struggling and _____ are separate for me now.

making it, being loved, surviving, performing well, having a good life, creating what I want in my life

The Filling-the-Cup Script

Living with ease has all positive outcomes for me now.
I am safe and protected when I live with ease.
I am loved and accepted when I live with ease.
I am nurtured and supported when I live with ease.
I use the right amount of effort for each task I perform.
I automatically know what it will take to _____ , and I do it as appropriate.
I trust life's process, and I flow with it as appropriate.
My life is simple and easy as appropriate.
My life is spontaneous and free as appropriate.
My life is _____ as appropriate.
I move forward in peace and joy.
I move forward _____ .

Studying

I created this script for a client who was taking a fire department exam to become Captain. He subsequently got all A's and B's in the college courses he was taking (he had always been a C student). However, he did not pass the fire department exam. Go figure!

The Emptying-the-Cup Script

Studying and I are one.
I release and forgive myself for studying.
I release and forgive myself for not studying.
I release and forgive myself for not knowing how to study effectively.
I release and forgive myself for _____.

having trouble learning, understanding, remembering

I release and forgive everyone who did not teach me how to study effectively.
I release and forgive _____.

What are your negative experiences around studying? Did someone force you, prevent you, compare you to someone else, make you feel guilt or shame?

I dissolve all imbalances on the soul level around studying.
I dissolve all imbalances on the soul level around test anxiety.
I dissolve all imbalances on the soul level around fearing studying.
I dissolve all imbalances on the soul level around judging studying.
I dissolve all imbalances on the soul level around my personal study style.
I dissolve all imbalances on the soul level around my personal study habits.
I dissolve all imbalances on the soul level around motivating myself to study.
I dissolve all imbalances on the soul level around studying too much.
I dissolve all imbalances on the soul level around studying too little.
I dissolve all imbalances on the soul level around cramming.
I dissolve all imbalances on the soul level around giving up when it gets hard.
I dissolve all imbalances on the soul level around rushing through studying.
I dissolve all imbalances on the soul level around thinking negatively about studying.
I dissolve all imbalances on the soul level around feeling negative about studying.
I dissolve my field of experience around studying.
I transform my vibrational patterns around studying.
I transcend studying, and I am at peace with it.
I surrender to studying, and I allow it in my life as appropriate.
I bring all past issues around studying to an elegant completion in total grace.
I dissolve all future issues around studying before they materialize.
I take total and complete responsibility for my studying abilities and patterns.
I allow and assign others total and complete responsibility for their studying abilities and patterns.
Studying and _____ are separate for me now.

The Filling-the-Cup Script

Studying has all positive outcomes for me now.
I am safe and protected when I study.
I am loved and accepted when I study.
I am nurtured and supported when I study.
I realize studying is a lifelong habit, and I develop it in grace.
I learn all I need to know about how to study.
I have the desire and follow-through to study the things that interest me.
I have the discipline and commitment to study the things I need to learn and know.
I establish an effective system for studying that works for me.
I set a schedule to study in small doses over a period of time, and I keep it.
I estimate the time I will study, and I organize my schedule accordingly.
I study during my productive study times.
I take into consideration the type of test so I learn the right things.
I preview the material to get an idea of what it is about.
I view the material to get a clear idea of what it says.
I imagine possible test questions as I view the material.
I make notes of anything I don't understand, and I find the explanation of it.
I review the material to assure it is locked in.
I summarize the material out loud as appropriate.
I outline the material and write questions and answers about it as appropriate.
I list key names, dates, words, and concepts and fill in pertinent information about them as appropriate.
I skim over my notes, highlight the main points, and organize them in a meaningful way for me.
I am tough with myself on sticking to my study schedule.
I study the right things at the right times.
I study in the right way for the right reasons.
I use the study techniques best suited to my learning style.
I maintain an alert and eager state of mind while I am studying.
I take breaks for relaxation and renewal.
I take satisfaction from studying and learning.
I enjoy learning new facts and skills.
I enjoy studying _____.
I enjoy learning about _____.

Sufi Code

I included this script to show how any religious or philosophical belief system can be incorporated into your *Change Your Mind* scripts.

Living the Sufi code and I are one.
I release and forgive myself for living the Sufi code.

I release and forgive myself for not living the Sufi code.

I release, forgive, and dissolve all false models of the Sufi code.

I dissolve all imbalances on the soul level around my sincerity to God.

I dissolve all imbalances on the soul level around extending justice to all.

I dissolve all imbalances on the soul level around being of service to my elders.

I dissolve all imbalances on the soul level around showing kindness to the young.

I dissolve all imbalances on the soul level around giving good counsel to friends.

I dissolve all imbalances on the soul level around having forbearance for my enemies.

I dissolve all imbalances on the soul level around being indifferent to fools.

I dissolve all imbalances on the soul level around having respect for the learned.

I dissolve my field of experience around living the Sufi code.

I transform my vibrational patterns around living the Sufi code.

I transcend the Sufi code, and I am at peace with it.

I surrender to the Sufi code, and I allow it in my life.

I bring all past issues around living the Sufi code to an elegant completion in total grace.

I dissolve all future issues around living the Sufi code before they materialize.

I take total and complete responsibility for my part in living the Sufi code.

I allow and assign others total and complete responsibility for living the Sufi code as appropriate.

Living the Sufi code has all positive outcomes for me now.

I am safe and protected when I live the Sufi code.

I am loved and accepted when I live the Sufi code.

I am nurtured and supported when I live the Sufi code.

It is natural and automatic for me to live the Sufi code.

It is easy and effortless for me to live the Sufi code.

I live the Sufi code day to day and moment to moment.

I am peaceful and fulfilled when I live the Sufi code.

Taxes

I did this script to motivate myself to complete my taxes on time. That year and subsequent years, I filed for an extension, which puzzled me. Now I understand the IRS chooses most audit cases in June and July, which means my late filing decreases my chances of being audited. I enjoy these kinds of surprise results!

The Emptying-the-Cup Script

Taxes and I are one.

I release and forgive myself for owing and paying taxes.

I release and forgive myself for not owing and not paying taxes.

I release and forgive everyone who did not teach me to pay my taxes.
Tax preparation and I are one.
I release and forgive myself for preparing my taxes.
I release and forgive myself for not preparing my taxes.
I release and forgive everyone who did not teach me how to prepare my taxes.
I release and forgive everyone who prepared my taxes wrong.
I release and forgive _____.

yourself, friends, family, accountants

I release and forgive everyone who _____.

gave me bad advice, the wrong instructions.

I dissolve all imbalances on the soul level around taxes.
I dissolve all imbalances on the soul level around fearing taxes.
I dissolve all imbalances on the soul level around judging taxes.
I dissolve all imbalances on the soul level around tax preparation.
I dissolve all imbalances on the soul level around fearing tax preparation and filing.
I dissolve all imbalances on the soul level around judging tax preparation and filing.
I dissolve all imbalances on the soul level around not understanding taxes.
I dissolve all imbalances on the soul level around not understanding filing requirements.
I dissolve all imbalances on the soul level around the IRS.

What are your feelings about the IRS—your experiences with it, beliefs about it, experiences with audits?

I dissolve my field of experience around taxes, tax preparation, and filing.
I transform my vibrational patterns around taxes, tax preparation, and filing.
I transcend taxes, and I am at peace with them.
I transcend tax preparation and filing, and I am at peace with them.
I surrender to taxes, and I allow them in my life as appropriate.
I surrender to tax preparation and filing, and I allow them in my life as appropriate.
I bring all past issues around taxes to an elegant completion in total grace.
I bring all past issues around tax preparation and filing to an elegant completion in total grace.
I dissolve all future issues around taxes before they materialize.
I dissolve all future issues around tax preparation and filing before they materialize.
I take total and complete responsibility for my taxes, tax preparation, and filing.
I allow and assign others total and complete responsibility for their taxes, tax preparation, and filing as appropriate.

Taxes and _____ are separate for me now.

overpayment, burden, hassle

The Filling-the-Cup Script

Preparing and filing my taxes have all positive outcomes for me now.
I am safe and protected when I prepare and file my taxes.
I am loved and accepted when I prepare and file my taxes.
I am nurtured and supported when I prepare and file my taxes.
It is easy and fun to work on my taxes.
I am alert and fully present when I work on my taxes.
I am disciplined and detail-oriented when I work on my taxes.
I flow with each stage and phase of my taxes, from the record keeping to the reporting.
I choose the best record-keeping system for me and my situation.
I change record-keeping systems as appropriate to streamline my tax work.
I maintain simple, effective systems and records for my tax work.
I bring in the right help with my taxes at the right time for the right reasons.
I enjoy working on my taxes, and I enjoy completing them on time.
It is easy to find the time to do my tax work.
The time I spend on my taxes flies by, and I complete it in grace.
I file my taxes at the right time in the right way.

Test Taking

When I was working with individual clients exclusively, a college student who wanted an A in statistics came to me. This script got her the desired A, and the word of mouth about her "test-taking methods" got me dozens of student clients. A recording of this script would make a great gift for any student.

The Emptying-the-Cup Script

Taking tests and I are one.
I release and forgive myself being good at taking tests.
I release and forgive myself for not being good at taking tests.
I release and forgive myself for _____.

stressing, failing tests, freezing up, feeling dumb, underperforming, cheating

I release and forgive the school system for stressing tests over experience and knowledge.
I release and forgive _____.

What are your school experiences with tests, teachers, and grades?

I release and forgive _____ for stressing tests over experience and skill.

What is your profession's testing/certification process?

I dissolve all imbalances on the soul level around taking tests.
I dissolve all imbalances on the soul level around fearing taking tests.
I dissolve all imbalances on the soul level around fearing what will be on a test.
I dissolve all imbalances on the soul level around anyone who scares me with tests.
I dissolve all imbalances on the soul level around judging taking tests.
I dissolve all imbalances on the soul level around everyone who judges me based on my test scores.
I dissolve all imbalances on the soul level around judging myself based on my test scores.
I dissolve all imbalances on the soul level around being angry about tests.
I dissolve all imbalances on the soul level around preparing for tests.
I dissolve all imbalances on the soul level around understanding test questions.
I dissolve all imbalances on the soul level around remembering what I studied.
I dissolve all imbalances on the soul level around recalling what I know.
I dissolve all imbalances on the soul level around answering test questions correctly.
I dissolve all imbalances on the soul level around fearing I won't know enough to pass.
I dissolve all imbalances on the soul level around taking tests too seriously.
I dissolve all imbalances on the soul level around not taking tests seriously enough.
I dissolve all imbalances on the soul level around thinking and feeling tests aren't fair.
I dissolve all imbalances on the soul level around thinking and feeling the brightest do the best on tests.
I dissolve all imbalances on the soul level around plunging into a test without previewing it.
I dissolve all imbalances on the soul level around beginning without understanding the instructions completely.
I dissolve my field of experience around taking tests.
I transform my vibrational patterns around taking tests.
I transcend taking tests, and I am at peace with it.
I surrender to taking tests, and I allow it in my life as appropriate.
I bring all past issues around taking tests to an elegant completion in total grace.
I dissolve all future issues around taking tests before they materialize.
I take total and complete responsibility for my test-taking ability.
I allow and assign others total and complete responsibility for their test-taking ability as appropriate.
Taking tests and _____ are separate for me now.

The Filling-the-Cup Script

I understand how important tests are in my life.
I accept the role they play and flow with it.
Taking tests has all positive outcomes for me now.
I am safe and protected when I take tests.
I am loved and accepted when I take tests.
I am nurtured and supported when I take tests.
I have excellent test-taking skills and techniques.
I enjoy taking tests, and I take tests easily and well.
I enjoy studying for tests, and I retain what I study easily.
I recall information that I need effortlessly.
I enjoy finding solutions to test questions.
My mind flows effortlessly while I am taking a test.
I am always prepared completely, and it shows in my performance.
It is fun for me to study and learn _____.
Questions about _____ are fun for me to answer.
I learn all I can about my tests in advance.
I determine the form of the exam and the material it will cover.
I learn the testing and grading systems and time frames.
I begin tests with enthusiasm, confidence, and calm.
I begin tests by reading and understanding the testing format and instructions.
I ask about anything I don't understand.
I understand the directions quickly and easily.
I follow all the instructions exactly and provide answers in the right form.
I survey and skim the test first, getting a preview of it.
I preview the test so I know what I need to do.
I get a sense of the complete test automatically.
I recognize the specific technique required by each type of test question.
I go through the entire test with care.
I pace myself accordingly.
I remain calm and relaxed as I begin working.
I start with the easiest part of the test for me.
I return to the tougher items and reread them.
I remain steady and stable throughout the test.
I see myself achieving competently.
I see myself completing each section on time.
I see myself well ahead of the time frames for the overall test.
My hand is loose and flexible throughout the test.
My breathing is deep, rhythmic, and relaxed throughout the test.
I see myself halfway through the test, and I am relaxed and refreshed.
I see myself halfway through the test, and I am confident and performing well.
I am at ease, and my physical body is relaxed and loose.
I am at peace, and my mind is flowing and responsive.

My mind is clear and sharp and makes connections quickly.
I am achieving well, and my path to success with this test is clear.
I continue to focus and concentrate easily.
I know the correct answers automatically, and I answer confidently.
I move through the questions easily.
I see the last question; I am smiling.
I give everything a final review to check my accuracy.
I give everything a final review to assure I did what I intended to do.
I know my material, and I have demonstrated it.
I _____.

pass, get my grade, get my certificate, get my degree

Time Management

This is a traditional approach to time management. (Written for the recording "Being Organized"—the *Success* series.)

The Emptying-the-Cup Script

Time management and I are one.
I release and forgive myself for managing how I spend my time.
I release and forgive myself for not managing how I spend my time.
I release and forgive everyone who told me _____.

I wasted time, dreamed my life away, didn't finish on time

I release and forgive all false models of managing time.
I dissolve all imbalances on the soul level around time management.
I dissolve all imbalances on the soul level around managing myself.
I dissolve all imbalances on the soul level around managing how I spend my time.
I dissolve all imbalances on the soul level around fearing time management.
I dissolve all imbalances on the soul level around fearing managing myself.
I dissolve all imbalances on the soul level around fearing time management tools.
I dissolve all imbalances on the soul level around judging time management.
I dissolve all imbalances on the soul level around judging managing myself.
I dissolve all imbalances on the soul level around judging how I manage my time.
I dissolve all imbalances on the soul level around judging time management tools.
I dissolve all imbalances on the soul level around resisting time management.
I dissolve all imbalances on the soul level around creating urgency and drama.
I dissolve all imbalances on the soul level around having an addiction to urgency.

I dissolve all imbalances on the soul level around the myth time is speeding up.

I dissolve all imbalances on the soul level around speeding up my life.

I dissolve all imbalances on the soul level around slowing down my life.

I dissolve all imbalances on the soul level around creating drama around deadlines.

I dissolve all imbalances on the soul level around using time for power and control.

I dissolve all imbalances on the soul level around using deadlines for power and control.

I dissolve all imbalances on the soul level around wasting my time.

I dissolve all imbalances on the soul level around wasting others' time.

I dissolve all imbalances on the soul level around allowing others to waste my time.

I dissolve all imbalances on the soul level around crisis situations.

I dissolve all imbalances on the soul level around unproductive meetings.

I dissolve all imbalances on the soul level around telephone interruptions.

I dissolve all imbalances on the soul level around unclear lines of authority and responsibility.

I dissolve all imbalances on the soul level around unclear instruction and communication.

I dissolve all imbalances on the soul level around indecision and procrastination.

I dissolve all imbalances on the soul level around lack of planning and clear objectives.

I dissolve all imbalances on the soul level around lack of clear priorities.

I dissolve all imbalances on the soul level around deadlines.

I dissolve all imbalances on the soul level around fearing deadlines.

I dissolve all imbalances on the soul level around judging deadlines.

I dissolve all imbalances on the soul level around my inability to say no.

I dissolve all imbalances on the soul level around _____.

I dissolve my field of experience around time management.

I dissolve my field of experience around managing myself and how I spend my time.

I transform my vibrational patterns around time management.

I transform my vibrational patterns around managing myself and how I spend my time.

I transcend time management, and I am at peace with it.

I transcend managing myself and how I spend my time, and I am at peace with it.

I surrender to time management, and I allow it in my life as appropriate.

I surrender to managing myself and how I spend my time, and I allow it in my life.

I bring all past issues around time management to an elegant completion in total grace.

I bring all past issues around managing myself and how I spend my time to an elegant completion in total grace.

I dissolve all future issues around time management before they materialize.

I dissolve all future issues around managing myself and how I spend my time before they materialize.

I take total and complete responsibility for my time management.

I take total and complete responsibility for managing myself and how I spend my time.

I allow and assign others total and complete responsibility for their time management as appropriate.

I allow and assign others total and complete responsibility for how they manage themselves and their time as appropriate.

The Filling-the-Cup Script

Managing myself and my time has all positive outcomes for me now.
I am safe and protected when I manage myself and my time.
I am loved and accepted when I manage myself and my time.
I am nurtured and supported when I manage myself and my time.
I am in control of my life and my time.
Time is a valuable asset, and I invest it wisely.
I plan my time and I follow my plan.
I enjoy being on time and completing things on time.
I have sufficient time to do everything I want.
I am reasonable and practical when I plan my time.
I allow time for the unexpected.
I allow time for thinking and reviewing.
I allow time for reflection and consideration.
I allow time for ideation and creativity.
I allow time for leisure and renewal.
I determine what is important and urgent, and I respond appropriately.
I determine what is urgent and not important, and I respond appropriately.
I determine what is important and not urgent, and I respond appropriately.
I determine what is not urgent and not important, and I respond appropriately.
I handle all my activities within this framework, and I excel at managing my time.
I identify my priorities each day and plan time to complete them.
I recognize my most productive times of each day.
I work on my top priorities during my most productive periods.
I handle visitors effectively and efficiently.
I handle telephone calls effectively and efficiently.
I take the calls that are urgent and important, screening the others.
I bunch outgoing calls to avoid interrupting my blocks of productive time.
I have a clear agenda before placing a call.

I stay to my agenda on phone calls as appropriate.
I limit the time I spend on a call based on its importance.
I design and maintain my work area for comfort and productivity, not ego and appearance as appropriate.
I keep the papers I need and use; I discard what I have read or will never read as appropriate.
I open my mail, scan it, deal with it, and discard it as appropriate.
I keep the catalogs I need and use; I discard others as appropriate.
I keep the books I need and use; I discard others as appropriate.
I keep _____ I need and use; I discard others as appropriate.

What do you accumulate that you don't need?

I enjoy using effective self-management techniques, and I integrate them into my daily life.
It is effortless and natural for me to manage myself and how I spend my time.
It is enjoyable and rewarding for me to manage myself and how I spend my time.
I manage myself and how I spend my time so I have time for the important things in life.
I manage myself and how I spend my time so _____.

I can enjoy the family, paint, fish, bowl, meditate, volunteer, travel, study.

Truth

Webster's dictionary defines truth as freedom from falseness. Raised to be truthful, I found myself out of step with societal conventions. As I delved into the subject, I moved into a new realm of spirituality that encompassed knowing and expressing truth—and, ultimately, living truth automatically. (Written for the recording "Grounding Your Spirituality"—the *Spirituality* series.)

The Emptying-the-Cup Script

Truth and I are one.
I release and forgive myself for knowing, expressing, and living truth.
I release and forgive myself for not knowing, expressing, and living truth.
I release and forgive myself and others for building a life on untruth.
I release and forgive all who punished or persecuted me for living truth.
I release and forgive myself for punishing or persecuting others for living truth.
I release, forgive, and dissolve all false sources and false truths in peace.
I release and forgive myself and others for any and all forms of denial of truth.
I release and forgive myself for taking as permanent what is really impermanent.
I release and forgive myself for taking as self-possessing what is without self.
I release and forgive myself for taking as pure what is impure.

I release and forgive myself for taking as pleasant what is really painful.

I dissolve all imbalances on the soul level around knowing, expressing, and living truth.

I dissolve all imbalances on the soul level around fearing knowing, expressing, and living truth.

I dissolve all imbalances on the soul level around judging knowing, expressing, and living truth.

I dissolve all addictive patterns that obstruct my knowing, expressing, and living truth.

I dissolve all codependent patterns that obstruct my knowing, expressing, and living truth.

I dissolve all counter-dependent patterns that obstruct my knowing, expressing, and living truth.

I dissolve all imbalances on the soul level around all mental domination that obstructs my knowing, expressing, and living truth.

I dissolve all imbalances on the soul level around all physical domination that obstructs my knowing, expressing, and living truth.

I dissolve all imbalances on the soul level around all emotional domination that obstructs my knowing, expressing, and living truth.

I dissolve all imbalances on the soul level around all spiritual domination that obstructs my knowing, expressing, and living truth.

I dissolve all imbalances on the soul level around everyone who expressed nontruth in any time or place.

I dissolve all imbalances on the soul level around myself for expressing non-truth in any time or place.

I dissolve all imbalances on the soul level around myself and others for expressing exaggeration and drama as truth.

I dissolve all imbalances on the soul level around myself and others for expressing fantasy and illusion as truth.

I dissolve all imbalances on the soul level around myself and others for expressing logic and reason as truth.

I dissolve all imbalances on the soul level around myself and others for expressing convention and custom as truth.

I dissolve all imbalances on the soul level around all false shared opinions established by worldly consent.

I dissolve all imbalances on the soul level around automatic views, habitual certainty, and foregone conclusions.

I dissolve all imbalances on the soul level around all false assumptions, mind systems, and paradigms.

I dissolve all imbalances on the soul level around all false intellectualization and justification.

I dissolve my field of experience and transform my vibrational patterns around knowing, expressing, and living truth.

I transcend knowing, expressing, and living truth, and I am at peace with it.

I transcend opinions, customs, and conventions as appropriate.

I surrender to knowing, expressing, and living truth, and I allow it in my life.

I bring all my past issues around knowing, expressing, and living truth to an elegant completion in total grace.

I dissolve all future issues around knowing, expressing, and living truth before they materialize.

The Filling-the-Cup Script

I recognize life as a perfect unfolding of events to learn and live truth.

I easily discern between knowledge, wisdom, and truth.

I find my truth through faith, open-mindedness, and openheartedness.

I am safe, loved and accepted when I know, express, and live truth.

I am nurtured, supported, and protected when I know, express, and live truth.

I am honored and respected when I know, express, and live truth.

Truth flows through me like a peaceful river.

Living my truth is a primary goal and accomplishment in my life.

Truth is the basis of my right action and magical efficiency.

I hold myself within the principle of truth and behold things clearly as appropriate.

I embrace the complexity of reality and accept the inexpressible as real.

I remember and relearn the wisdom and truth of the ages.

I am disciplined in my openness to truth and humble in my perceiving of truth.

I honor each path to truth and follow the one best suited for me.

I neither fear nor fix my mind upon knowing truth; I simply become truth in action.

I joyously serve truth and I live it in simple harmony.

I allow truth to come forward from the core of my being.

I dissolve the distance between knowing truth and living truth in one gentle step.

I receive revelations in the proper time and season.

I absorb and assimilate truth in peaceful, healthy ways for me.

I attract others who seek truth and are willing to live it.

I form a link in the chain of truth, passing it through me in perfect ways.

I live truth in ways that are evolutionary for myself and others.

I form relationships based on truth, simplicity, and love.

I maintain congruity between my words and behavior in all times and places.

I move forward, knowing what I feel, expressing what I mean, and doing what I say.

Expressing truth has all positive outcomes for me and for others.

I am divinely guided when and how to express truth.

I express truth at perfect times in perfect ways.

I maintain aligned content, timing, and context in my expressions.

I maintain consistency in my word choice, tonality, and nonverbal body language.

I express truth in refined, cultivated, sensitive ways as appropriate.
I express truth in helpful, kind, gentle ways as appropriate.
I express truth in supportive, nurturing, loving ways as appropriate.
I express truth in direct, concise, sparse ways as appropriate.
I express truth in corrective, confrontative, refuting ways as appropriate.
I express truth in strong, firm, unyielding ways as appropriate.
I express truth without blame, judgment, or doggedness.
I express truth without dogma, arrogance, or pride.
I express truth in balance and harmony, with simplicity and compassion.
I express truth in universally understandable ways.
My expressions of truth are vibrational charges that support positive changes in the world.
I detach from thought and opinion to live my truth as appropriate.
I live an unhindered and unadulterated view of reality.
I direct my personality to serve my soul in truth.
I stand firmly in the power of truth.
I believe in my truth in the face of false opposition.
I accept direct perception and inference as my sources of truth.
I accept trustworthy scripture and testimony as my sources of truth.
I express my knowing through doing as appropriate.
I am a perfect demonstration of truth in action moment to moment.
I demonstrate my truth through right energy, right action, and right living.
I bring all my thoughts, words, and actions into perfect alignment with Truth and Love.
I live my truth through moral discipline and patience.
I live my truth through meditation and insight.
I live my truth as the observer, the process of observing, and the observed.
I live in a state of knowing, expressing, and living truth.
I live and love within truth, and truth lives and loves through me.
I claim my divine power and harmony that comes from living my truth.

Twelve Steps

This is an adaptation of the twelve-step program used by Alcoholics Anonymous and its offshoot programs for eaters, debtors, gamblers, and so on. Modify it to fit your personal situation.

The Emptying-the-Cup Script

Addiction and I are one.
I release and forgive myself for being addicted.
I release and forgive myself for not being addicted.
I release and forgive myself for being addicted to _____.

drama, alcohol, food, cigarettes, excitement, sex, drugs, work, TV, the Internet, playing the stock market

I release and forgive _____ for modeling addiction to me.
I release and forgive _____ for starting me on my addiction.
I release, forgive, and dissolve all false messages about addiction.
I dissolve all imbalances on the soul level around addiction.
I dissolve all imbalances on the soul level around my addiction to _____.

drama, alcohol, food, cigarettes, excitement, sex, drugs, work, TV, the Internet, playing the stock market

I dissolve all imbalances on the soul level around fearing addiction.
I dissolve all imbalances on the soul level around fearing _____.
I dissolve all imbalances on the soul level around judging addiction.
I dissolve all imbalances on the soul level around judging myself for being an addict.
I dissolve all imbalances on the soul level around judging _____.
I dissolve all imbalances on the soul level around denying my addiction.
I dissolve all imbalances on the soul level around my mental causes of addiction.
I dissolve all imbalances on the soul level around my physical causes of addiction.
I dissolve all imbalances on the soul level around my emotional causes of addiction.
I dissolve all imbalances on the soul level around my spiritual causes of addiction.
I dissolve my field of experience around addiction.
I dissolve my field of experience around trying to get what I want in dysfunctional ways.
I dissolve my field of experience around trying to get my needs met in dysfunctional ways.
I dissolve my field of experience around _____.

What is your addiction?

I transform my vibrational patterns around addiction.
I transform my vibrational patterns around trying to get what I want in dysfunctional ways.
I transform my vibrational patterns around trying to get my needs met in dysfunctional ways.
I transform my vibrational patterns around _____.

What is your addiction?

I transcend addiction, and I am at peace with it.
I transcend _____, and I am at peace with it.

What is your addiction?

I surrender to addiction, and I allow it in my life as appropriate.
I bring all past issues around addiction to an elegant completion in total grace.
I bring all past issues around _____ to an elegant completion in total grace.
I dissolve all future issues around addiction before they materialize.
I dissolve all future issues around _____ before they materialize.
I take total and complete responsibility for my addiction.
I take total and complete responsibility for _____.
I allow and assign others total and complete responsibility for their addiction as
   appropriate.
Addiction and _____ are separate for me now.

The Twelve-Steps Script

Healing my addiction has all positive outcomes for me now.
_____ has all positive outcomes for me now.

admitting my addiction, being honest about my addiction

I am safe and protected when I heal my addiction.
I am safe and protected when I _____.

admit my addiction, tell my family, tell my friends, seek help

I am loved and accepted when I heal my addiction.
I am loved and accepted when I _____.

enter a treatment center, go to meetings

I am nurtured and supported when I heal my addiction.
I am nurtured and supported when I _____.

change my way of life and living

I acknowledge my life has become unmanageable.
I acknowledge my _____ has become unmanageable.

What is your addiction?

I dissolve my field of experience around my life being unmanageable.
I transform my vibrational patterns around my life being unmanageable.
I know a higher power can restore me to wholeness and health.
I know a higher power can restore me to sanity.
I dissolve my field of experience around believing a higher power can restore me to
   sanity.
I transform my vibrational patterns around believing a higher power can restore
   me to sanity.
I surrender my will and my life to that higher power as appropriate.
I trust the higher power to guide me through the process to a life of wholeness and
   health.

I trust the higher power to guide me through the process to a life of honor and integrity.

I trust the higher power to guide me through the process to a life of _____.

I dissolve my field of experience around surrendering to a higher power to restore me to wholeness and health.

I transform my vibrational patterns around surrendering to a higher power to restore me to wholeness and health.

I make an honest and complete self-inventory of who I am.

I make a searching and courageous inventory of the way I live.

I dissolve my field of experience around making a self-inventory of who I am and the way I live.

I transform my vibrational patterns around making a self-inventory of who I am and the way I live.

I admit the exact nature of my wrongs to myself.

I admit the exact nature of my wrongs to a higher power.

I admit the exact nature of my wrongs to others.

I release and forgive myself for these wrongs.

I know the higher power releases and forgives me for these wrongs.

I am entirely ready to have the higher power remove these wrongs.

I transcend these wrongs.

I dissolve my field of experience around admitting the exact nature of my wrongs.

I transform my vibrational patterns around admitting the exact nature of my wrongs.

I am ready to live free of my shortcomings.

I am ready to live free of my defects of character.

I sincerely ask the higher power to remove my shortcomings.

I release my shortcomings and defects of character completely.

I transcend my shortcomings and defects of character.

I dissolve my field of experience around being ready for a higher power to remove my shortcomings and defects of character.

I transform my vibrational patterns around being ready for a higher power to remove my shortcomings and defects of character.

I identify all persons I have harmed as appropriate.

I release and forgive myself for harming others.

I release and forgive myself for harming _____.

I know the higher power forgives me for harming others.

I transcend harming others.

I dissolve my field of experience around harming others.

I transform my vibrational patterns around harming others.

I make direct amends to all persons I have harmed as appropriate.

I am at peace with the people I have harmed.

I dissolve my field of experience around making amends to those I have harmed.

I transform my vibrational patterns around making amends to those I have harmed.

Being wrong has no power over me.
I know when I am wrong, and I admit it openly.
I dissolve my field of experience around admitting when I am wrong.
I transform my vibrational patterns around admitting when I am wrong.
I improve my conscious contact with higher power daily.
My feeling of oneness with higher power increases daily.
I pray and meditate regularly.
I pray and meditate for the power to live for higher purpose.
I am one with these principles.
I practice these principles in my daily life.
I share who I am with others at all appropriate times in appropriate ways.
I share my message with others at all appropriate times in appropriate ways.
I live these principles, and it shows.
I live in peace and harmony, love and forgiveness.
I live in clarity and honesty, health and balance.
I live in _____.
I live my higher purpose daily.

Wealth

My definition of wealth includes mental, physical, emotional, spiritual, and financial well-being. For me, this script includes those. (Written for the recording "Opening to Wealth"—the *Money* series.)

The Emptying-the-Cup Script

Creating, accumulating, and maintaining wealth and I are one.
I release and forgive myself for creating, accumulating, and maintaining wealth.
I release and forgive myself for not creating, accumulating, and maintaining wealth.
I release and forgive my mother and father for their issues with prosperity, abundance, and wealth.
I release and forgive my family for creating, accumulating, and maintaining wealth.
I release and forgive my family for not creating, accumulating, and maintaining wealth.
I release and forgive my family for not teaching me how to create, accumulate, and maintain wealth.
I release, forgive, and dissolve all false models and messages around creating, accumulating, and maintaining wealth.
I dissolve all imbalances on the soul level around family and generational models and patterns of wealth.

I dissolve all imbalances on the soul level around societal and cultural models and patterns of wealth.

I dissolve all imbalances on the soul level around gender and age models and patterns of wealth.

I dissolve all imbalances on the soul level around fearing and judging creating and accumulating wealth.

I dissolve all imbalances on the soul level around fearing and judging managing and maintaining wealth.

I dissolve all imbalances on the soul level around fearing and judging the experiences and consequences of wealth.

I dissolve all imbalances on the soul level around fearing and judging power and responsibility.

I dissolve all imbalances on the soul level around fearing and judging freedom and independence.

I dissolve all imbalances on the soul level around fearing and judging choice and free will.

I dissolve all imbalances on the soul level around fearing and judging security and stability.

I dissolve all imbalances on the soul level around fearing and judging leadership and being in charge.

I dissolve all imbalances on the soul level around fearing and judging being out front and making things happen.

I dissolve all imbalances on the soul level around fearing and judging free time, boredom, and having nothing to do.

I dissolve all imbalances on the soul level around associating wealth with pain, loss, and limitation.

I dissolve all imbalances on the soul level around associating wealth with being betrayed and persecuted.

I dissolve all imbalances on the soul level around associating wealth with separation and isolation.

I dissolve all imbalances on the soul level around associating wealth with dishonesty and treachery.

I dissolve all imbalances on the soul level around associating wealth with struggle and hard work.

I dissolve all imbalances on the soul level around associating wealth with insensitivity and arrogance.

I dissolve all imbalances on the soul level around associating wealth with selling my soul.

I dissolve all imbalances on the soul level around blocks to creating, accumulating, and maintaining wealth.

I dissolve all imbalances on the soul level around doubts about creating, accumulating, and maintaining wealth.

I dissolve all imbalances on the soul level around ambivalence around creating, accumulating ,and maintaining wealth.

*I dissolve all imbalances on the soul level around conflicts around creating, ac-
cumulating, and maintaining wealth.*

*I dissolve my field of experience and transform my vibrational patterns around
creating, accumulating, and maintaining wealth.*

*I transcend creating, accumulating, and maintaining wealth, and I am at peace
with it.*

*I surrender to creating, accumulating, and maintaining wealth, and I allow it
in my life.*

*I bring all past issues around creating, accumulating, and maintaining wealth
to an elegant completion in total grace.*

*I dissolve all future issues around creating, accumulating, and maintaining
wealth before they materialize.*

*I take responsibility for my part in creating, accumulating, and maintaining
wealth.*

*I allow others responsibility for their part in creating, accumulating, and main-
taining wealth.*

The Filling-the-Cup Script

I am safe and protected when I am prosperous and wealthy.

I am loved, supported, and nurtured when I am prosperous and wealthy.

I am accepted, honored, and appreciated when I am prosperous and wealthy.

I am calm, serene, and centered with prosperity and wealth.

I am grateful for the abundance, prosperity, and wealth I already have.

*I maintain a wealthy state of mind moment to moment, and I am filled with
wealth-consciousness and intention.*

*I focus my attention and intention on creating, accumulating, and maintaining
wealth as appropriate.*

*I bring all my thoughts, feelings, and actions into alignment with wealth on all
levels.*

I recognize the many forms and expressions of abundance, prosperity, and wealth.

*I move from a superficial to a profound relationship with money, prosperity, and
wealth.*

*I understand the true nature of prosperity and wealth, and I am clear on what
wealth means to me.*

*I have positive reasons to be wealthy, and they are in alignment with my life's
purpose.*

*I understand being wealthy is an art, and I master it in creative, joyful, caring,
sharing ways.*

*I understand wealth creates richness of choice, and I accept choosing well requires
clarity and discernment.*

I attain and maintain clarity and discernment in all positive ways.

I make the journey from limitation to unlimited choice in one easy step.

I understand wealth creates abundance of freedom, and I accept being truly free means being authentic.

I embrace freedom as a path to authenticity, and I attain and maintain both in harmony and grace.

I understand wealth creates power, and I accept that true power is expressed through responsibility, right action, and right use of resources.

I am responsible in the right way at the right time for the right reasons.

I engage in right action and right use of resources at all times and places.

I understand wealth is a catalyst for change, and I use it appropriately.

I engage in personal and global transformation at the right time in the right way.

I understand the processes and time frames of creating wealth, and I flow with them.

I master the principles of creating, accumulating, and maintaining wealth.

I have the determination and commitment to create, accumulate, and maintain wealth.

I have the courage and heart to create, accumulate, and maintain wealth.

I have the self-discipline and persistence to create, accumulate, and maintain wealth.

I develop and maintain the knowledge, skills, and abilities to create and accumulate wealth.

I develop and maintain the knowledge, skills, and abilities to manage and maintain wealth.

I develop and maintain empowering thoughts and feelings to create, accumulate, and maintain wealth.

I develop and maintain effective strategies and actions to create, accumulate, and maintain wealth.

I leverage my resources to create the conditions that bring wealth to me with ease.

I leverage my resources to create, accumulate, and maintain wealth in all appropriate ways.

I take practical, effective steps to create, accumulate, and maintain wealth.

I redirect the way I earn, spend, and invest to create, accumulate, and maintain wealth.

I recognize wealth opportunities and possibilities, and I take right action on them.

I create wealth opportunities and possibilities, and I take right action with right resources.

I create and accumulate wealth in the right way at the right time for the right reasons.

I manage and maintain wealth in the right way at the right time for the right reasons.

I create, accumulate, manage, and maintain wealth easily and effortlessly.

I deserve prosperity and wealth, and I feel the peace and joy of living a life of wealth.

Being wealthy is natural and easy for me now, and I welcome it.
I open to, allow, and embrace prosperity, abundance, and wealth as my personal law.
I reimagine and reinvent myself as a prosperous and wealthy person on all levels.
I recognize and accept wealth as a means, not a master.
I put no limits on wealth in my life, and wealth in my life puts no limits on me.
I use wealth to increase the quality of life for myself and others.
I create, accumulate, and maintain wealth without creating scarcity on any level.
My wealth serves me, my family, my community, and my world.

Weight Loss

Weight loss is a complex issue, and I get mixed results with clients. Interestingly, many people lose more weight listening to the "Releasing Your Past" recording than they do listening to a weight-loss recording. That makes for interesting theorizing!

The Emptying-the-Cup Script

Losing weight and I are one.
I release and forgive myself for losing weight.
I release and forgive myself for not losing weight.
I release, forgive, and dissolve all my old responses to losing weight.
I release and forgive myself for not being able to lose weight before.
I release and forgive myself for finding it hard to change my thinking, actions, and lifestyle.
I release and forgive everyone who didn't teach me to take good care of my body.
I release and forgive everyone who taught me poor eating habits.
I release and forgive everyone who gave me food instead of love.
I dissolve all imbalances on the soul level around losing weight.
I dissolve all imbalances on the soul level around fearing losing weight.
I dissolve all imbalances on the soul level around fearing not losing weight.
I dissolve all imbalances on the soul level around fearing _____.

being weighed, trying on new clothes, wearing shorts, dressing in a locker room, seeing myself in a mirror, letting my partner see me naked

I dissolve all imbalances on the soul level around judging losing weight.
I dissolve all imbalances on the soul level around judging my body.
I dissolve all imbalances on the soul level around judging myself for _____.

my weight, my body size and shape

I dissolve all imbalances on the soul level around my addiction to _____.

food, sugar, carbohydrates, caffeine

I dissolve all imbalances on the soul level around my emotional addictions that support poor eating habits.

I dissolve all imbalances on the soul level around my psychological addictions that support poor eating habits.

I dissolve all imbalances on the soul level around my mental addictions that support poor eating habits.

I dissolve all imbalances on the soul level around physical addictions that support poor eating habits.

I dissolve all imbalances on the soul level around cravings.

I dissolve all imbalances on the soul level around _____.

Are there known physical causes for your weight? hormonal imbalances, glandular imbalances, acid/base imbalances

I dissolve all imbalances on the soul level around my obstacles to losing weight naturally and automatically.

I dissolve all imbalances on the soul level around my weight fluctuations up and down.

I dissolve all imbalances on the soul level around being impatient about losing weight.

I dissolve all imbalances on the soul level around getting discouraged about losing weight.

I dissolve all imbalances on the soul level around _____.

What are your experiences around weight-loss attempts in the past?

I dissolve all imbalances on the soul level around substituting one appetite for another.

I dissolve all imbalances on the soul level around eating to feel loved, accepted, and validated.

I dissolve all imbalances on the soul level around eating to feel safe, secure, and in control.

I dissolve all imbalances on the soul level around eating to relax.

I dissolve all imbalances on the soul level around eating to _____.

When do you eat? What is going on in your life when you reach for food?

I dissolve all imbalances on the soul level around snacking.

I dissolve all imbalances on the soul level around snacking while I'm _____.

When do you snack—reading, working, watching TV?

I dissolve all imbalances on the soul level around eating in secret.

I dissolve my field of experience around losing weight.

I transform my vibrational patterns around losing weight.

I transcend losing weight, and I am at peace with it.

I surrender to losing weight, and I allow it in my life as appropriate.
I bring all past issues around losing weight to an elegant completion in total grace.
I dissolve all future issues around losing weight before they materialize.
I take total and complete responsibility for my weight loss.
I allow and assign others total and complete responsibility for their weight loss.
I recognize my barriers to losing weight, and I dissolve them.
I recognize food's relationship to my past, and I dissolve it.
I stay fully conscious and responsible around my food choices.

The Filling-the-Cup Script

Losing weight has all positive outcomes for me now.
I am nurtured and supported while I lose weight.
I am safe and protected while I lose weight.
I am loved and accepted while I lose weight.
I am peaceful and calm while I lose weight.
I am _____ while I lose weight.

energetic, self-assured, confident

Reaching my weight-range goal is exciting, energizing, satisfying, and fulfilling.
I have the desire and commitment to lose weight.
I have the courage and discipline to lose weight.
I have the knowledge and ability to lose weight.
I have the nonstop determination to reach my desired weight range and maintain it.
I have a specific, healthy, desired weight range.
Everything I need to lose weight is inside me, and I draw on it in grace.
I set my weight-range goals, and I review them each day.
I achieve my weight-range goals one day at a time, and I am successful each day.
It is easy for me to stay on my plan to obtain my weight range in all healthy ways.
The weight-loss process is easy and fun for me.
I lose weight the smart way to be healthy for my lifetime.
I assure I am getting all the nutrition I need while I lose weight.
Developing healthy eating habits becomes easier each day.
I stay on a healthy eating plan and maintain my healthy weight easily.
Each day, I automatically and successfully eat more and more healthfully.
I make a take-charge lose-weight contract with myself, and I keep it easily.
I choose the best method for losing weight for me, my body, and my lifestyle.
I lose weight systematically, and I keep it off permanently.
I am aware of my eating habits and how they affect my weight.
I am willing to change my eating habits, and I do so effortlessly.
I identify my emotional eating triggers, and I stay ahead of them.
I identify my physical eating triggers, and I stay ahead of them.

I overcome my addiction to food in healthy ways.
I am free of cravings for foods that add unhealthy weight.
I satisfy my physical appetites in healthy and healing ways.
I satisfy my emotional appetites in healthy and healing ways.
I satisfy my mental appetites in healthy and healing ways.
I eat slowly and chew thoroughly.
I easily resist social pressure to eat.
I easily resist _____ pressure to eat.

family, partner, social, party, holiday

I control my between-meal snacks effortlessly.
When I snack, it is on healthy food.
I do everything I need to do to achieve my healthy weight.
I see myself at my healthy weight, and I achieve it in healthy ways.
It is easy for me to stay on my plan to maintain my healthy weight.
I reward myself at each step of my successful weight-loss program.
I enjoy the process of reaching and maintaining my healthy weight.
I allow sufficient time for the process of reaching and maintaining my healthy weight.
It is fun for me to reach and maintain my healthy weight.
I allow time to reach my healthy weight.
I know the benefits of losing weight, and I review them regularly as appropriate.
I eat the foods and amounts that maintain my healthy weight.
I eat and drink what I need when I need it.
I enjoy eating and drinking in ways that are healthy for me.
Each day is easier for me to stay at a healthy weight.
I maintain a healthy weight for the rest of my life.
I have a positive attitude about what I eat, when I eat, and how I eat.
I take control of my life and my habits, and I feel good about myself.
I realize my body functions are a miracle unto themselves, and I respect them.
I love my physical body and treat it with the respect it deserves.

Weight Loss: Dieting

For this script, I have taken the approach that diet is the healthy way we eat every day.

The Emptying-the-Cup Script

Dieting and I are one.
I release and forgive myself for dieting.
I release and forgive myself for not dieting.
I release and forgive myself for staying on diets.

I release and forgive myself for not staying on diets.
I release and forgive myself for associating diets with _____.

self-denial, deprivation, hardship

I dissolve all imbalances on the soul level around dieting.
I dissolve all imbalances on the soul level around fearing dieting.
I dissolve all imbalances on the soul level around judging dieting.
I dissolve all imbalances on the soul level around defining diet as a weight-loss program only.
I dissolve all imbalances on the soul level around _____ diets.

crash, fad, popular, unhealthy, perfect

I dissolve all imbalances on the soul level around regular and consistent dieting.
I dissolve all imbalances on the soul level around my eating habits.
I dissolve all imbalances on the soul level around eating _____.

junk food, fried foods, desserts, snacks

I dissolve all imbalances on the soul level around cheating on my diet.
I dissolve all imbalances on the soul level around _____.

binging, giving myself treats, comforting myself with food, overindulging

I dissolve all imbalances on the soul level around disappointments with results from diets.
I dissolve all imbalances on the soul level around impatience with results from diets.
I dissolve all imbalances on the soul level around _____ with results from diets.
I dissolve all imbalances on the soul level around eating foods that cause my body to degenerate.
I dissolve my field of experience around diets.
I transform my vibrational patterns around diets.
I transcend dieting, and I am at peace with it.
I surrender to dieting, and I allow it in my life as appropriate.
I bring all past issues around dieting to an elegant completion in total grace.
I dissolve all future issues around dieting before they materialize.
I take total and complete responsibility for my diet.
I allow and assign others total and complete responsibility for their diet as appropriate.
Dieting and _____ are separate for me now.

The Filling-the-Cup Script

Dieting has all positive outcomes for me now.
I am safe and protected when I diet.

I am loved and accepted when I diet.
I am nurtured and supported when I diet.
I give myself permission to become a new me physically and in all ways.
I understand dieting is a lifelong way of eating to be healthy.
I am committed to healthy dieting for the remainder of my life.
I see my diet as a lifelong routine to maintain my health.
I see my diet as a learning experience—about me, my body, and my health.
I develop and follow a healthy diet that gets easier over time.
I make a commitment to live by my new eating rules as appropriate.
I allow myself occasional lapses without guilt or self-recrimination as appropriate.
I see each lapse as a short detour to my goal, and I go on.
I correct myself without guilt or self-condemnation.
I integrate my lapses into my healthy life, and I go on, focusing on my healthy diet.
My daily diet is healthy for me.
My daily diet is low in sodium, sugar, and fat as appropriate.
My daily diet is moderate in protein as appropriate.
My diet is high in fiber and complex carbohydrates as appropriate.
I eat the foods that cause my body to thrive.
I change my tastes to create a preference for healthy food.
I maintain a vigilant awareness of my diet and eat accordingly.
I transform my desire for perfection to a commitment to progress.

Weight Maintenance

The Emptying-the-Cup Script

Maintaining my healthy weight and I are one.
I release and forgive myself for maintaining my healthy weight.
I release and forgive myself for not maintaining my healthy weight.
I release and forgive myself for regaining weight I have lost.
I release and forgive myself for _____.
I dissolve all imbalances on the soul level around maintaining my healthy weight.
I dissolve all imbalances on the soul level around fearing not maintaining my healthy weight.
I dissolve all imbalances on the soul level around judging not maintaining my healthy weight.
I dissolve my field of experience around maintaining my healthy weight.
I transform my vibrational patterns around maintaining my healthy weight.
I transcend maintaining my healthy weight, and I am at peace with it.
I surrender to maintaining my healthy weight, and I allow it in my life as appropriate.

*I bring all past issues around maintaining my healthy weight to an elegant com-
pletion in total grace.*
*I dissolve all future issues around maintaining my healthy weight before they ma-
terialize.*
I take total and complete responsibility for maintaining my healthy weight.
*I allow and assign others total and complete responsibility for maintaining their
healthy weight as appropriate.*
Maintaining my weight and _____ are separate for me now.

giving up eating out, social events, holiday meals

The Filling-the-Cup Script

Maintaining my healthy weight has all positive outcomes for me now.
I am safe and protected when I maintain my healthy weight.
I am loved and accepted when I maintain my healthy weight.
I am nurtured and supported when I maintain my healthy weight.
My mind automatically keeps me in my healthy weight range.
My eating automatically keeps me in my healthy weight range.
My habits and lifestyle automatically keep me in my healthy weight range.
It is natural and effortless for me to maintain my healthy weight.
*I renew my goal to live right, eat right, and maintain my healthy weight regu-
larly.*

Working

All of us work in some way—as a nonsalaried homemaker, a wage earner,
a contractor, a self-employed person, and so forth. We have a lot of programming around working, and this script is to support our finding freedom
and satisfaction in our work. (Written for the recording "Achieving Right
Livelihood"—the *Money* series.)

The Emptying-the-Cup Script

Working and I are one.
I release and forgive myself for working and for not working.
I release and forgive myself for enjoying working and for not enjoying working.
*I release, forgive, and dissolve all false models and messages about work and
working.*
I dissolve all imbalances on the soul level around work and working.
*I dissolve all imbalances on the soul level around family and generational pat-
terns of work and working.*
*I dissolve all imbalances on the soul level around societal and cultural patterns
of work and working.*

I dissolve all imbalances on the soul level around gender and age patterns of work and working.

I dissolve all imbalances on the soul level around fearing and judging work and working.

I dissolve all imbalances on the soul level around associating work and working with pain.

I dissolve all imbalances on the soul level around dishonoring honest labor.

I dissolve all imbalances on the soul level around having a dysfunctional relationship with work.

I dissolve all imbalances on the soul level around having an addictive relationship with work.

I dissolve all imbalances on the soul level around going unconscious around work and working.

I dissolve all imbalances on the soul level around repeating my unresolved family issues at work.

I dissolve all imbalances on the soul level around replaying childhood conflicts at work.

I dissolve all imbalances on the soul level around creating drama around work and working.

I dissolve all imbalances on the soul level around engaging in others' drama around work and working.

I dissolve all imbalances on the soul level around knowing and following the rules of work and working.

I dissolve all imbalances on the soul level around confusing working hard with safety and security.

I dissolve all imbalances on the soul level around confusing working hard with acceptance and belonging.

I dissolve all imbalances on the soul level around confusing working hard with recognition and status.

I dissolve all imbalances on the soul level around confusing working hard with success.

I dissolve all imbalances on the soul level around doing the wrong work or working the wrong way.

I dissolve all imbalances on the soul level around working at the wrong time or for the wrong reasons.

I dissolve all imbalances on the soul level around false expectations about work and working.

I dissolve all imbalances on the soul level around false standards of productivity and success.

I dissolve all imbalances on the soul level around past successes and failures with work and working.

I dissolve all imbalances on the soul level around toxic, oppressive, and abusive work and work environments.

I dissolve my field of experience and transform my vibrational patterns around work and working.

I dissolve my field of experience and transform my vibrational patterns around myths, illusions, and fantasies about work and working.

I transcend work and working, and I am at peace with them.

I surrender to work and working, and I allow them in my life as appropriate.

I bring all past issues around work and working to an elegant completion in total grace.

I dissolve all future issues around work and working before they materialize.

I take total and complete responsibility for my part in work and working.

I allow and assign others total and complete responsibility for their part in work and working.

The Filling-the-Cup Script

I understand and accept the true nature of work and the role it plays in my life.

I choose work that enriches me and provides abundance in all areas of my life.

I use my favorite knowledge, skills, and abilities in an enjoyable, productive, and profitable way.

I give myself permission to be paid for having fun and enjoying myself.

I accept that the world of work can be illogical, biased, and unpredictable.

I accept hiring, promotion, and firing may have nothing to do with qualifications and performance.

I accept employers and employees may treat me well or badly regardless of my performance or the stated rules.

I accept my job may go on forever, or it may end abruptly.

I respect the gifts I bring to the world of work, and I choose work and workplaces that respect those gifts.

I bring a sense of meaning and value to my work, and I work with an attitude of gratitude, excellence, and service.

I perform at the highest level possible with the least amount of stress and negativity.

I respect my boss, coworkers, and subordinates, and they respect me as appropriate.

I am grateful for the work I am doing, and I recognize how it serves my growth.

Wrestling

I wrote this script for the Alaska Pacific University wrestling team the first year it was formed. That year, the team placed number two in the United States. It will give you an idea of how a sports performance script can be written.

The Emptying-the-Cup Script

Wrestling and I are one.
I release and forgive myself for wrestling.
I release and forgive myself for not wrestling.
I release and forgive myself for winning at wrestling.
I release and forgive myself for not winning at wrestling.
I release and forgive _____.

What is your issue around wrestling—do you agree with your coach, is anyone pushing you to wrestle and/or win, trying to stop you from wrestling?

I dissolve all imbalances on the soul level around wrestling.
I dissolve all imbalances on the soul level around winning.
I dissolve all imbalances on the soul level around losing.
I dissolve all imbalances on the soul level around developing my strength.
I dissolve all imbalances on the soul level around developing my skill.
I dissolve all imbalances on the soul level around _____.

What is your block around wrestling?

I dissolve my field of experience around wrestling.
I transform my vibrational patterns around wrestling.
I transcend wrestling, and I am at peace with it.
I transcend winning, and I am at peace with it.
I surrender to wrestling, and I allow it in my life as appropriate.
I surrender to winning, and I allow it in my life as appropriate.
I bring all past issues around wrestling to an elegant completion in total grace.
I take total and complete responsibility for my wrestling performance as appropriate.
I allow and assign others total and complete responsibility for their wrestling performance as appropriate.

The Filling-the-Cup Script

Wrestling has all positive outcomes for me now.
I am safe and protected when I wrestle.
I am loved and accepted when I wrestle.
I am supported and nurtured when I wrestle.
I enjoy wrestling, and I am good at it.
I am completely relaxed and loose when I wrestle.
I am always in good body position.
I keep my weight over my legs.
I keep my elbows tight to my sides.

I keep my hands behind my knees in the proper position.
I concentrate on my opponent at all times.
I stay close to my opponent.
I hear my opponent's breathing.
I hear my own breathing, which is deep and regular.
I move toward my opponent.
I lower my altitude and jolt my opponent hard.
I run the pipeline successfully.
My forehead is in his stomach.
My hands are locked loosely on his leg.
I step quickly to my right.
I drop my hips and step straight back.
My head is up.
My hips are lower than my shoulders.
I feel the power of my body pressing down on his leg.
I see my opponent hit the mat.
I attack instantly and break him down.
I easily control his hips.
I move quickly to break him down.
I look for a pin situation.
I see his near arm pop up.
I bar it and start my pinning situation.
I bar his close arm; I trap his far arm.
I start around his head.
I keep my weight down on my opponent.
I keep my weight into my opponent.
I maintain motion and good body control.
I feel my pressure and weight pushing him down.
My weight is all down on his shoulder and head.
I'm out in front covering his head with my body.
My opponent is on his back.
The official is looking for the pin.
The referee is slapping the mat.
I win; I win again.
Winning has all positive outcomes for me now.
I am safe and protected when I win.
I am loved and accepted when I win.
I am nurtured and supported when I win.

Writing

This script is in response to client requests.

The Emptying-the-Cup Script

Writing and I are one.
I release and forgive myself for writing.
I release and forgive myself for not writing.
I release and forgive myself for _____.

struggling with writing, not being able to express myself clearly, poor spelling, poor grammar, not knowing what to say

I release and forgive myself for being too critical of my writing.
I release and forgive everyone who was too critical of my writing.
I dissolve all imbalances on the soul level around writing.
I dissolve all imbalances on the soul level around fearing writing.
I dissolve all imbalances on the soul level around judging writing.
I dissolve all imbalances on the soul level around procrastinating about writing.
I dissolve all imbalances on the soul level around _____.

What are your writer's blocks?

I dissolve my field of experience around writing.
I transform my vibrational patterns around writing.
I transcend writing, and I am at peace with it.
I surrender to writing, and I allow it in my life as appropriate.
I bring all past issues around writing to an elegant completion in total grace.
I take total and complete responsibility for writing and what I write.
I allow and assign others total and complete responsibility for their writing and what they write.

The Filling-the-Cup Script

Writing has all positive outcomes for me now.
I am safe and protected when I write.
I am loved and accepted when I write.
I am nurtured and supported when I write.
I enjoy writing, and it is fun to write.
I take pleasure putting ideas into words.
I have a natural talent and ability to express myself in writing.
I feel satisfaction seeing my thoughts in print.
I flow with ideas and ways to express them.
I have a natural flow with language.
Simple, clear expression is natural for me.

I am motivated to write, and I do it.
I enjoy beginning new writing projects, and I do so as appropriate.
I enjoy completing existing writing projects, and I do so as appropriate.
My enthusiasm and motivation carry me through each project to completion.
I stay highly motivated from the beginning to the end of each project.
I create writing time easily and effortlessly.
I make writing schedules, and I keep to my schedules.
I block out time for my writing regularly.
I maintain my writing time free and clear.
I organize my writing space effectively for me and my style.
I work well in any environment as appropriate.
I work well with any medium—typewriter, computer, tape recorder.
I organize my materials easily and quickly.
I focus my thoughts and proceed effortlessly.
I know my material, and I present in the best way for me.
I know my audience, and I present my material in the most effective way for them.
I write at the right level for my audience.
My attention stays on the task while I am writing.
I feel good as my work unfolds.
I trust my work to be good as appropriate.
I flow from the beginning of my writing time to the end.
I maintain my momentum through completion.
I achieve within the appointed time easily and effortlessly.
It is fun to make my deadlines.
I love to edit my work and improve it.
I know when to edit and when to leave my writing as it is.
I feel natural and relaxed when I write.
I am a good writer and it shows in my work.

For fiction writing, add sections on story lines, characters, dialogue, settings, etc. If you are selling your work, add sections on being recognized, selling, making, money, etc.

Bibliography

Akpinar, S., G. A. Uleft, and M. Itil. "Hypnotizability Predicted by Computer-Analyzed EEG Pattern." *Biological Psychiatry* 3 (1997): 387–92.

Albert, I., G. A. Cicala, and J. Siegel. "The Behavioral Effects of REM Sleep Deprivation in Rats." *Psychophysiology* 6 (1970): 550–60.

Albrecht, Karl. *Brain Power.* Englewood Cliffs, NJ: Prentice-Hall, 1980.

Amato, I. "Muscle, Melodies and Brain Refrains." *Science News* Vol. 135 (1989): 202.

Anch, A. M., et al. *Sleep: A Scientific Perspective.* Englewood Cliffs, NJ: Prentice-Hall, 1988.

Atwater, F. H. *The Hemi-Sync Process.* Faber, VA: The Monroe Institute, 1997 <http://www.monroeinstitute.org/research>.

Barabasz, A., and M. Barabasz. "Attention Deficit Hyperactivity Disorder: Neurological Basis and Training Alternatives." *Journal of Neurotherapy.* Vol. 1 (Summer 1995).

Bateson, G. *Steps to an Ecology of Mind.* San Francisco: Chandler Pub. Co. 1972.

Beasley, Victor. *Your Electro-Vibratory Body.* Edited by Christopher Hills. Boulder Creek, CA: University of the Tree Press, 1975.

Beningron, J. H., and H. C. Heller. "Does the Function of REM Sleep Concern non-Rem Sleep or Waking?" *Progress in Neurobiology* 44 (1994): 433–49.

———. "Restoration of Brain Energy Metabolism as the Function of Sleep." *Progress in Neurobiology* 45 (1995): 347–60.

Benson, Herbert. *The Relaxation Response.* New York: Morrow, 1975.

Bentov, Itzhak. *Stalking the Wild Pendulum.* New York: Dutton, 1977.

Blakeslee, Thomas R. *The Right Brain: A New Understanding of the Unconscious Mind and Its Creative Powers.* New York: Berkley Books, 1983.

Bloch, V., E. Hennvin, and P. Leconte. "Relationship Between Paradoxical Sleep and Memory Processes." *In Brain Mechanisms in Memory and Learning: From the Single Neuron to Man.* Edited by M. A. Brazier. New York: Raven Press, 1979.

Brady, D. Brian. "Binaural-Beat-Induced Theta EEG Activity and Hypnotic Susceptibility." Northern Arizona University, May 1997.

Brown, Mark. *Left Hand, Right Hand.* Newton Abbott [Erg.]: David & Charles, 1978.

Bryant-Tuckett, R., and L. H. Silverman. "Effects of Subliminal Stimulation of Symbiotic Fantasies on the Academic Performance of Emotionally Handicapped Students." *Journal of Counseling Psychology* 31, 3 (1984): 295–305.

Budzynski, Thomas. "Tuning In on the Twilight Zone." *Psychology Today* 11 (August 1977): 38–44.

Buzan, Tony, and Terence Dixon. *The Evolving Brain.* Newton Abbott [Erg.]: David & Charles, 1978.

Cade, C. M., and N. Coxhead. *The Awakened Mind.* New York: Delacorte Press/Eleanor Friede, 1979.

Carter, G. *Healing Myself.* Norfolk, VA: Hampton Roads, 1993.

Castaldo, V., V. Krynicki, and J. Goldstein. "Sleep Stages and Verbal Memory." *Perceptual and Motor Skills* 39 (1974): 1023–30.

Caton, R. "The Electrical Currents of the Brain." *British Medical Journal* 2 (1875): 278.

Chance, Paul. "Music Hath Charms to Soothe a Throbbing Head." *Psychology Today* 21 (February 1987): 14.

Changeux, Jean-Pierre. *Neuronal Man: The Biology of Mind.* New York: Oxford University Press, 1986.

Chopra, Deepak. *Quantum Healing.* New York: Bantam, 1989.

Cousins, Norman. *Head First: The Biology of Hope.* New York: Dutton, 1989.

Crane, R. Adam, and Richard Soutar, Ph.D. *Mindfitness Training: Neurofeedback and the Process.* Writers Club Press, 2000.

Davidson, Keay. "Subliminal Learning or Wishful Thinking?" *San Francisco Examiner* A-1: 1990.

Davidson, R. J., G. E. Schwartz, and D. Shapiro. *Consciousness and Self-Regulation. Advances in Research,* Vol. 3. New York: Plenum Press, 1980.

Davis, Joel. *Endorphins: New Waves in Brain Chemistry.* Garden City, NY: Dial Press, 1984.

DeMoss, Robert T. *Brain Waves Through Time: 12 Principles for Understanding the Evolution of the Human Brain and Man's Behavior.* New York: Plenum Press, 1999.

deQuincey, C. "Consciousness All the Way Down?" *Journal of Consciousness Studies* 1, 2 (1994): 217–29.

Dixon, N. F. *Subliminal Perception, The Nature of a Controversy.* New York: McGraw-Hill, 1971.

Dixon, Norman. "Subliminal Perception and Parapsychology, Points of Contact." *Parapsychology Review* 10, 3 (May/June 1979): 1–6.

———. *Preconscious Processing.* New York: John Wiley & Sons, 1981.

Dossey, Larry. "Healing, Energy, and Consciousness: Into the Future or a Retreat to the Past?" *Subtle Energies* 5, 1994: 1–33.

Dossey, Larry. "Where in the World is the Mind?" Unpublished paper presented at the Third International Empathy Conference, Guadalajara, Mexico, 1989.

Dryden, Gordon, and Jeanette Vos. *The Learning Revolution.* Carson, CA: Jalmar Press, 1994.

Dujardin, K., A. Guerrien, and P. Leconte. "Sleep, Brain Activation, and Cognition." *Physiology & Behavior* 47 (1990): 1271–78.

Dumas, R. A. "EEG Alpha-Hypnotizability Correlations: A Review." *Psychophysiology* 14 1997: 431–38.

Edrington, D. "A Palliative for Wandering Attention." This report is available from the Monroe Institute. 1985.

Empson, J. A. C. *Human Brainwaves: The Psychological Significance of the Electroencephalogram.* New York: Stockton Press, 1986.

Empson, J. A. C., and P. R. F. Clark. "Rapid Eye Movements and Remembering." *Nature* 227 (1970): 287–88.

Fehmi, Lester F., and George Fritz. "Open Focus: The Attentional Foundation of Health and Well-Being." *Somatics* (Spring 1980): 24–30.

Ferguson, Marilyn. *The Brain Revolution.* New York: Bantam, 1973.

——. *The Aquarian Conspiracy.* Los Angeles, CA: Tarcher, 1987.

Filmore, Charles. *Jesus Christ Heals.* Kansas City, MO: Unity School of Christianity, 1987.

Fishbein, W. "Interference with Conversion of Memory from Short-Term to Long-Term Storage by Partial Sleep Deprivation." *Communications in Behavioral Biology* 5 (1970): 171–75.

——. "Disruptive Effects of Rapid Eye Movement Sleep Deprivation on Long-Term Memory." *Physiology & Behavior* 6 (1971): 279–82.

——. "Memory Consolidation in REM Sleep: Making Dreams Out of Chaos." *Sleep Research Society Bulletin* 2 (1995): 53–58.

——. "Sleep and Memory: A Look Back, a Look Forward." *Sleep Research Society Bulletin* 1 (1996): 55–56.

Fishbein, W., and B. M. Gutwein. "Paradoxical Sleep and Memory Storage Processes." *Behavioral Psychology* 19 (1977): 425–64.

Foulkes, D., et al. "Processing of Memories and Knowledge in REM and NREM Dreams." *Perceptual and Motor Skills* 68 (1989): 365–66.

Garfield, Lael M. *Sound Medicine: Healing with Music, Voice and Song.* Berkeley, CA: Celestial Arts, 1987.

Gawain, Shakti. *Creative Visualization: Use the Power of Your Imagination to Create What You Want in Your Life.* Revised edition. San Rafael, CA: New World Library, 1955.

Giannitrapani, D. *The Electrophysiology of Intellectual Functions.* New York: Karger, 1985.

Glaser, G. H. *EEG and Behavior.* New York: Basic Books, 1963.

Gleick, James. *Chaos: Making a New Science.* New York: Viking, 1987.

Green, Elmer, and Alyce Green. *Beyond Biofeedback.* Ft. Wayne, IN: Knoll Publishing, 1989.

Greenstein, Y. J., C. Pavlides, and J. Winson. "Long-Term Potentiation in the Dentate Gyrus Is Preferentially Induced by Theta Rhythm Periodicity." *Brain Research* 438 (1988): 331–34.

Gutwein, B. M., and W. Fishbein. "Paradoxical Sleep and Memory 1, Selective Alterations Following Enriched and Impoverished Environmental Rearing." *Brain Research Bulletin* 5 (1980): 9–12.

——. "Paradoxical Sleep and Memory 2, Sleep Circadian Rhythmicity Following Enriched and Impoverished Environmental Rearing." *Brain Research Bulletin* 5 (1980): 105–9.

Hartmann, E., and W. C. Stern. "Desynchronized Sleep Deprivation: Learning Deficit and Its Reversal by Increased Effects of Amitriptyline." *Psychopharmacologia* 33 (1972): 585–87.

Helmstetter, Shad. *What to Say When You Talk to Yourself.* New York: Pocket Books, 1987.

Henley, Sue. "Cross-Modal Effects of Subliminal Verbal Stimuli." *Scandinavian Journal of Psychology* 16 (1975): 30–36.

Hennevin, E., et al. "Processing of Learned Information in Paradoxical Sleep: Relevance for Memory." *Behavioral Brain Research* 69 (1995): 125–35.

Hennevin. E., B. Mars, and C. Maho. "Memory Processing in Paradoxical Sleep." *Sleep Research Society Bulletin* 1 (1995): 44–50.

Herman, Art. Interview, May 1990, President, Teachnology, Santa Barbara, CA.

Hobson, J. A. *The Dreaming Brain.* New York: Basic Books, 1988.

Hobson, J. A., R. Stickgold, and E. F. Pace-Schott. "The Neuropsychology of REM Sleep Dreaming." *NeuroReport* 9 (1998): R1–R14.

Hord, D. J., et al. "Feedback for High EEG Alpha Does Not Maintain Performance or Mood During Sleep Loss." *Psychophysiology* 14 (1976): 58–62.

Horne, J. A., and M. J. McGrath. "The Consolidation Hypothesis for REM Sleep

Functions: Stress and Other Confounding Factors—a Reveiw." *Biological Pyschology* 18 (1984): 165–84.

Hubbard, Barbara Marx. *Conscious Evolution: Awakening Our Social Potential.* Novato, CA: New World Library, 1998.

Hurley, Thomas J., Jr. "Inside the Black Box: New Cognitive View of the Unconscious Mind." *Noetic Sciences Review* (Winter 1987): 22–25.

Hutchison, Michael. *Megabrain: New Tools and Techniques for Brain Growth and Mind Expansion.* New York: Ballantine Books, 1986.

———. *Mega Brain Power: Transform Your Life with Mind Machines and Brain Nutrients.* New York: Hyperion, 1994.

Johnson, Harold, and Charles W. Eriksen. "Preconscious Perception: A Reexamination of the Poetzl Phenomenon." *Journal of Abnormal and Social Psychology* 62, 3 (1961): 497–503.

Johnson, R. K., and R. G. Meyer. "The Locus of Control Construct in EEG Alpha Rhythm Feedback." *Journal of Consulting and Clinical Psychology* 42 (1974): 913.

Jones, B. E. "The Neural Basis of Consciousness Across the Sleep-Waking Cycle, Consciousness: In at the Frontiers of Neuroscience." *Advances in Neurology* 77 (1998): 75–94.

Joseph, Lawrence E. *Gaia: The Growth of an Idea.* New York: Bantam, 1990.

Joudry, Patricia. *Sound Therapy for the Walkman.* St. Denis, Sask., Canada: Steele and Steele, 1978.

Jourdain, Robert. *Music, the Brain, and Ecstasy.* New York: Morrow, 1997.

Kalat, James, W. *Biological Psychology.* Belmont, CA: Wadsworth, 1984.

Kamiya, J. "Operant Control of the EEG Alpha Rhythm and Some of Its Reported Effects on Consciousness." In *Altered States of Consciousness,* edited by C. T. Tart. Garden City, NY: Doubleday, 1969.

Karni, A., et al. "Dependence on REM Sleep for Overnight Improvement of a Perceptual Skill." *Science* 265 (1994): 679–82.

Kenyon, Tom. *Brain States.* Naples, FL: United States Publishing, 1994.

Key, Wilson Bryan. *The Age of Manipulation: The Con in Confidence and the Sin in Sincere.* Lanham, MD: Madison Books, 1993.

Kihlstrom, J. F. "The Cognitive Unconscious." *Science* 237 (1987): 1445–52.

Koob, George, and Floyd E. Bloom. "Behavior Effects of Neuropeptides: Endorphins and Vasopressin." *Annual Review of Physiology* (1982).

Kupfer, D. J., and M. B. Bowers, Jr. "REM Sleep and Central Monoamine Oxidise Inhibition." *Psychopharmacologia* 27 (1972): 183–90.

Larson, J., and G. Lynch. "Patterned Stimulation at the Theta Frequency Is Optimal for the Induction of Hippocampal Long-Term Potentiation." *Brain Research* 368 (1986): 347–50.

Leconte, P., E. Hennevin, and V. Bloch. "Duration of Paradoxical Sleep Necessary for the Acquisition of Conditioned Avoidance in the Rat." *Physiology and Behavior* 13 (1974): 675–81.

Lester, Henry A. "The Response to Acetylcholine." *Scientific American* (February 1977).

Lindsley, D. B. "Psychological Phenomenon and the Electroencephalogram." *Electroencephalography and Clinical Neurophysiology* 4 (1952): 443.

Locke, Steven, and Douglas Colligan. *The Healer Within: The New Medicine of Mind and Body.* New York: Dutton, 1986.

London, P., J. T. Hart, and M. P. Leibovitz. "EEG Alpha Rhythms and Susceptibility to Hypnosis." *Nature* 219 (1968): 71–72.

Lubar, J. F. "Discourse on the Development of EEG Diagnostics and Biofeedback for Attention-Deficit/Hyperactivity Disorders." *Biofeedback and Self-Regulation* 10, 8 (1991): 201–25.

Lynch, Gary, and Michael Baudry. "The Biochemistry of Memory: A New and Specific Hypothesis." *Science* 224 (1984): 1057–63.

McAuliffe, Kathleen. "Brain Tuner." *Omni* January 1983.

―――. "Get Smart: Controlling Chaos." *Omni* February 1990: 42–92.

McConnell, James V., et al. "Subliminal Stimulation." *American Psychologist* 12 (1958), 229–42.

Maquet, P., et al. "Functional Neuroanatomy of Human Rapid-Eye Movement Sleep and Dreaming." *Nature* 383 (1996): 163–66.

Martindale, C. "Creativity, Consciousness, and Cortical Arousal." *Journal of Altered States of Consciousness* 3 (1978): 69–87.

Mikuriya, T. H. "Interhemispheric Alpha Rhythm Synchronization: A Voluntary Altered State of Consciousness." *American Journal of Clinical Biofeedback* 2 (1979): 22–25.

Miller, Mark Crispin. "Hollywood: The Ad." *Atlantic Monthly.* April 1990: 1–54.

Monroe, R. *The Hemi-Sync Process.* Monroe Institute Bulletin #PR31380H, 1982.

Moore, Timothy E. "Subliminal Advertising: What You See Is What You Get." *Journal of Marketing* 46 (Spring 1982): 38–47.

Moss, Thelma. *The Probability of the Impossible.* London: Routledge & Kegan Paul, 1974.

Muzio, J. N., et al. "Retention of Rote Learned Meaningful Verbal Material and Alteration in the Normal Sleep EEG Pattern." *Psychophysiology* 9 (1972): 108.

Nadel, L., and M. Moscovitch. "Memory Consolidation, Retrograde Amnesia and the Hippocampal Complex." *Current Opinions in Neurobiology* 7 (1997): 217–27.

Natale, Jo Anna. "Are You Open to Suggestion?" *Psychology Today* (September 1988): 28–30.

Ochs, L. "Electroencephalographic Disentrainment Feedback (EDF)." 1993 (electronically published manuscript available from the author, Len Ochs, Ph.D., 3490 Silver Spur Court, Concord, CA 94518 or by E-mail at 72040.3433@compu serve.com).

O'Regan, Brenda. "The Hidden Mind: Charting Unconscious Intelligence." *Noetic Sciences Review* (Winter 1987): 21.

Ornstein, Robert E. *The Psychology of Consciousness.* San Francisco, CA: W. H. Freeman, 1972.

Ostrander, Sheila, and Lynn Schroeder. *Superlearning.* New York: Delacorte, 1979.

―――. *Superlearning 2000.* New York: Delacorte, 1994.

―――. *Supermemory: The Revolution.* New York: Carroll & Graf, 1991.

Parker, Jonathan. *Bibliography of Subliminal Research.* Gateways Research Institute, 1990.

Parker, K. A. "Effects of Subliminal Symbiotic Stimulation on Academic Performance: Further Evidence on the Adaptation-Enhancing Effects of Oneness Fantasies." *Journal of Counseling Psychology* 29, 1 (1982): 19–28.

Pearlman, C. "Latent Learning Impaired by REM Sleep Deprivation." *Psychonomic Science* 25 (1971): 135–36.

―――. "REM Sleep and Information Processing: Evidence from Animal Studies." *Neuroscience & Biobehavioral Reviews* 3 (1979): 57–68.

Pearlman, C., and M. Becker. "Brief Posttrial REM Sleep Deprivation Impairs Discrimination Learning in Rats." *Physiological Psychology* 1 (1973): 373–76.

―――. "REM Sleep Deprivation Impairs Bar-Press Acquisition in Rats." *Physiology & Behavior* 13 (1974): 813–17.

Pelletier, K. R., and E. Peper. "Developing a Biofeedback Model: Alpha EEG Feedback as a Means for Pain Control." *The International Journal of Clinical and Experimental Hypnosis* 25 (1977): 361–71.

Penfield, W. *The Mystery of the Mind.* Princeton: Princeton University Press, 1975.

Peniston, E. G., and P. J. Kulkowski. "Alpha-Theta Brainwave Training and Beta-endorphin Levels in Alcoholics." *Alcoholism: Clinical and Experimental Research* 13, 2 (1989): 271–79.

―――. "Alcoholic Personality and Alpha-Theta Brainwave Training." *Medical Psychotherapy* 3 (1990): 35–37.

Pines, Maya. *The Brain Changers: Scientists and the New Mind Control.* New York: Harcourt Brace Jovanovich, 1973.

Pinker, Steven. *How the Mind Works.* New York: Norton, 1997.

Plotkin, W. B., "The Alpha Experience Revisited: Biofeedback in the Transformation of Psychological State." *Psychological Bulletin* 86 (1979): 1132–48.

Plotkin, W. B., and R. Cohen. "Occipital Alpha and the Attributes of the 'Alpha Experience.'" *Psychophysiology* 13 (1976): 16–21.

Poole, W. "The Healing Power of Music." In *The Heart of Healing*, edited by K. Butler and E. Fox. Atlanta: Turner Publishing, 1993.

Pribram, Karl. *Languages of the Brain.* Englewood, NJ: Prentice-Hall, 1971.

Prigogine, Ilya, and Isabelle Stengres. *Order Out of Chaos: Man's New Dialogue with Nature.* New York: Bantam, 1984.

Rao, K. R., and J. Freola. "Electrical Activity of the Brain and ESP: An Exploratory Study of Alpha Rhythm and ESP Scoring." *Journal of Indian Psychology* 2 (1979): 118–33.

Ray, Sondra. *The Only Diet There Is.* Berkeley, CA: Celestial Arts, 1995.

Rechtschaffen, A. "Current Perspectives on the Function of Sleep." *Perspectives in Biology and Medicine* 41 (1998): 359–90.

Roney-Douglas, Serena. "The Interface Between PSI and Subliminal Perception." *Parapsychology Review* 12, 4 (July/August 1981): 12–18.

Russell, Peter. *The Brain Book.* New York: E.P. Dutton, 1979.

Sackein, H. A., I. K. Packer, and R. C. Gur. "Hemisphericity, Cognitive Set, and Susceptibility to Subliminal Perception." *Journal of Abnormal Psychology* 86, 6 (1977): 624–30.

Sagales, T., and E. F. Domino. "Effects of Stress and REM Sleep Deprivation on the Patterns of Avoidance Learning and Brain Acetycholine in the Mouse." *Psychopharmacologia* 29 (1973): 307–15.

Saul, J. J., H. David, and P. A. Davis. "Psychologic Correlations with the Electroencephalogram." *Psychosomatic Medicine* 11 (1949): 361.

Schacter, D. L. "EEG Theta Waves and Psychological Phenomena: A Review and Analysis." *Biological Psychology* 5 (1977): 47–82.

———. *Searching for Memory: The Brain, the Mind, and the Past.* New York: Basic Books, 1996.

Schroeder, Lynn, and Sheila Ostrander. Subliminal Report: What You Don't Know Can Help You—or Hurt You. Booklet #010, Superlearning, 1985.

Schurtman, R., J. R. Palatier, and E. S. Martin. "On the Activation of Symbiotic Gratification Fantasies as an Aid in the Treatment of Alcoholics." *The International Journal of Addictions* 17, 7 (1982): 1157–74.

Schwartz, G. E., and D. Shapiro, eds. *Consciousness and Self-Regulation: Advances in Research.* Vol. 1. New York: Plenum Press, 1976.

Schwartz, Marvin, and Michael A. Rem. "Does the Averaged Evoked Response Encode Subliminal Perception?" *Psychophysiology* 12, 4 (1975): 390–94.

Sheldrake, Rupert. *The Presence of the Past: Morphic Resonance and the Habits of Nature.* New York: Vintage Books, 1988.

Shevrin, Howard. "Subliminal Perception and Dreaming." *The Journal of Mind and Behavior* 7 (1986).

———. "Brain Wave Correlates of Subliminal Stimulation, Unconscious Attention, Primary and Secondary Process Thinking, and Repressiveness." *Psychological Issue* 8, 2 (1971): 149–62.

———. "Does the Average Evoked Response Encode Subliminal Perception? Yes, a Reply to Schwartz and Rem." *Psychophysiology* 12, 4 (1975): 395–98.

Shevrin, Howard, William H. Smith, and Dean E. Fitzler. "Average Evoked Response and Verbal Correlates of Unconscious Mental Processes." *Psychophysiology* 8, 2 (1971): 149–62.

Shiromani, P., B. M. Gutwein, and W. Fishbein. "Development of Learning and Memory in Mice After Brief Paradoxical Sleep Deprivation." *Psysiology and Behavior* 22 (1979): 971–78.

Shulman, Lee M., Joyce Shulman, and Gerald P. Rafferty. *Subliminal: The New Channel to Personal Power.* Santa Monica, CA: Infobooks, 1990.

Silverman, Lloyd H. "A Comprehensive Report of Studies Using the Subliminal Psychodynamic Activation Method." *Psychological Research Bulletin* 20, 3 (1980): 1–22.

———. "Unconscious Oneness Fantasies: Experimental Findings and Implications for Treatment." International Forum for Psychoanalysis, 1, 2 (1984): 107–54.

Silverman, Lloyd H., and Frank M. Lachmann. "The Therapeutic Properties of Unconscious Oneness Fantasies: Evidence and Treatment Implications." *Contemporary Psychoanalysis* 21, 1 (1985): 91–115.

Silverman, Lloyd H., Frank M. Lackmann, and Robert H. Milich. *The Search for Oneness.* New York: International University Press, 1982.

Silverman, Lloyd H., and Doris K. Silverman. "A Clinical-Experimental Approach to the Study of Subliminal Stimulation." *Journal of Abnormal Social Psychology* 69, 2 (1964): 158–72.

Silverman, Lloyd H., et al. "Effect of Subliminal Stimulation of Symbiotic Fantasies on Behavior Modification Treatment of Obesity." *Journal of Consulting Clinical Psychologists* 46, 3 (1978): 432–51.

Smith, C. "Sleep States and Learning: A Review of the Animal Literature." *Neuroscience & Biobehavioral Review* 9 (1985): 157–68.

———. "Sleep States and Memory Processes." *Behavioral Brain Research* 69 (1995): 137–45.

———. "Sleep States, Memory Processes and Synaptic Plasticity." *Behavioral Brain Research* 78 (1996): 49–56.

Smith, C., and S. Butler. "Paradoxical Sleep at Selective Times Following Training Is Necessary for Learning." *Physiology and Behavior* 29 (1982): 469–73.

Smith, C., and G. Kelley. "Paradoxical Sleep Deprivation Applied Two Days After the End of Training Retards Learning." *Physiology and Behavior* 43 (1988): 213–16.

Smith, C., and L. Lapp. "Increases in Number of REMS and REM Density in Humans Following an Intensive Learning Period." *Sleep* 14 (1991): 325–30.

Smith, C., and G. M. Rose. "Evidence for a Paradoxical Sleep Window for Place Learning in the Morris Water Maze." *Physiology and Behavior* 59 (1996): 93–97.

———. "Posttraining Paradoxical Sleep in Rats Is Increased After Spatial Learning in the Morris Water Maze." *Behavioral Neuroscience* 111 (1997): 1197–1204.

Somekh, D. E., and J. M. Wilding. "Perception Without Awareness in a Dichoptic Viewing Situation." *British Journal of Psychology* 64, 3 (1973): 339–49.

Starr, Douglas. "Brain Drugs." *Omni* February 1983.

Staubli, U., and G. Lynch. "Stable Hippocampal Long-Term Potentiation Elicited by 'Theta' Pattern Stimulation." *Brain Research* 435 (1987): 227–34.

Stern, W. C. "Acquisition Impairments Following Rapid Eye Movement Sleep Deprivation in Rats," *Physiology and Behavior* 7 (1971): 345–52.

Swann, R. S., et al. *The Brain—A User's Manual.* New York: Putnam, 1982.

Tart, C. T., ed. *Altered States of Consciousness.* Garden City, NY: Doubleday, 1969.

———. *States of Consciousness.* New York: Dutton, 1975.

Taylor, Eldon. *Subliminal Communication: Emperor's Clothes or Panacea?* Las Vegas, NV: Just Another Reality. 1990.

"Therapeutic Effect of Oneness Fantasy." *Perspective* (4), A.R.E. Press, December 1985.

Tilley, A. J., and J.A.C. Empson. "REM Sleep and Memory Consolidation." *Biological Psychology* 6 (1978): 293–300.

Tomatis, Alfred A. *The Conscious Ear.* Barrytown, NY: Station Hill Press, 1991.

Trevisan, Louise Ann. *Beyond the Sound: A Technical and Philosophical Approach to Music Therapy.* Porterville, CA: Nowicki/Trevisan, 1978.

Vertes, R. P. "An Analysis of Ascending Brain Stem Systems Involved in Hippocampal Synchronization and Desynchronization." *Journal of Neurophysiology* 46 (1981): 1140–59.

———. "Brainstem Control of the Events of REM Sleep." *Progress in Neurobioloby* 22 (1984): 241–88.

———. "A Life-Sustaining Function for REM Sleep: A Theory." *Neuroscience & Biobehavioral Reviews* 10 (1986): 371–76.

———. "Memory Consolidation in REM Sleep: Dream On." *Sleep Research Society Bulletin* 1 (1995): 27–32.

Watson, Audrey. *Movement and Drama in Therapy: The Therapeutic Use of Movement, Drama, and Music.* Boston, MA: Plays, Inc., 1973.

Weinstein, Sidney. "A Review of Brain Hemisphere Research." *Journal of Advertising Research* 22, 3 (1982): 59–63.

Weinstein, Sidney, Curt Weinstein, and Ronald Drozkenko. "Brain Wave Analysis." *Psychology and Marketing* 1, 1 (Spring 1984): 1742.

Weinstein, Sidney, Valentine Appel, and Curt Weinstein. "Brain Activity Responses to Magazine and Television Advertising." *Journal of Advertising Research* 20, 3 (1980): 57–63.

Westerlundh, Bert. "Subliminal Influence on Imagery: Two Exploratory Experiments." *Psychological Research Bulletin* 25 (1985): 6–7.

Williams, P. "EEG Alpha Feedback: A Comparison of Two Control Groups." *Psychosomatic Medicine* 39 (1977): 44–47.

Winson, J. "The Biology and Function of Rapid Eye Movement Sleep." *Current Opinion in Neurobiology* 3 (1993): 243–48.

———. "Interspecies Differences in the Occurrence of Theta." *Behavioral Biology* 7 (1972): 479–87.

———. "Loss of Hippocampal Theta Rhythm Results in Spatial Memory Deficit in the Rat." *Science* 201 (1978): 160–63.

———. *Brain and Psyche: The Biology of the Unconscious.* Garden City, NY: Doubleday, 1985.

———. "The Meaning of Dreams." *Scientific American.* November 1990: 42–48.

Wise, Anna. *The High Performance Mind: Mastering Brainwaves for Insight, Healing and Creativity.* New York: Jeremy P. Tarcher/Putnam, 1997.

Wittrock, M. C., et al. *The Human Brain.* Englewood Cliffs, NJ: Prentice-Hall, 1977.

Yates, A. J. *Biofeedback and the Modification of Behavior.* New York: Plenum Press, 1980.

Zaidel, E. "Academic Implications of Dual-Brain Theory." In *The Dual Brain.* New York: Guilford Press, 1985.

Zenhausen, Robert, and Karen Hansen. "Differential Effect of Subliminal and Supraliminal Accessory Stimulation on Task Components in Problem-Solving." *Perceptual and Motor Skills* 38 (1974): 375–78.

Index of Scripts

Action   90

Aging   92

Anger   93

Assertiveness   96

Betrayal   99

Boundaries   101

Budgeting   103

Careers   104

Change   107

Childhood   109

Commitment   110

Communication   112

Completing: Projects/Tasks   115

Concentration   116

Confidentiality   118

Conflict Resolution   120

Conscious Evolution   122

Control   125

Creative Problem Solving   127

Creativity   130

Dating   132

Debt   135

Delegation   137

Deserving   139

Divorce   141

Exercising   145

Expectations   147

Family Dysfunction   149

Family—Loving   151

Fear   154

Feedback   157

Feelings   160

Forgiving   164

Global Citizenship   166

Goals   168

Gratitude   171

Grieving   173

Guilt   174

Healing: Christian   176

Health: General   178

Holographic Universe   182

Humor   183

Inner Peace   186

Intelligence   189

Intimacy   192

Intuition   195

Letting Go   197
Listening   200
Manifesting   203
Meditation   206
Moving On   208
Neatness   209
Negativity   212
Passive-Aggression   213
Perfectionism   214
Performing Well   216
Personal Power   218
Prayer   220
Prejudice   222
Prosperity   223
Public Speaking   225
Quit Smoking   227
Sales Calls/Cold-calling   231
Self-love   235

Shame   238
Spirituality   240
Strategic Thinking   242
Struggle   245
Studying   246
Sufi Code   248
Taxes   249
Test Taking   251
Time Management   254
Truth   257
Twelve Steps   260
Wealth   264
Weight Loss   268
Weight Loss: Dieting   271
Weight Maintenance   273
Working   274
Wrestling   276
Writing   279

Teri Mahaney, Ph.D.

is an expert in identifying and changing unconscious patterns that control individual and organizational behavior.

Teri is

. . . a recognized leader in several fields, which include educational leadership, high performance management, and personal transformation. She has been honored as an International Leader in Achievement, an Outstanding Woman of the Year, and is listed in *The World Who's Who of Women*.

. . . a widely experienced professional woman. Her careers include college dean and professor, counselor/mentor, workshop leader, white-water guide, high-ranking state government official, and small business owner.

. . . a highly respected management trainer for corporate and government clients. She has worked with thousands of participants in her training sessions, which range from conducting brain-mapping workshops for CEOs to teaching white-water rowing to at-risk teens to presenting supervisory and management training for improved performance.

. . . an avid learner. Her formal college degrees are in educational leadership and management, black studies, and small business ownership. Her eclectic informal studies include Eastern philosophy and religion, the mind/body connection, and nontraditional healing methods.

. . . a "walk your talk" counselor, Teri's life is a continuous exploration of different approaches to truth and transformation. She takes great pleasure in sharing her insights, approaches, and practical solutions for a better life. She is available for speaking and workshop engagements.

For a free catalog of SuperSleep™ products and services,
call 800.762.9937 or visit www.changeyourmind.com.